A GAY SYNAGOGUE IN NEW YORK

▼

A Gay Synagogue in New York

MOSHE SHOKEID

UNIVERSITY OF PENNSYLVANIA PRESS   PHILADELPHIA

First published 1995 by Columbia University Press
Copyright © 1995 Columbia University Press
Preface and Epilogue copyright © 2003 University of Pennsylvania Press
All rights reserved
Printed in the United States of America on acid-free paper

Published by
University of Pennsylvania Press
Philadelphia, Pennsylvania 19104-4011

Library of Congress Cataloging-in-Publication Data
Shokeid, Moshe.
    A gay synagogue in New York / Moshe Shokeid.
        p.   cm.
    Originally published : New York : Columbia University Press, c1995.
    Includes bibliographical references and index.
    ISBN 0-8122-1840-X (pbk. : alk. paper)
        1. Congregation Beth Simchat Torah (New York, N.Y.)   2. Jewish
    gays—New York (State)—New York—Religious life.   3. Homosexuality—
    Religious aspects—Judaism.   I. Title.
    BM225.N52 B487   2002
    289'.086'64097471—dc21   2002032031

▼

To
Mel Rosen,
Carl Bennett,
Walter Schwartz,
and Rob Cooper—
Martin,
Edward,
Harry,
and *Paul*.
Tragically, they cannot
witness the work
to which they
generously contributed.

▼

CONTENTS

▼

When the original edition of *A Gay Synagogue in New York* went out of print, I was certain it had not come to the end of its useful life. I believed there was a growing interest in issues of homosexuality, spirituality, and Judaism. I also believed the study was representative of the research venues available to students of anthropology looking for challenging new fields in urban environments. For this reissue, I have left the ethnography intact but added an epilogue that briefly presents the changes that have taken place in the synagogue since I completed my initial observations. I thank my editors at Columbia University Press for their dedicated work on the first edition. I am grateful in particular to Roger Sanjek at Queens College, who encouraged me to proceed with a new edition, to Peter Agree of the University of Pennsylvania Press, who took on the project, and to Edward Pass— "Mark," in my text—for his comments on the epilogue.

▼

ACKNOWLEDGMENTS

I was able to carry out my research at Congregation Beth Simchat Torah (CBST) during the spring of 1989 as Dorot Visiting Professor at New York University's Department of Anthropology and during the summer and fall of 1990 as Visiting Scholar at the Department of Anthropology of the Graduate Center of the City University of New York. The invitation to spend the fall term of 1992 at the Department of Social Anthropology of Stockholm University enabled me to write several of these chapters. My stay during the summer of 1993 at the Center for Jewish Studies of the Graduate Center of the City University of New York enabled me to complete a few more chapters. I thank Dale Eickelman, Tomas Gerholm, Ulf Hannerz, Paul Ritterband, and Annette Weiner for their support and interest. I am also grateful for the grants extended to me by the Memorial Foundation for Jewish Culture and the Lucius N. Littauer Foundation, both of New York.

I thank Samuel Heilman and Roger Sanjek of Queens College, CUNY, and Shlomo Deshen of Tel Aviv University, who read the manuscript and generously contributed their suggestions and comments. Edward Pass—"Mark," in my text—was more than my first-draft editor: this would have been another book without his efforts (and if up to him, yet another). Ann Miller, my editor at Columbia University Press, consistently encouraged my writing. Susan Pensak, the manuscript editor for Columbia University Press, made incisive comments and carefully prepared the final version. The Faculty of Social Sciences at Tel Aviv University assisted me in preparing the manuscript for publication; I thank Roslyn Langbart, Sylvia Weinberg, and Pamela Yacobi for the typing and retyping.

▼

I consider this book, however, in large measure a tribute to the congregants at CBST, who welcomed me with warmth and openness and whose stories, words, and deeds make up this work. I hope I have not offended anyone with my portrayal.

Finally, I am deeply indebted to Ora, Nadav, and Noam, my wife and sons, who supported my project and, albeit grudgingly, tolerated my absences and travels. They never questioned the importance of my work in a field that, in not a few quarters, still prompts whispers and disdain. I am very proud of them.

March 1994

▼

A GAY SYNAGOGUE IN NEW YORK

▼

CHAPTER ONE

A Journey to CBST

1. Choice of Field

How did a mainstream Israeli anthropologist come to study a gay synagogue in New York? And what social and cultural baggage did he bring along that might affect his observations? While for many years anthropologists divulged very little about themselves, the development of reflexivity in the wake of the publication of Malinowski's diaries in 1967 has made these questions pertinent if not indispensable. In my previous ethnographic studies I have been forthright about my motives and possible biases,[1] but never before was I conscious so early in my work that I would be expected to make my position clear. I could see that expectation in the eyes of my "subjects," colleagues, and friends. Homosexuality is not yet considered an ordinary field for mainstream anthropologists. These ordained reporters of "other" societies have for the most part remained committed to the dominant societal ethos. They have been tolerated, even privileged, as researchers of the exotic, gaining status as adventurers in remote continents, but they have been careful to avoid areas considered sensitive to their home society.

During a sabbatical in New York, 1982–84, studying Israeli immigrants, I was asked by a colleague in the sociology department, at Queens College[2] to advise a doctoral student who was doing research on a gay synagogue in Manhattan. In order to get a better idea of the field, I suggested I join the observer at a service. I had no idea what a gay synagogue would be like.

▼

My knowledge of homosexuality was limited to the stereotypes typical to my generation of Israeli society, modified by a few direct observations. The first of these only reinforced the stereotype: a man exposing himself in a public toilet in Jerusalem and wordlessly suggesting sexual contact. The second occurred when, in my late twenties, I was onboard an Israeli liner on my first trip to Europe to pursue graduate studies in Britain. I noticed a fellow Israeli, handsome, self-confident, and continually surrounded by admiring women. One inclement evening when most passengers were confined to their cabins, I met him strolling on deck. We struck up what became a lengthy conversation, which concluded with his telling me he was gay. This revelation confounded my stereotype of homosexuals as miserable, if not criminal, characters easily identified by their effeminate manner.

A more profound experience occurred two years later when a close female friend from our undergraduate days together wrote me in Britain to tell of her recent discovery that she was a lesbian. I was taken aback, having always assumed that we would someday pursue what seemed to me our mutual attraction. But more than that, her revelation challenged a myth rooted in the deepest layers of my education: the perception of myself, my friends, my generation, as true sabras—the new idealized men and women, robust, self-assured, without flaws and defects, destined to create the next brave Jewish generation.

Later, in 1967, my friend took a break from her studies in the United States and joined me for a week in London. Taking me in tow, she searched out the center of gay life on Kings Road, explorations that led me far from the social and cultural environment I had known until then. I later returned to several of these locales on my own, to test my feelings and observe a new world, but never felt comfortable in them. That same feeling persisted when I subsequently explored gay pubs in Manchester as well as gay sites on my first trip to the United States. As fantastical as some of these seemed, I couldn't join the party. It was not my "thing."

With these few experiences as a prelude, I remember my great surprise upon reaching CBST. I found a real synagogue with a group of men and women that looked as ordinary as an Israeli Modern Orthodox congregation. Attending one service was enough for me to conclude that this was not another scene of anonymous relationships. I was no less moved by the style of the service and the melodies, which reminded me of the synagogue of my boyhood. The visit to CBST was the first time, after many years, that I had been back to an Ashkenazi synagogue since enrolling in a secular high school at age fourteen and giving up religious life completely.[3] My visit convinced me that the ethnographic literature on gays in Western society was inadequate in its concentration on fields of anonymous sex. I thought that other promising topics within the field of homosexuality were waiting for anthropologists in their own society if they could only break free from the fear of losing respectability. (I was also affected, at that time, by reading Herdt's extraordinary ethnography *Guardians of the Flutes* [1981], dealing with ritualized "homosexuality" in New Guinea.) But for myself, I was still working on my book on Israeli immigrants—*yordim*—and assumed it would soon be introduced in a Ph.D. dissertation.

Six years later, in 1989, I was spending the spring term at NYU and considered the possibility of doing research. I was not inclined to expand my work among Israeli immigrants and was looking for a field close to my Washington Square apartment. To my surprise, I discovered that the research on CBST had never been completed and thought, Why not give it a try? Eventually, I returned to New York for the summer and fall of 1990 to complete a year of observation. I also attended services during subsequent short visits to New York.

I undertook the study of CBST with the conviction that it was consistent with my interest in social minorities. But more than that, I took advantage of the freedom inherent in the anthropologist's career to choose one's field of research by the call of one's imagination. I probably sacrificed some of my reputation as a specialist in Middle Eastern studies. Some voiced surprise at my unexpected choice, believing perhaps that it offered an outlet for a suppressed identity. If that were the case, then I had already expressed, through my professional life, three hidden identities: that of a Moroccan Jew (1971), an Israeli Arab (1982), and a *yored* (1988). I have no regrets. Above all, I have enjoyed the opportunity of meeting so many interesting individuals.

Ironically, in May of 1993, as I was writing the last chapters of this book, my obscure field received international attention following the denial of CBST's request to march in the annual Salute to Israel Parade on Fifth Avenue. The controversy, which divided the Jewish establishment, was widely covered in the New York and Israeli media. Eventually, CBST and its supporters held their own separate celebra-

3

▼

tion at Central Synagogue, a few blocks from the parade route. As the *Daily News* reported (May 10, 1993): "The divided celebration had politicians—past, present, and future—rushing to appear at both functions." My choice of a field—considered eccentric, if not bizarre, by colleagues and friends—had suddenly lost its obscurity.

Anthropologists have usually studied people from remote worlds who were somehow disadvantaged compared to their own social, economic, or cultural position. At CBST I had the unusual experience of studying articulate, well-educated—frequently professional—people with whom I shared ethnic roots and cultural sentiments. Most were equally economically advantaged, some much more so. If my Hebrew was superior to theirs, in the lingua franca of our time mine was that of the colonized, not the colonizer.

2. The Ethnographer's Presentation of Self

My immediate and continuing dilemma at CBST was how to introduce myself. Should I, when meeting a new congregant, explain my sexual identity and my research intentions? I was concerned that, if I did, my presence might be resented, destroying any chance for normal social interaction. Alternatively, my exposition might be derided as that of a closeted homosexual interested in the synagogue but unwilling to acknowledge his identity. I decided to begin as I had during my study of the yordim. I gave only basic information: my name, my profession, and positions at NYU and Tel Aviv University. This was enough for the more perceptive of my early acquaintances to foresee the potential consequences of my attendance. After a Sabbath morning service on my second visit, that information given to a small group of congregants prompted the service leader, Simon, to comment: "You might find an interesting story here." This was the beginning of a friendship that bore a tremendous impact on my work. Simon often reminded me of Doc, the informant in Whyte's classic *Street Corner Society* (1955) who introduced the Harvard student to the society of an Italian youth gang. Simon was ready for my appearance as narrator of CBST's story. He encouraged me to write the book he would have loved to write himself. As he told me later, he was scared that AIDS would wipe out his generation and he wanted the story of the synagogue to survive. He came to believe I could be relied on to be their witness.

My credibility was happily enhanced when, shortly after my arrival, reviews of my book on the yordim appeared in publications (e.g., *Judaism, West Side Spirit*) Simon and other congregants read. I then decided to give copies of the book itself to Simon, Aaron (leader of the Talmud class), and a few other congregants I had met, assuming they would thus understand my project as well as my personal situation. I preferred them to learn about me from my book, believing that if they liked my narrative on the Israelis, they would accept me and spare me a confession of my motives.

In this I was both right and wrong. To my dismay, a few did not notice the personal details presented on the book's jacket or in my own introduction. Others who did were initially upset, but ultimately forgave me my early silence on personal matters. This was typically the case. Once my unexpected identity was revealed, most of my close acquaintances did not change their trusting attitude toward me. They continued to joke about sexual matters in my presence and shared intimate subjects with me. I was never segregated from social interaction. "You feel comfortable in our community," was the way one member articulated what was probably a common understanding of my attraction to CBST.

But there were other occasions early in my stay when I was expected to introduce myself in a clear, forthright manner. This was the case at my first session with a discussion group on gay and lesbian issues. After hearing me briefly introduce myself, Martin, the group leader, asked if I had joined the synagogue because of my professional interest or because I shared with them the problems of gay people. Feeling on the spot, I told the group of ten men and women, honestly, that I believed all men and women carried the potential for being attracted to members of their own sex. I told them that I wanted to know gay people and understand their lives, which I could not do in the less hospitable locales I had explored. I remarked that anthropologists, who are supposed to be at the forefront of liberalism, neglected the study of homosexuality—even when it showed up in their own field—in order to avoid suspicion that they were themselves gay. Later in the same meeting when another member asked what I thought was the etiology of homosexuality, I ascribed it mainly to cultural and environmental conditioning. Martin disputed this view but let the issue rest. Later, I mentioned my family and my relationship with my children. Whatever the group concluded, they accepted me, and, in time, I enjoyed the warm friendship of several of the participants and of Martin in particular.

▼

Even without an overt statement on my part or the presentation of my newly published book, my close friends soon came to know my personal story. Those who observed me closely realized I didn't use my attendance to look for potential partners and politely avoided opportunities presented. Others noticed my physical awkwardness in confronting the hugging and kissing so common among friends and acquaintances at CBST. Simon told me he could sense very early that I was different by my stiff reaction to those signs of affection. "You were not appreciative," he observed. (In fact, only toward the end of my stay was I able to reciprocate freely with these simple demonstrations of friendship, which so strongly displayed the bonding among the congregants.) But some of my acquaintances took a while to grasp my identity. Ze'ev only learned that I had a family months after we first met. When the subject finally came up during a dinner we shared before a synagogue service, he concluded, "You are a different person from the one I knew half an hour ago." Nevertheless, that late revelation did not impair our relationship.

As for my research intentions, I myself was not sure at the outset I would end up writing a book on CBST, not being obligated by any grant. Only at a later stage in my study did I openly voice a plan to do so. Nonetheless, there were those who from the beginning of our friendship expected that such a book would result. Simon, as I have described, hoped for it. Aaron saw a continuity between my book on the yordim and the one he believed I would write on the synagogue: both were about the search for Judaism and a lost sense of community. Martin, when he saw me arrive for Thanksgiving dinner at his lover's home carrying my book on the yordim, immediately held it up and loudly announced to the guests: "Moshe Shokeid's book on the homosexuals at CBST!" But only a few days earlier I had confronted a delicate situation with Joel, former chair of the Religious Committee, who had been very friendly from my first days in the synagogue and an important source of information on its affairs. To my great surprise, I learned he was angry upon discovering from a comment Larry made that I was doing research on CBST. I couldn't believe that he had not realized it long ago. He complained to both Larry and Simon that I had not requested the board's permission. They replied in my defense that approval wasn't necessary because I hadn't asked for confidential board records. I was concerned by Joel's unexpected reaction and imagined myself being thrown out of the synagogue. But when I met him later the same day to clarify my intentions, Joel was satisfied enough to continue offering his help.

It is difficult to assess the impact of my Israeli identity on this project. I believe it buttressed my position as an insider/outsider, making me both close and distant. I was Jewish and therefore a full partner to a major component of the identity of the participants, regardless of my sexual persona. My Israeliness added interest to my presence and offered a neutral basis for communication with most congregants. The congregation was strongly supportive of Israel, and many congregants had visited, or had friends or relatives, there. That I was a good informant on Israel and not politically neutral led to lively conversations. My Israeliness added to the ambiguity of my status at CBST and helped to mitigate the unresolved issues of my presence.

3. Integrating Into the Field

During my initial attendance at Friday evening services I felt uncomfortably isolated. I would take a seat in a remote corner apart from other congregants until the vacant seats near me were occupied by later arrivals or by acquaintances who wished to join me. Before and after the service I would kill time awkwardly standing at the hospitality table pretending to read literature I was already familiar with while waiting for someone to talk to. Not knowing the rules of the game, and self-conscious of my nongay sexual identity, I was reluctant to initiate social interactions lest they be misconstrued as come-ons. And I was likewise leery of monopolizing the time of those who initiated conversations with me, lest they ultimately discover they had wasted their time.

I soon discovered I was much better able to communicate and develop close relationships in smaller gatherings such as the Sabbath morning services, committee meetings, volunteer efforts, courses and trips sponsored by the Education Committee, etc. The relationships I developed in these contexts later facilitated my social interaction at the crowded services, as I gradually became a familiar face. After a while I was called to the bimah (pulpit) to read—rather than chant—portions of the Torah or haftarah using the pronunciation of modern Hebrew. These instances were both a service novelty and a special honor.

A clear sign of my growing comfort with the congregation was manifested soon after I returned in the summer of 1990. The service

▼

leader, an old acquaintance, suggested that I read a prayer dedicated to the State of Israel. As I was reading the phrase "Bless the leaders of Israel with wisdom and courage," I took the liberty of expressing my resentment of the then Likud government by adding "of which they are seriously lacking." As I continued reading the prayer, I heard the murmur of laughter and whispered comments from those who noticed my improvisation of the text. Though my "leftist" convictions were not particularly popular at CBST, I felt sufficiently at ease to express them publicly. As I wrote in my notes, "I have thus claimed an independent position."

A few weeks later came a more serious test of my field position. Mark invited me to the Gay Pride Parade—to watch, if not participate. Gleefully, he promised that if I marched I could fulfill an anthropologist's dream: to experience life as his subjects experience it—to feel the discomfort of being a member of a stigmatized group. As we were standing along Central Park South, the CBST contingent came marching by. Mark waded into the slow-moving group to greet his neighbors Naomi and Susan, and to my surprise announced he was joining them. Given little time to reflect, I felt I had no choice. I gingerly stepped out into the street. As we rounded the corner onto the fully packed Fifth Avenue, I tried to find refuge under my hat, pulling my miserably thin cap down as far as it would go over my head. Naomi, watching my embarrassment, told me she went through a similar experience on her first parade, trying to escape photographers and looking for a "safe side" of the street.

Mark was obviously amused, but pleased with my willingness to join in. He told me that the first time he marched, a number of years ago, he felt he was doing something daring, and that everyone was looking at him. Now he was annoyed that they weren't. He described the parade as a group therapy session in which, for one day, gays are emboldened to openly proclaim an identity many keep hidden throughout the year. Someone overhearing our conversation added: "It is a reaffirmation of our identity." Martin, now board chair, was delighted to see me among his flock. "Once you have come out in the march, it is final," he told me. Saul, his predecessor, warned me, laughingly, that my picture would be seen on Israeli television.

An important opportunity to integrate into the inner circle of CBST was the invitation to several parties given by leading members. Simon was very helpful in securing the first of these, particularly the Rosh

Hashanah party given by Morris celebrating CBST's eighteenth year. Through my own social skills I was later invited to parties given by Harvey and Norman as well as those of the Talmud circle. My participation at these events moved me from a position of marginality to one of social visibility.

9

Gradually, as in other fields, I developed close relationships with many individuals whose voices are represented in this work. In my conversations with congregants, sixty of whom are mentioned by name, I refrained from disturbing the natural ambience by recording or writing notes in their presence. For a long time I wrestled with the question of whether to conduct formal interviews at CBST. To do so would conflict with my initial strategy of avoiding presenting myself as a researcher, an outsider. But later as I became more confident with my position in the synagogue, I accepted Simon's counsel that I supplement my data by interviewing active members. This approach proved beneficial. Interestingly, the greatest success was with Leon, a former board chair, who I had always felt had ignored me, brushing off Simon's attempts to involve me in their company. But he agreed to a formal interview and invited me to his home. He was very open about the synagogue's history, principal players, and major issues. We both obviously enjoyed the session, and he later told Simon he regretted I hadn't taped it.

As part of that same late strategy, I gave a lecture on my study of the yordim after a Friday night service. The lecture was announced in the *Synagogue News*, offering me at the time the widest visibility as a serious academic.

In addition to observation and interviews, I made use of written records and published materials: prayer books, supplementary handouts, *drashah* (sermon) texts, the complete text of the first commitment ceremony, committee minutes, etc. Invaluably, Martin made available the complete set of *Gay Synagogue News* since its first issue in 1974. In a desire to broaden my perspective, I visited other gay institutions and organizations in New York. These included services at the two Catholic congregations, Dignity Big Apple and Dignity New York, meetings of the Gay Fathers Forum, the Bisexual Pride Group, and Act Up–AIDS Coalition. I also visited popular gay bars, clubs, bookstores, movie theaters, restaurants, and the few remaining saunas.

My relationships in the synagogue reveal, however, a discrepancy when one compares the web of connections I maintained with men

▼

versus women. Although I gradually established close relationships with a growing number of women—Naomi, Susan, Judy, Jean, Rose, and Carol, in particular—on the whole I was more exposed to opportunities for friendships with men. The attendance of men at the synagogue during my stay usually outnumbered that of women, and men were more actively engaged in the many tasks as committee members, ritual leaders, etc. But apart from that I was at the start somewhat hesitant about approaching the lesbian participants and embarrassed at hanging around them. No doubt I could more naturally join the company of men at activities outside the synagogue and easily probe among them into delicate issues such as sexuality and mating. Nevertheless, had I stayed at CBST for a longer period, I believe, the extent of my ties with women might have almost equaled my network of male friends. That inhibition, however, has also been reported in other situations of female/male audiences observed by male researchers, and even under circumstances where women were equally open about sexual behavior.[4]

I assume my book might therefore disappoint readers who rightly expect an equal presentation of the experiences and viewpoints of gay men and lesbian congregants in the various contexts of the following chapters. True, I could probably better exploit the data I collected on women in order to maintain a more satisfactory parity in the presentation of the lesbian constituency. I refrained from that strategy. A calculated construction of the text for the sake of equal gender representation would have detracted from my own notion of ethnographic integrity. But, whatever the sources of strength or shortcomings of my project, I have no doubt CBST and its audience could be introduced through different perspectives instigated by the unique identities and personal experiences of other observers.

4. Informants and the Ethnographic Text

Anthropologists have traditionally escaped review of their work by the people they studied. In most cases their subjects were unable to read their manuscripts because of differences in language, education, and culture. Instead, anthropologists have sought validation by "peer review" from their respective schools and rarely have given more than lip service to validation from the "native's point of view." Clifford's prediction (1983:140) that anthropologists will increasingly have to share their texts with their indigenous collaborators has not yet materialized. This is not to say we should leave the "natives" with the final decision on the depiction and meaning of their behavior. Social life everywhere exists as part of an ongoing process of negotiation and discourse between often contradictory interpretations. But the "natives' " assessment of the ethnographer's portrayal is not irrelevant, least of all when they are as articulate and self-aware as those at CBST.

Already, in my work on the yordim, I was tempted to offer a copy of my manuscript to a key informant, but finally opted against that course, avoiding the possible need to deal with his unhappiness at his portrayal. I reasoned that any ethnography, even one disciplined by a strict empirical tradition—as I felt mine to be, was a work of imagination, a creation of art. Would Leonardo have changed the Mona Lisa's smile had she objected to that enigmatic expression on her face?

My apotheosized conjecture about Leonardo and his model was brought to earth when I decided to present a first paper on the synagogue at a fall 1990 meeting of the Association for Jewish Studies in Boston. The subject was the Talmud class. I felt I could not deliver that lecture without first showing the work to Aaron. He was the leader of the Talmud circle, and, despite changing his name, Aaron's identity could not be disguised. But more than that, I had great respect for Aaron's deep human understanding and was anxious for his judgment on my observations and interpretations. Equally important, Aaron was well aware of my project, and I felt an obligation to share it with him. After reading the paper, Aaron was impressed, overall, with the way I had captured the atmosphere and personal relationships of the Talmud class, but was surprised at the resentment I had portrayed among other congregants toward his group. He was also unhappy with my metaphorical comparison of the Talmud disciples to drag queens in their impact on the larger community. Despite his reservations, I felt confirmed in my basic presentation of the material: I believed he underestimated the antipathy toward Orthodoxy among many of the congregants at CBST; as for my metaphor, I could sympathize with his uneasiness, but felt the creative license to employ its imagery.[5]

In another incident, I actively sought out the "natives' " view as a corrective for my own. In early 1990 *Gay Synagogue News* published the drashah Ze'ev had delivered the prior Rosh Hashanah: "I've always been amused when I hear some Jews, I among them, talk to other Jews; we say 'blow the shofar' . . . with the warmth of informal tone, the

▼

familiar (nonpublic), personal, affectionate manner. This linguistic familiarity identifies it in the inner circle of our special things."

I was puzzled when I read this. Had Ze'ev consciously intended to relate shofar blowing to a "blow job," or had I imposed this interpretation on his text? Simon was not impressed by my reading but suggested we solicit other opinions. Jack and Joel, current and past chairs of the Religious Committee, assumed there was no sexual connotation. Isaac, an academic, disagreed as did a congregant who was both an ordained rabbi and social worker. "When a gay man writes about blowing the shofar, it is fairly clear he made a sexual allusion," the latter declared. Three other congregants at first refused to consider the possibility of sexual innuendo, but later confessed unease. Martin, among them, told us he had tried to dismiss the sexual allusion when he first saw the newsletter, believing there were occasions when sexual thoughts were improper. The editor of Gay Synagogue News explained he didn't want to think about it, but added: "Obviously, it carries a sexual inference even if Ze'ev hadn't meant it. I have five thousand thoughts on my mind every minute and one of them is always sexual. Naturally, whenever 'to blow' is mentioned, a sexual thought goes through my mind."

Finally, we approached Ze'ev himself. He denied a sexual intent, but after considering the matter was inclined to agree that whenever "blowing" is mentioned a sexual innuendo is inescapable.

What seemed equally inescapable to me was that this unresolved confrontation of meanings suggested some of the problems inherent in the ethnographic process. It is not only the deficiency of the ethnographer in transcribing the observed behavior but no less the multiple meanings that the observed themselves impose on their own texts.

Simon was another key informant to whom I presented a major portion of my manuscript for comment. Simon's major reservation about my text was the depiction of the congregants' behavior in terms of "performance." That common anthropological mode of presentation struck him as demeaning. I accommodated his view and deleted that metaphor whenever it seemed unnecessary. He also pointed out several instances in which I had revealed personal details congregants might find unbecoming or compromising to their identity. In response to Simon's fear I called several congregants and was surprised to learn, in fact, how unconcerned they were at the prospect of their possible identification. Some even expressed a preference to be presented by their full name, a mark of self-assertion.[6] Simon's other minor corrections saw him continuing in his role as a guide anxious to make me get my data "right." I was pleased to receive his favorable verdict, as I had been with Aaron's opinion on my Talmud class paper. Both had been instrumental in my study, facilitating my entry into their field in a way similar to the first people I had met in earlier ethnographic projects (Shokeid 1988b).

13

Another "native" who played an important role in my work was Mark. We had met socially at the home of a couple with whom we were both close friends. Mark had known the wife for many years; her Israeli husband had been a key informant in my work on the yordim. Mark and I would chat together on art, theater, and politics at the couple's frequent gatherings. I welcomed the opportunity to speak to someone whose focus was not Israel; he was happy to find someone with whom to speak English. Though I, in time, came to know that Mark was both Jewish and gay, neither this nor my study of CBST—of which he was unaware—was ever discussed between us. One evening, a few months after our introduction, I was attending a lecture at CBST by Knesset member Shulamit Aloni when Mark came up and said hello. He, it turned out, was a nominal member of the synagogue and had received the lecture announcement. Now that a new topic had opened between us, Mark was happy to share his knowledge of the gay world outside CBST and expressed interest in my study of the synagogue. I have already mentioned his role in later instigating my participation in the Gay Pride march.

Sometime after our accidental meeting at CBST I asked Mark if he would take a look at the galleys of a paper I was publishing on a subject unrelated to gay life. He agreed and whited out a couple of typos. I again called on his facility with English on a draft of another article unrelated to the synagogue, and a third time when I prepared the paper on the Talmud class. By now his role had become that of a full-fledged manuscript editor, and in the last instance, involved in my CBST study. From his initial retouching he had moved to a role—as he himself humorously defined—not unlike that of the editor of the first *Othello* in Yiddish who presented:

"Sheykspir ibergezetst, fartaytsht, un farbersert" [Shakespeare translated, touched up and improved.]

By some tacit, unspoken understanding, Mark and I had made a pact to complete the manuscript together. It was on my part a process

▼

of pleasure and agony combined. He proved a severe critic with no tolerance for an anthropological jargon that only adds to the professional mystique. He insisted on a direct style and saw no reason why even ambiguity should not be clearly communicated. He also often suspected me of expressing mainstream ideology and stereotypes, a theme that resulted in hectic arguments and textual alterations

Mark's involvement gave me the assurance that I was listening to a voice from the field in a way I had never done before. Mark was an outsider/insider at CBST. He was a member, but not engaged in its daily life. His perspective was essentially that of the wider, New York Jewish gay world. Therefore my first reader and judge was not a detached colleague. Likewise, Aaron and Simon offered an insider's critique of my work. At last I could truly practice my own words: "Anthropologists and their informants are inextricably bound together in producing an ethnographic text that integrates the impact of their unique personalities, their social incongruities, and dreams (1988b:45)."

One last question remains: can an outsider really understand the intricacies of gay lives and penetrate their inner world? That issue was rarely raised when anthropologists studied alien societies in the third world or even as they later turned their attention to fields within the borders of their own society. But in recent years anthropologists have increasingly concerned themselves with the construction of the ethnographic reality as a discourse between and betwixt the "native's" and the observer's points of view: Geertz (1973), Rabinow (1977), Crapanzano (1977), Dumont (1978), Clifford and Marcus (1986), for example. However, for better or worse, the ethnographer as alien cannot be erased from the past and future annals of anthropology without eradicating them altogether. Anthropology was born in sin by a stranger who went out to discover virgin cultures.

Nevertheless, the problem of authenticity in reports by strangers seems to be particularly acute in the area of gay studies. The long history of repression and the clear avoidance of the study of gay life by mainstream anthropologists have left its mark. How can the "heterosexual colonizers" put themselves in the place of oppressed gay and lesbian people and comprehend their experiences? A clear sign of that resentment among scholars has been the recent decision to change the name of the Anthropology Research Group on Homosexuality to SOLGA—the Society of Lesbian and Gay Anthropologists. But we have no evidence that insiders are necessarily free of flawed observations, personal ideological perspectives, individual biases as well as internalized self-resentment (Shokeid 1989). I will not attempt, a priori, to justify my choice of field and prove my credentials to study it. I had no trace of Moroccan ancestry when I decided to study Jews from the Atlas Mountains in an Israeli village, nor any Arab ancestry when I studied Arabs in an Israeli city, but no one questioned my right or ability to undertake these projects. I can only quote Gates's (1991:30) comment on several celebrated autobiographies of Native American and Black American figures discovered to have been written not by "natives" but by white outsiders, and bigots at that

15

> The lesson of the literary blindfold test is not that our social identities don't matter. They do matter. And our histories, individual and collective, do affect what we wish to write and what we are able to write. But that relation is never one fixed determinism. No human culture is inaccessible to someone who makes the effort to understand, to learn, to inhabit another world.

CHAPTER TWO

From Tearoom to Sanctuary: Introduction

"The Explosion of Gay Things"

Among "the explosion of gay things" in the 1970s, as Adam (1985) termed it, was the gay religious movement. Its beginning can be traced to the founding of the Metropolitan Community Church in Los Angeles by the Reverend Troy Perry in 1968.[1] MCC's members were drawn from a myriad of denominations, some later going on to form congregations in their own religious persuasions.

The first gay synagogue, Beth Chayim Chadashim ("House of new life"), was one of these, founded in Los Angeles in 1972 and meeting, initially, in a hall rented from MCC.[2] The next year, the second gay synagogue was formed: Congregation Beth Simchat Torah—the subject of this study—in New York City. Since then, this gay Jewish movement has grown to twenty institutions in metropolitan centers across North America, ranging in size from a few dozen to over a thousand members.[3]

Critics who have written on the gay religious phenomenon have interpreted it variously. As radical or conservative; permanent or transitory. Shandler (n.d.), analyzing the presentation of gay synagogues through their names and logos, sees them as nonconfrontational, marking in Duberman's (1990) words, "a shift within the gay world from a need to rebel to a need to belong" (105). Kosmin and Lachman, similarly, see it in part as "a search for societal respectability" (1993:231). In Enroth's view "MCC and other gay religious groups are merely an extension of the gay life-style and the secular gay sub-culture" (1974:356), not a profound religious phenomenon. Thumma (1991) argues that the evangelical organization he studied draws people who are suffering from an identity crisis, and "once the dissonance is resolved or reduced, they disappear" (344). For Irle (1979), however, the issue is more fundamental. All religions arise from a need to provide ultimate meaning for the human condition. Sexuality is a basic human condition. Therefore, as the visibility and presence of homosexuality increase, organized religion will inevitably have to address it.

17

Whatever the meaning and prospects of the gay religious movement, events in the last few years have borne out Irle's projection. Homosexuality has emerged as a central issue in organized religion in America, and most religious bodies have needed to examine their position toward it—often heatedly. Gay and lesbian Jews have themselves entered this discourse.[4]

Among the branches of Judaism, all have engaged in this examination[5] and adopted public positions, confronting the traditional Levitican injunction: "You shall not lie with a man as one lies with a woman; it is an abomination [to'evah] . . . they shall be put to death and the fault is theirs alone" (18:22, 20:13)—about which Rebecca Alpert writes: "In our encounter with Leviticus, we experience the pain and terror and anger that this statement arouses in us. We imagine the untold damage done to generations of men, women, and children who experienced same–sex feelings and were forced to cloak or repress them" (1989:69).

In this religious discourse the most common defense of homosexual claims—typically found among the liberal branches of Judaism—rests on a distinction between homosexual acts as the Torah sees them and the modern concept of gay life.[6] For example, Leviticus is seen as proscribing the ritual practices of pagan cults, which included various forms of sexuality, that therefore are irrelevant to modern same-sex love relationships. Such reinterpretation is seen as consistent with the long tradition of adapting Halakhah (Jewish law) to changing circumstances.

Even among the more traditional Jewish thinkers, a need to explain their position has arisen. Rabbi Herschel Matt (1978) of the Conservative movement applied to homosexuals the Halakhah category of me'ones (uncontrollable compulsion), which allows violations

▼

of law by those unable to control their actions because of threat of punishment or temporary mental illness.

Typical of the Orthodox position was Norman Lamm (1974), president of Yeshiva University, who wrote an extensive responsum affirming the prohibition against homosexuality advocated in the biblical text, interpreting it as "morally repugnant" and a "grave sin." He could not find any support in Jewish religious terms for homosexual claims, which, in his view, reject the divine plan of human anatomy, family, and reproduction. Lamm, nevertheless, opposed any civil penalty for such behavior, invoking a psychological understanding of homosexuality as a disease in order to encourage compassion for its victims.

However, it is not only the biblical dictate of *to'evah* that made it so difficult for Jewish mainstream denominations to accommodate homosexuals among their ranks but as much the central position of the family in Jewish society and its ethos of reproduction. In the eyes of traditionalists homosexual men and women challenge the basic unit of the Jewish social fabric, often considered far more important than most other communal institutions, including the synagogue.[7]

These examinations have undergirded the public positions formally taken, in recent years, by the several branches of Judaism. Conservative Judaism's position was articulated in resolutions adopted by the Committee on Jewish Law and Standards of the Rabbinical Assembly in 1990 and 1992. The first, supporting tolerance, contains four points:

> (1) Support full civil equality for gays and lesbians in our national life. (2) Deplore the violence against gays and lesbians in our society. (3) . . . Gays and lesbians are welcome as members in our congregations. (4) Call upon our synagogues . . . to increase understanding and concern for our fellow Jews who are gays and lesbians.

The second, demarcating ritual participation, declares:

> (a) We will not perform commitment ceremonies for gays or lesbians. (b) We will not knowingly admit an avowed homosexual to our rabbinical or cantorial schools or to the Rabbinical Assembly or the Cantors' Assembly. . . . (c) Whether homosexuals may function as teachers or youth leaders in our congregations and schools will be left to the rabbi authorized to make

halakhic decisions. . . . (d) Similarly, the rabbi of each Conservative institution . . . will formulate policies regarding the eligibility of homosexuals for honors within worship and for lay leadership positions. (e) . . . Gays and lesbians are welcome in our congregations, youth groups, camps and schools.

In the Reform movement, the largest branch of Judaism,[8] the Union of American Hebrew Congregations (UAHC) General Assembly voted to support the Human Rights Bill for gays and lesbians in 1977. In a 1987 resolution, it declared that open lesbians and gays were fully accepted for membership and participation in Reform synagogues. And in 1990 the Central Conference of American Rabbis took the final step of declaring, in reference to its rabbinical school, "The written guidelines state the College-Institute considers sexual orientation of an applicant only within the context of a candidate's overall suitability for the rabbinate." (Although open gay and lesbian students are currently working toward ordination, for which they are eligible, their ultimate job prospects will depend on the willingness of congregations to hire them.) The movement has also admitted several gay synagogues to membership, including Beth Chayim Chadashim in Los Angeles.

The Reconstructionist movement—by far the smallest and least traditional—has for years supported open lesbians and gays, and a 1993 report by the Reconstructionist Commission on Homosexuality strongly endorses the full embrace of those who, it assumes, represent 7–8 percent of the American Jewish community. The report accepts gay and lesbian rabbis, supports rabbis who choose to officiate at same–gender commitment ceremonies, and encourages educational programs about issues relating to Judaism and homosexuality.

Among the institutions representing the Orthodox movement, Agudath Israel of America has publicly taken strong stands against the extension of nondiscrimination laws in New York City and New York State to gays and lesbians, as well as against the New York City school system teaching, in their view, "that all forms of personal lifestyle and interpersonal relationship share moral equivalence."[9] A phone call to the National Council of Young Israel requesting a public policy statement on homosexuality elicited the reply: "I don't want to waste a minute on that. There is a *passuk* [verse] in the Torah: it is an abomination!"[10]

▼

The Ethnography of Synagogues

For many generations the synagogue has represented the major institution of Jewish communal life. It has been the stage for social, political, cultural, and religious activity. The individual's achievements and failures were publicly announced in this forum. And those who broke away from the norms, beliefs, and aspirations of Jewish society were expelled or themselves departed from the synagogue.

The synagogue in traditional Jewish society has also upheld the ethos of family life by emphasizing the norms and expectations of adulthood and the continuity of generations. But the family, as an autonomous unit, has not had an institutional role per se in the synagogue. In America, however, new forms of Jewish worship and synagogue activity have evolved a new institutional role for the family. The Jewish Center movement, as first designed by Mordecai Kaplan, endowed the American Reform, Conservative, and Reconstructionist synagogue with social functions that co-opted many provided by the family and the traditional Jewish community. But that new organizational arrangement has not deprived the family of its central position. On the contrary, it has provided it with a new support system. As suggested by many observers, the American synagogue is far more than a center of religious activity; its scope includes entertainment, education for young and old, social activities, etc.[11]

Despite the significant number of Jewish anthropologists, and the voluminous published material in Jewish studies, the ethnographic literature on synagogues is quite limited. This is surprising given the central place that Glazer (1957) and other social scientists have ascribed to the synagogue in the totality of organized American Jewish life, and its centrality to Jewish identity. Liebman went so far as to claim that "pure Jewish secularism has no legitimacy in America" (1983:269).[12] Two ethnographies, however, are particularly pertinent for this study: Samuel Heilman's *Synagogue Life* (1973) and Riv-Ellen Prell's *Prayer and Community* (1989). They also make an interesting juxtaposition, having been based on observations made in the same period of the early 1970s, but in totally different settings: a Modern Orthodox synagogue and a Havurah minyan. Both institutions represent the evolution of American Jewry in recent generations.

Heilman defined his project in Goffman's interactionist tradition: "the study is more about behavior within a conveniently bordered and clearly defined setting, which just happens to be an Orthodox synagogue" (x). Wishing to prove that there is no institution that cannot be studied by modern sociological methodologies, Heilman, in fact, produced an important document on Jewish life in America.

Having to live close enough to the synagogue to walk to it on the Sabbath, Heilman's Orthodox congregants also experience each other as neighbors and friends, a social determinant absent in Conservative, Reform, and Reconstructionist congregations. Heilman explored the web of obligations and tributes, through which the entire membership is uniquely bonded, that also serves as a mechanism of social control. He found that this synagogue community was also the arena in which the congregants' identity in American society is molded, an identity with two foci: modernity and Orthodox Judaism. Heilman writes: "In a sense, one might describe that existence as one characterized by shifting involvements. . . . At any moment, the modern Orthodox Jew must be prepared to shift his involvement from the Orthodox Jewish to the modern secular world and vice versa" (266). Heilman concluded, however, that modernity was not yet threatening Orthodoxy, and that for the subjects of his study their ultimate identity was still their Jewish one.

The Havurah congregation Prell studied was part of a movement of small, informal, home-based prayer groups that dated from the founding of the first of these in Boston in 1968.[13] They reflected a disenchantment among educated, third-generation Jews with their successful parents' monumental, suburban—typically Reform or Conservative—synagogues, which were seen as imitations of mainstream Protestant American society. Prell writes: "The synagogue was expressive of Americanization and served as a bridge between worlds and a medium for formulating identity in part through decorum" (61). No longer needing confirmation of their Americaness, Havurah members sought greater participation and personal meaning in prayer through informal, face-to-face, gatherings that also provided a sense of true community.

Prell argued that the Havurah looked back to the European synagogue as a source for its Jewish heritage, but, in fact, her group shared little with Heilman's Modern Orthodox synagogue. Their differences probably accounted for the group's disintegration, which Prell recorded, as well as the movement's lack of viability as an independent offshoot: the informality, voluntary participation, liturgical inno-

▼

vation, and absence of social control were not prescriptions for institutional survival. Instead, during the 1980s, the Havurah style of informal, egalitarian worship was incorporated by many mainstream synagogues as an additional prayer gathering. Prell judged this not as a failure but as proof of the strength of American Judaism: protesting against its Americanization, Havurah members had reinvented Judaism and reaffirmed their unique identity as American Jews.

Heilman and Prell's ethnographies are interesting in and of themselves but they are also pertinent, in a number of respects, to the gay synagogue that is the subject of this study. Its founding in the early 1970s sets it in the same time frame as Heilman and Prell's research. The tension between intimacy and formality, volunteerism and institutionality reflected in the Havurah movement was frequently played out in the history of CBST. Both Havurah and CBST presented theological and social challenges to institutional Judaism, though with significant differences, however. Unlike the Havurah, the gay synagogue movement stood in direct confrontation to the family-based congregation to which all branches of Judaism were committed. But despite their challenge to the Jewish establishment—both Orthodox, and initially more liberal as well—CBST members did not share the Havurah's bitter rejection of their parents' synagogue "decorum," or institutional basis. As I shall describe in later chapters, they wanted to recreate and innovate Judaism, theologically and socially, but within the framework of a synagogue. Heilman's synagogue study is pertinent because not a few of the founders of CBST, as well as its core members, came from traditional Jewish backgrounds not unlike that of Heilman's congregation.

Homosexuality is absent from these ethnographies of the "sacred." It may be found, though not in abundance, among the ethnographies of the "profane."

The Ethnography of Homosexuality

The earliest ethnographically oriented studies of homosexuality were not undertaken by anthropologists, who—unlike their daring ancestors in the field, Malinowski and Margaret Mead, in particular—shied away from human sexuality,[14] but by groundbreaking sociologists and psychologists interested in "deviant behavior." This work of the 1960s and 1970s, pioneered by Evelyn Hooker (e.g., 1967) and followed by Hoffman (1968), Humphreys (1970), Warren (1974),

Plummer (1975), Delph (1978), Levine (1979), and others, focused on the furtive behavior of male homosexuals in their search for sex.[15] As Hoffman characterized it, "The need to manage information about one's deviant activity leads to much of the anonymous promiscuity of the gay world" (1968:179).

23

Among these works was the first full-fledged book on specific homosexual behavior, Laud Humphreys's audacious *Tearoom Trade* of 1970, an observation of the activity at a public toilet. Its microsociological approach to the study of nonverbal communication was rooted in the emerging methodology of Goffman's symbolic interactionism. As Lee Rainwater pointed out in the preface to his student's work, Humphreys did not attempt to analyze in any detail the personal meaning of the activity he observed. (Something Rainwater thought might be possible if the subjects were given sufficient assurance of anonymity.) Humphreys kept his own identity as a researcher secret throughout his study and rarely communicated with the "tearoom's" patrons about their life experiences. He did seek to learn more about his subjects by tracking them down through their license plate numbers and attempting to conduct interviews without acknowledging his earlier observation. He found that they came from all strata of society and could likely as not be the next-door neighbor, the loyal family man, or the churchgoer. Not being able to afford the price of acknowledging their homosexuality, "tearoom" sex was, in Humphreys's view, a rational solution.

Two years after *Tearoom Trade* Esther Newton published the first major anthropological work on gay life in America, *Mother Camp* (1972), which studied female impersonators. Newton's choice of that field revealed the special role of the drag queen in gay society: "The drag queen symbolizes all that homosexuals say they fear the most in themselves, all that they feel guilty about; he symbolizes, in fact, *the* stigma" (103).

Unlike Humphreys, Newton *was* able to penetrate the inner life of her subjects as well as explore the significance of the drag queen for its gay observers on emotional and symbolic levels.[16] Her work also touched upon issues of gay identity and communality. Meanwhile both sociologists and anthropologists continued to study the field of anonymous sex, expanding their purview beyond Humphreys's tearoom to cruising sites in parks, streets, bars, and, in particular, gay baths.[17] Delph, in *The Silent Community* (1978), analyzed this world

▼

of the "public eroticist," as he termed him, a world Rechy had portrayed in popular fiction (e.g., 1977). That tendency, however, was not out of tune with the view expressed by close observers (e.g., Adam 1992; Forrest 1994); for most gay men a sense of community has continuously been centered on the commercial scene, which expanded tremendously in the post-Stonewall period. Not surprisingly, Adam commented (1992:176) that the scene was also "presenting the best-known face of gay life to those least engaged with it."

In 1980 Kenneth Read, an anthropologist who made his reputation with previous work in New Guinea, published *Other Voices*, a major ethnographic study of a lower-class gay bar. While to my mind a remarkable piece of work, with its subtle presentation of what Read defined as "rituals of stigmatization" and "rites of intensification"—the gender jokes, games, and curses by which the patrons at once humiliate each other and reject the dominant culture's definition of gender—his field was so far removed from the mainstream gay urban experience as to be only marginally relevant. His bar, in a gay backwater, was populated by the socially and economically disadvantaged[18]—"failures," as Read termed them, in America's culture of achievement—who viewed gay liberationists as "freaks." His own work was also disadvantaged—doubly *retardataire*—by having been researched, and first drafted, many years before its publication, allowing him to claim "homosexuals seem the least likely to organize successfully on a national level" (5), or, "the 'bond' of male homosexuality is not associated with a complex of shared values, mores, and patterned ways of behavior that are subsumed . . . by the concept of 'culture' " (11).

In the introduction to his work Read made a confession that offers an insight into the development of gay studies in anthropology: the omission of his observation of homosexual practices from his earlier research in New Guinea.

> The gaps in my record of the Gahuku cannot be retrieved now and I advise skepticism in accepting my statement (Read 1955) that homosexual practices did not exist. . . . As a "legitimate" study, homosexuality remained the "vice without a name" . . . and even homosexual members of the profession, who might have been expected to be more aware than their straight colleagues, were prudently deeply closeted. (184–85)

If Read's portrayal of a gloomy gay existence energized mainly by the search for immediate sexual gratification did not have a wide impact, another New Guinea anthropologist's work a year later aroused great interest: Herdt's *Guardians of the Flutes* (1981). This fascinating and   25 acclaimed ethnography presented a strong case in favor of the social construction of sexuality, in general, and homosexuality, in particular. Starting at a young age and continuing until marriage, boys in the New Guinea Sambian[19] society engage in oral sex, but, rather than leading to adult homosexuals, this stage in a long rite of passage nurtures the development of an aggressive heterosexuality. Not only was Herdt's work provocative in its implication for the variable social meaning of homosexuality, but it revealed the evasive behavior of many researchers in New Guinea whose omission of this sexual phenomenon was now conspicuous. A growing number of anthropological studies of homosexuality among third world societies followed in Herdt's wake.[20]

A corresponding growth in gay ethnography, however, did not occur in contemporary American studies. Mains, not a professional anthropologist, but working in an ethnographic mode, published a study of the leather community in 1984; the leather and S&M world of the Mineshaft bar was later reconstructed by Brodsky (1993).

The major scholarly development in this era was not, in fact, in gay male studies, but in the emerging genre of lesbian ethnography. Deborah Wolf as early as 1979 had, somewhat gingerly, drawn a picture of the lesbian community in San Francisco. Krieger (1983) studied lesbian identity and community in a small Midwestern university town. Most recently, Kennedy and Davis (1993) published a major study of the growth of the lesbian community in Buffalo, exploring the evolutionary developments affecting lesbian identity and community formation (e.g., the emergence of lesbian bars in the 1940s; the appearance of a new butch style in the 1950s; the subsequent disappearance of butch-fem erotics, etc.). Regarding the construction of identity, the authors conclude that their data "suggest that lesbian identity is multiple and changes according to particular historical conditions" (384). Of community building, the authors demonstrate the important role of working-class lesbians in the development of an exclusive social space, the bar, around which a society could coalesce.

What does one make of this slim body of ethnographic work, begun late, dominated initially by sociologists and psychologists, and, in reference to males, rather narrowly focused on anonymous

▼

sexuality? Stephen Murray (1984) sees this as a reflection of the theoretical approaches dominant at the time. He attributes the initial avoidance of homosexual life as a research area to the functionalist sociological paradigm—and Parsonian theory in particular—which had little place for those groups that did not fit neatly into its construct of a harmonious social system. In Murray's view the breakdown of that theory in the face of the turbulent 1960s and 1970s opened the door to new theoretical perspectives and fields of research. Symbolic interactionism, in particular, with its research concentration on small units of anonymous behavior at once fostered studies of homosexual behavior and limited their scope.

Herdt (1992) has pointed out an important development in the field: "Scholars of 'homosexuality' are more and more gays or lesbians themselves" (5). But a review of the literature suggests that this has not led to a greater focus on ethnographic research in America, and my impression is that a number of these anthropologists have been drawn into studying the history of the gay movement, the politics of gay rights, and the crisis of AIDS. The last, in particular, has shifted interest and funds from traditional ethnographic projects to such applied research as how to change the sexual behavior of gay males or identifying the needs of persons with AIDS.[21]

Whatever the reason, no comprehensive community study of the lives of gay men has yet been produced. By the term *community study* I do not mean a traditional ethnography of a group of people who share a full life cycle system encompassing residence, work, sociability, spirituality, etc., but, borrowing from the community studies model, an exploration of the life experience of individuals and groups who share an institution or an activity in a way that presents them as fully acting personae.[22] I am not underestimating research in a bar, a bath, or a public toilet, but their masked actors have no past or present beyond their furtive search for sex. Except for Humphreys's method of tracking the "tearoom" patrons and interviewing them with a questionnaire unrelated to their covert life, most of the symbolic interactionist research completely lacked their subjects' voices. Though intending to demonstrate the humanity of homosexual behavior and, in fact, contributing immensely to our understanding of gay life, these studies left their subjects as one-dimensional sexual males, puppets in a shadow theater.

In the context of this literature a study of an institution—com-

posed of women and men—where sex is not the first agenda, and through whose evolving life the lives of its members are illuminated, may find a place. *Tearoom Trade* observed what seemed to represent an inner truth of gay life as performed in a space naked of the ele- 27
mentary forms of societal decorum and protocol. I posit that the attraction of gays and lesbians to the synagogue's sanctuary, a territory of exemplary decorum and prescribed conventions, is no less representative of an inner truth of their being.

Space and Identity: "The House of the New Theft"

In a number of the studies referred to above the nexus between social space, community, and identity was explored. This was clearly so in the lesbian community studies, but even in the gay male studies, which tended to focus on the codes of communication developed between strangers looking for company or sex, the meeting ground and excitement of the shared activity taking place there were increasingly perceived as promoting gay communality and identity.[23] Warren (1974:17) wrote, in almost Durkheimian style: "A community that is secret and stigmatized must quite literally have walls: places and times set apart from other places and times in which the community can celebrate itself." Delph's title, *The Silent Community*, refers to his belief that his "public eroticists" felt a sense of community with one another. Newton makes a similar point in her recent work, *Cherry Grove, Fire Island* (1993), which traces the history of that gay and lesbian enclave. Referring to the wooded area of anonymous male sex, the "Meat Rack," Newton writes:

> Sexuality stripped of social condition can foster *communitas*, the diffuse but powerful feeling of group solidarity transcending the usual social divides. In other words, group sex in the Rack, whatever else it was, was a powerful factor in the creation of gay nationalism. (184)

Newton's reference to nationalism raises the issue of the "ethnicity" of homosexuality. Under the influence of Foucault, who argued against identity politics, European gay scholars have tended to dismiss the idea of a "nationalism" based on a shared sexual orientation.[24] On the other hand, American gay scholars, anthropologists included, have been far more supportive of the claim of gay identity in terms close to that of ethnic representation. [25]

▼

The claim for public recognition of a gay and lesbian group identity has been a radical one, however—differing, as it does, from the
usual bases upon which group identity is legitimized in contemporary society: the primordial bonds of kinship, ethnicity, nationality,
and religion as well as the shared interests and sentiments of class,
ideology (e.g., political party), etc.

The "homelands" from which these claims were first forged and
advanced were the bars, the baths, and other locales that provided a
territorial basis and a relatively safe space for collective activities and
the experience of communitas.[26] In this context it was not surprising
that the spark of the gay rights movement, the "gay Bastille," was the
rebellion of a group of drag queens against the invasion of their territory, the Stonewall Bar, by the police.[27]

Important as they were to gay community and gay identity, however, these gay venues were defensively removed from legitimized,
mainstream territory. Bars and baths were particularly gay arenas.
That framing of gay spaces not only offered protected zones for acting out sexual desires but also bounded their participants' experiential realms from spilling over out of the gay into the nongay.[28] The
emergence of gay synagogues, as much as that of gay churches, signi-
fies a movement out of this physical and mental differentiation. For
while they embody a social segregation akin to other gay establishments, they symbolically represent a movement into what was heretofore deemed exclusively mainstream territory: institutionalized religion, and Judaism in particular. They represent, as well, a claim by
their participants to full status as moral personae. That this religious
co-optation marks an encroachment onto mainstream Judaism turf
can be sensed by the resistance to it contained in a letter to the editor
of the *Journal of Reform Judaism* written by Rabbi Jacob Petuchowski,
mockingly referring to the Los Angeles synagogue Beth Chayim
Chadashim as "Beth Gneva Chadasha," "House of the new theft"
(1985:125).[29]

By way of analogy I would point to the Gay Pride Parade, which is
New York City's second largest, and has proceeded uneventfully for
years down fifty blocks in the center of Manhattan. As powerful a
statement of gay power as this is, the occupation of the abandoned
Fifth Avenue on a Sunday afternoon does not impinge on the territorial and symbolic turf of particular constituencies. But when two
dozen Irish gays and lesbians ask to participate in the St. Patrick's Day

Parade, or CBST in the Salute to Israel Parade, the result is grand con-
sternation, threats of termination of the event by its sponsors, and
ultimate rejection.

As much as CBST represents a symbolic movement into new terri-   29
tory, to its core membership it may also suggest a new evolution in
gay identity. Much of the analysis of identity in the social science literature on homosexuality reviewed above—as well as in my own
work—is cast in terms of Goffman's concept of "stigma": members of
a group stigmatized by society tend to ghettoize themselves and adopt
that dimension of their existence as the major component of their
identity. Weeks, for example, argues that to say, "I am gay," "I am a lesbian" is "to privilege sexual identity over other identities, to say in
effect that how we see ourselves sexually is more important than class,
or racial, or professional loyalties" (1991:68). This view is shared by
others who maintain that gays often organize their self–identity
around their sexual identity.[30] However, for members of CBST—particularly those most deeply involved in it—the issue of identity may
be subtler and more complex. To what extent do the multiple identities implicit in the institution of a gay synagogue reflect themselves in
the members' own identities? Are these identities at odds, completely
compartmentalized, or complementary and mutually reinforcing?
These are issues to which this work is addressed.

My study of CBST may be defined in terms close to the interpretive
and symbolic traditions in anthropology. Since Durkheim, the study
of religion has observed the role of rituals and symbols as vehicles for
the invocation and display of cosmological ideas, social sentiments,
human dilemmas and needs. It has also come to recognize that these
rites have the power to effect behavior and transform social reality. I
intend to explore these ideas in a contemporary urban field, among a
group of men and women who have chosen to confront acute existential problems embedded in their "modern world" within the
framework of their ancestors' realm of primordial attachments, religious beliefs, and cultural sentiments.

Like Geertz's Balinese who, in his view, experience their cultural
ethos and private sensibility through a ceremonial event,[31] one could
suggest that the CBST congregants in this study, in a collectively sus-
tained symbolic structure, were addressing their unique existential
position and their innermost desires. But, following Victor Turner,
one could also posit that through this "ritual process"—all the reli-

▼

gious and social activities that are the content of our observations—the congregants were also creating a new social persona with a new type of communitas,[32] that of lesbian and gay American Jews.

This new persona, however, has never been a simple alloy of its Jewish and gay elements. As shall be seen, its blending was continually negotiated and debated in various synagogue arenas—from the bimah, in the social hall, in committees, at local restaurants, and private homes—anywhere feverish arguments could be waged: What is our special streak of Judaism? Where do we stand between ultra-Orthodox and Reconstructionist? Is the synagogue's ritual too traditional or too innovative? How much should the gay agenda be part of the liturgy? What is the policy on commitment ceremonies? Whom do we address first, a social or a religious community? These and many other "gay" versus "Jewish" dilemmas composed the discourse I witnessed, a discourse expressed at times in anger or in laughter, in tones of achievement or of disappointment.

CBST has changed greatly since its first days in 1973. It has changed even more since I completed my observation in 1991 (for example, the dramatic growth of the lesbian constituency). These transformations offer an indication of the ongoing process of both individual and communal identity formation. I hope my construction of the synagogue's past and present reality and my presentation of its members, its acting personae, constitute more than an outsider's personal perspective. I would like to believe that the ethnographer's voice, and his interpretive ambition, have not drowned out the voices of the women and men I was so anxious to know and understand from their own point of view.

In the previous chapter I explored the personal circumstances that led me to study CBST. But my choice of fieldwork in a gay synagogue, as well as the framework and style of ethnographic presentation, also reveal my reaction to the professional malaise displayed and experienced as one reviews the anthropological agenda of recent years (e.g., Stocking 1992; Shokeid 1992). Fieldwork—"the *sine qua non* both for the testing of theory and for making new discoveries" (Fortes 1978:24) or "a *sine qua non* for full status as an anthropologist" (Stocking 1992:13)—has considerably lost its magic and authority.

The ethnographic project, which for many decades energized the development of modern anthropology, has become the butt of deconstructionist fashion. Anthropologists seem to stand on trial, insecure patients at the mercy of enthusiastic doctors happy to devour their ethnographic texts and prove their empirical deficiencies and intellectual naïveté. That "postmodern" agenda claims authority from prestigious forums with cheering crowds at major professional events and publications. Why should smart young novice anthropologists waste their time and energy on a difficult but dubious journey erroneously intended to engage them in the life of other people, often remote from home and deprived of its comforts?

I take the risk of proclaiming again the great pleasure and the potential contribution of the ethnographic project when applied to novel fields that explore the human condition in remote societies or those closer to home. In spite of our shortcomings as participant observers and the temporality of the theoretical tools we employ, I believe that the anthropologist's task to introduce his or her fieldwork experiences and ethnographic narrative, in a vocabulary intelligible to wide audiences, still remains our major vocation. If not for that, who needs anthropology?

CHAPTER THREE

The History of CBST

The First Years: From Shopping Bag to Religious Committee

On February 8, 1973, a small classified ad appeared in the *Village Voice*:

GAY SYNAGOGUE
Friday Night Service and Oneg Shabbat
Feb. 9 at 8:00 PM,
360 West 28th street
(basement entrance)

As the evening of the service approached, Jacob Gubbay hurried home from work, excitedly gathered up candlesticks, siddurs and a few well-worn yarmulkas, and went off to find a challah. But here he hit a snag: he'd forgotten that being Shabbas, all the Jewish bakeries were closed. Just as he was about to give up, he remembered a little Italian grocer who kept a few challahs on hand for his Jewish customers. Now, with only minutes before the service was to begin, Jacob raced across town. . . .

The first evening went off beautifully. True, the religious aspect was a bit shaky. But what we lacked in know-how, we made up in spirit.

(Adapted from CBST's Eleventh Anniversary Show, February 1984)

Only ten people attended that first service—establishing what would ultimately become the largest gay synagogue in America—but their number "grew almost weekly." Those who lived through the early days tell a similar story of CBST's unlikely founder, Jacob Gubbay, a resident alien Indian Jew, whose daring was recalled in the 1984 Anniversary Show. On the way to placing his ad, a friend encounters him and warns:

33

"Look, you of all people should realize your position. I mean, you're from India, you know all about Untouchables. Well here, it's us gay people who are the Untouchables. I'm telling you, man, if the immigration department finds out you're gay, they'll put you on the first plane back to Bombay."

"I appreciate your concern, but I'm going through with it," Jacob replies.

"Okay. It's your funeral."

But if CBST celebrates his tenacity and credits its existence to his courage, Jacob Gubbay himself remains essentially a figure cloaked in mystery, an exotic Jew from outer space whose life is only dimly known. Among those who knew him Aaron could say little about Jacob's background beyond: "He was am ha'aretz [uneducated in Judaism], but he wanted gay Jews to have a place to pray." Pressed for more details he concluded, with characteristic mysticism: "God has all sorts of messengers."

Another early congregant provided the fullest portrait of this messenger in a reminiscence of CBST's founder:

I first met the founder of our synagogue [Jacob Gubbay] in early 1973 when I anxiously responded to an advertisement in the *Village Voice* announcing a Friday night Erev Shabbat service being held at the Church of the Holy Apostles on 29th Street. On my arrival, I was warmly greeted in the courtyard by a short, impish figure who had a sallow complexion, delightful smile and a marvelous Indian accent. He put me at ease immediately by his ingratiating manner and personal warmth.

Jacob explained to me that he decided to found the gay synagogue to answer the deep need of lesbian and gay Jews to daven [pray] to the G-d of Abraham and Sarah in their own secure and loving space.

I later learned that Jacob was the scion of the world-renowned

▼

philanthropic, Sephardic family of Gubbay-Sassoon, which originated in Baghdad and later flourished in Bombay, India.[1]

Describing the Episcopal church in which the fledgling synagogue met for the first two years, he continued: "In those early days we met in the kindergarten playroom of the Church Rectory and some of our members had no place to sit other than on tiny kiddy chairs!" Not only did the Church of the Holy Apostles provide sanctuary for the congregation, but in many respects the church itself was the genesis of the synagogue. The early congregant explained:

Jacob told me that originally the Church, especially the Pastor, Father Weeks, had graciously welcomed the Jewish gays and lesbians to their Christian services. . . . Later, a few Christian members felt there were too many Jews at the Sunday services and suggested the Jews conduct their own worship service. This inspired Jacob to place that unique advertisement and to subsequently schlep his famous shopping bag filled with two challahs, a kiddush cup, and Shabbes candleholders on those cold February nights.

About a year after founding CBST, Jacob Gubbay left New York and moved to Australia, where he attempted to form another gay synagogue.[2] As befits the progenitor in a myth of creation, little or nothing is known of his later life. If Jacob's departure did not have a profound effect on the collective memory of the synagogue, it was because another congregant, who had joined early on, had by then become the major figure in the synagogue, and would leave his mark on its ritual for many years to come.

Aaron, a good-looking man in his early thirties, had grown up in an Orthodox community in Brooklyn. He had undertaken advanced studies in a prestigious yeshiva and could have expected a successful rabbinical career. But he had come to realize these prospects could not accommodate a homosexuality of which he was increasingly aware and that he was unable to suppress. He had abandoned the yeshiva, enrolled in a liberal arts college, and sought the opportunities available in the gay world. But, as he told me many years later, he found he was uncomfortable with the sexuality he discovered in the bars, baths, parks, and other cruising grounds of the late 1960s and early 1970s. His search for a more compatible society brought him to the gay church. There he met his lover, who was active in religious affairs, and who encouraged Aaron to return to his own spiritual roots.

Aaron's personality and background perfectly suited the needs of CBST's fragile experiment. He had the education and training of an 35 Orthodox rabbi but the spirit and style of a Hasidic rebbe. Almost immediately, he was acknowledged the synagogue's spiritual leader. The Gentile lover of a leading congregant remembered: "When we joined the synagogue there was a very intimate atmosphere. The congregation was small. . . . The rabbi [Aaron] used to sit up front and it was his style which prevailed."

Everyone I met who had known Aaron spoke of him with unusual admiration, and praised the magical atmosphere of his services. One congregant described his impact:

> Aaron is a true rebbe. He extended the Sabbath service with songs and gaiety; we refused to let him go home. It was so wonderful, you thought you were alone in the world, the only homosexual on earth; then you got to the synagogue and saw these people of all ages happily engaged in prayers. I think at least 20 percent were not gay [but came because they were charmed by Aaron's service].

A younger man, who joined the synagogue after being thrown out of his parents' house when they discovered he was gay, similarly described the synagogue's first years: "In those days the synagogue was something extraordinary. Aaron had charisma and the synagogue had a special *heimish* [homelike, cozy] atmosphere. You came out from the reality of gay life in the bars, baths, and parks, and here was a sort of an extended family."

Aaron incorporated music, dance, and candlelight to imbue his services with a mystical atmosphere. Many congregants nostalgically recalled the communal dance that snaked through the dimly lit hall. The music that contributed to the enchantment initially included rock but was later replaced by Hasidic melodies and songs.

If I had any doubts about the congregants' memories of the mysticism of those Sabbath services, they were dispelled by looking at the first siddur (prayer book) Aaron compiled for CBST. In it Aaron prefaced the opening Friday evening prayer, Lecha Dodi, with a two-paragraph introduction entitled "Notes on the Dance." It begins:

▼

We welcome the Sabbath bride with dance as the mystics did in Safed of old. The Zohar [major thirteenth-century work of Jewish mysticism] teaches that immediately preceding the Barchu, the *nishama yiteira*, the additional soul, comes upon us. Only by making ourselves a proper receptacle will we feel and become aware of this spiritual gift. Our Dance then both welcomes the bride and prepares us for spiritual heights.

Further evidence of Aaron's rhetorical skill, as well as his charisma, is found in an excerpt from the invocation he delivered to the 1975 International Conference of the MCC Churches in Dallas:

Prayer is a verbal expression of the heart's condition. It can be a petition for deeply felt needs and also a declaration of truly felt joy. Let us do the second kind of prayer tonight, for all of us are part of a great miracle which has happened in the past few years and is still happening. Yes, we were afflicted for thousands of years . . . and then, we have witnessed a redemption no less wonderful than the deliverance from the Egyptian bondage of our ancestors.[3]

The president of the conference is quoted commenting: "he had never before heard a Hebrew brother preach like a Pentecostalist.' "

Aaron was not the only important member to join the synagogue during its first year. Two academics—Edward, a classicist, and Gilbert, a Bible scholar—in particular, assisted him in leading the congregation. Other early members went on to became active and influential in the synagogue's ritual and political affairs, remaining so as late as my arrival at CBST, sixteen years after its founding. But Aaron indelibly stamped the synagogue with his personality and the style of his religious leadership. In later years a few ordained Reform and Conservative rabbis joined the congregation as members, but they never gained the respect and affection bestowed upon Aaron. For many years Aaron was the only one who was ever deemed to be—and actually called—the synagogue's rabbi.[4] However, his Black gentile lover was less happy with *rebbetzin* (rabbi's wife), by which he was sometimes called. Nevertheless, he became an important part of the folklore surrounding the synagogue's early years. During the 1984 Anniversary Show the narrative of CBST's history continues:

At about the same time [as the first services begun by Jacob Gubbay], we had the good fortune to acquire a rabbi. And not just a rabbi, but an honest to goodness Hasid from Williamsburg. Complete with his own rebbetzin . . . well, sort of. Oy, what a reception we gave him!

Similar feelings of nostalgia and affection were expressed in the June 1989 *Gay Synagogue News*, which recalled the first time the synagogue participated in the Gay Pride Parade: "The following year [1974] about twenty of us bravely marched . . . up 6th Avenue. Our rabbi, Aaron, and his 'rebbetzin,' Johnny, were with us." 37

Those who had known him, described Aaron's lover as personable, helpful, and well-liked. That he came from a non-Jewish culture and was hence an "alien" befitted the myth of creation. The anomaly of his presence symbolized the anomaly of their project and their challenge to the Jewish establishment as well as the uncharted nature of the religious path they would trod. They no doubt took amused satisfaction in what one might call Jewish camp.

Those first years were remembered by the old-timers for their creativity. "Ideas were flying about," is how the first editor of *Gay Synagogue News* described it. Discovering their Judaism and homosexuality, many participants were also discovering each other through intimate relationships. "People were trying each other out." The feeling of creativity and intimacy was enhanced by the inclusion of additional foci of communal activity. Morris, an affluent and generous member, invited the congregants to take the Sabbath meal at his home after the Friday services—a happy conclusion to the evening's activities. Another member founded a Zionist *chug* (circle) that remained active until he immigrated to Israel. Hebrew sing-alongs were a popular activity. A Yiddish class, begun by a university teacher, attracted the core membership and effected close relationships between the participants.

These communal activities as well as the captivation of the services themselves, which Aaron conducted, drew new congregants to the synagogue. By the end of the first year CBST consisted of about fifty dedicated members. By the end of the second year membership had doubled, and the first issue of *Gay Synagogue News* (November 1974) already declared the urgent need for larger, permanent quarters for the quickly expanding congregation. Given this rapid expansion and level of activity, a move was inevitable.

In July 1975 this milestone was reached. The congregation moved from the Church of the Holy Apostles to its own leased quarters in the

▼

Westbeth Artists Complex, along the Hudson River in the West Village. *Gay Synagogue News* (July 1975) reported:

> Our new quarters will be about three times as large as the community room at the Holy Apostles, which we have so dramatically outgrown. . . . We will have exclusive, 24-hour-a-day use.
> . . . It was conceded that Westbeth constitutes a frontier between a fashionable residential area and a notorious cruising ground. . . . Blessed are you Lord, our God, King of the Universe, who has kept us alive and preserved us and enabled us to reach this season!

In 1977, when the congregation accepted the offer of a five-year lease on a larger space in the same complex, *Gay Synagogue News* could happily exclaim: "After forty years of wandering, the children of Israel reached the Promised Land. After only four years of wandering, our congregation has found a home."

The Westbeth Complex has remained the synagogue's home to this day. Although many members had hoped to see the synagogue one day move into a facility it owns—and considerable funds have been raised for that purpose—the favorable terms of its lease and other advantages of space and location have given the Westbeth address a sense of permanence. And after several renovations, a feeling of intimacy and comfort, as well.

Another important issue, which took a full year of deliberation, was finally settled in March 1978: the synagogue's name. According to the founders' story, Jacob Gubbay had, in fact, chosen the name "Torah V'Simcha" for the new congregation. This name makes a subtle reference to gayness, *simcha* being "happiness, gaiety, joy." The lawyer handling the synagogue's incorporation as a nonprofit organization, however, thought this name out of keeping with others, which typically include a reference to an institution. Acting on his own at the last minute, he transposed the original and came up with "Congregation Beth Simchat Torah" (House of gladness in the Torah). While grammatically correct, it became a source of embarrassment, as discussed in *Gay Synagogue News* of August 1977:

> *Simchat Torah* is the name of a holiday and shuls are not normally named after holidays. Many individuals both within our group and outside of it have questioned the name, laughed about it, and finally put it down to our ignorance of, or lack of

concern for, Jewish learning and Jewish tradition. . . . We do not want anyone to get the idea that gay Jews are ignorant Jews or are disdainful in their approach to Judaism.

As a congregant explained to me, "It's funny to name a synagogue after a holiday, imagine 'Beth Purim!' "

Faced with these doubts, the Board of Trustees decided to let the membership consider a name change. A committee was appointed to review alternatives and, from seventeen submitted, selected three to present to the congregation: "Shira Hadasha" (New song), "Orah V'Simcha" (Light and joy), and "Torah V'Simcha" (Torah and joy). But when the entire congregation finally met to make their selection, they voted overwhelmingly to keep the old name, Congregation Beth Simchat Torah.

> After a year of thought and discussion, some of those who at first favored a change decided that the concept of "gladness in the Torah" was appropriate after all, and that the negative reaction in the community had never been widespread, as far as we know. Our inability to choose from among the excellent alternative names suggested by different members also helped decide the issue (*Gay Synagogue News*, March 1978).

Why did the congregants retain the old name in spite of its strange, if not amusing, construction when they could easily have chosen a more poetic and respectable one? As much as they wished to accommodate and impress Jewish public opinion, that unusual name had become a symbol of their successful enterprise, unique precisely because of its strangeness. It had become an affectionate trademark too precious to give up only for the sake of respectability. The issue was never raised again.

But if, in the question of its name, the congregation ultimately opted for continuity, within a year an event occurred that marked a profound break in the history of the synagogue. Aaron, who had become so greatly identified with CBST, and whose personality and style had stamped it, left the congregation, closing the chapter one might entitle "The Myth of Creation."

Was Aaron rejected by the lay leadership that had gradually gained power in running the synagogue? Had he become out of tune with the religious expectations and social aspirations of the rank and file in a rapidly expanding congregation? Was Aaron himself disenchanted

39

▼

with his own creation? The various explanations for Aaron's departure typically combine all these suggestions. It seems, however, that the major impetus for Aaron's withdrawal was the spiritual transformation he himself had undergone.

Aaron's arrival at the synagogue was the beginning of a process that eventually brought him back to Orthodoxy. But as he was gradually changing he hoped to move the congregation with him by exposing it to the wealth of Jewish tradition and the importance of fulfilling the mitzvot (commandments). The changes he sought were both in the institutional ritual of CBST and in the lives of its members.

An indication of Aaron's thinking is contained in a plea made to the congregation at the conclusion of a sermon a year and a half before his departure:

> It is to the danger of stagnation and ultimate descent that we, at CBST, must turn our thoughts. Almost all of us went through a period of exhilaration during our first few years in the shul. We rediscovered our Judaism. We committed ourselves, with qualifications, to a Friday night Shabbat. . . . How do we move from the non-demanding bourgeois religion to vital Yiddishkeit? How do we create a Jewish community worthy of its name? What can our community do to re-ignite the *pintele Yid* [the seed of Jewishness] in our souls? (*Synagogue News*, August 1977).

Aaron always emphasized this desire to create a community at CBST that would stand in contrast to the cruising scenes of gay life. However, his conception of community was from the very start intertwined with his evolving concept of Judaism. He told me frankly, "I had a vision of a community whose Judaism I could be comfortable with."

Three months later the November 1977 issue of the *Synagogue News* announced the introduction of a new Sabbath service, 10:30 A.M. the first Saturday morning of each month: "The tone will be intimate and joyous . . . with singing, reading, and a Torah service. At 12:00 noon, we will share a Shabbat kiddush."

But the attendance at the monthly Sabbath service never grew beyond a small group of dedicated congregants and occasional visitors. It rarely numbered more than fifteen men and women and often fell short of a minyan (quorum of ten).

Aaron considered his inability to attract a larger constituency for this service a major failure, one reflecting on the congregants as well. He felt that the Friday evening service attracted a large crowd because it fit in with the members' social routine. "But who is cruising on a Saturday morning?" In the same vein, he complained that while he was wrestling with the challenge of maintaining a steady participation in the shul's religious activities and a growing commitment to Judaism, the congregants were exchanging notes on the number of "tricks" they had had since they last met.

Aaron was opposed in the direction he wished to move the synagogue by the lay leadership. He told me about his falling out with Morris. Morris, who retained a leading position at CBST even as he emerged as a prominent figure in New York's gay community, was equally dedicated to the idea of a synagogue community, which he saw as a substitute for the family many congregants had lost. He promoted the tradition of congregational dinners and coined the phrase "a family that eats together cleans together," which became a motto for the synagogue's communal aspirations, suggesting the mutual obligations between members of an extended family. But Morris's perception of a community was basically secular. Judaism in his view was a common bond, a basis for comfortable sociability and shared spirituality but not a goal in itself. When he discovered that one of his favorite congregants had, under Aaron's influence, begun to strictly observe Sabbath rules and regulations, he was alarmed, and reacted—in Aaron's words—as if he had lost a son.

To Leon, chairman of the Board of Trustees, Aaron had become a liability to the synagogue's development. Leon argued that at that time it was almost impossible to exist at once in both the gay and traditional Jewish worlds: "Being gay was not Jewish. For the Jewish world, you had to be straight looking; for the gay world, we couldn't look and speak like Aaron with his 'Brooklyn' style. We moved to mainstream Judaism in order to satisfy the gay community."

This viewpoint was echoed by a young man who hadn't witnessed the events, but told me: "The rabbi was very authoritative and he finally left with all those who wanted a *shtiebel* [a small traditional synagogue]." Dov, who was present at the time and remained close to Aaron, came to the same conclusion: Aaron was moving in the direction of a *shtiebel*.

▼

While the frustration at being unable to move the congregation with him, and his lack of support from the board, contributed to Aaron's decision, both he and others cited a specific disagreement that precipitated his departure: when to light the Sabbath candles. Aaron asked to have the candles lit on Friday afternoon just before the start of the Sabbath at sundown. But the congregants wished to observe this ceremony, even though its performance later in the service was a violation of Orthodox Sabbath rules. Aaron told me there was no objection to his own growing Orthodoxy, "because it was okay for the rabbi," but not so for the synagogue. His request was denied.

According to Leon, he went to see Aaron in his apartment and tried to resolve the situation. Aaron told him he loved the synagogue, which had helped him to find his identity, but was not satisfied with it any longer. Leon, on his part, explained that the congregants were also anxious to see changes, but not in the direction of growing traditionalism. "It was clear—Aaron had to leave!"

Aaron, on his part, was not interested in a fight. On the contrary, it had become apparent that he was on the verge of a new beginning, one reflected in his personal life as well. He had separated from his Gentile lover and become involved in what was to be a long-term relationship with an Orthodox man. His life changed completely as he fully conformed to the rituals of Orthodox Judaism.

The January 1979 *Synagogue News* opened with the announcement: "After over five years of serving as our dedicated (and unpaid) spiritual leader . . . Aaron has relinquished some of his responsibilities for religious and ritual affairs. . . . The Board of Trustees has created a Ritual Committee with Larry as Interim Chairperson."

Aaron ceased to lead, or even attend, services at CBST. He did continue as teacher of the Talmud class he had established in 1973, and has conducted its Tuesday meetings to this day.

To some Aaron's departure was an untimely end to an era of intimacy in the synagogue's short history. A member whose departure followed Aaron's commented: "Since Aaron left I could not come again. We are a lost people." Another congregant lamented: "When Aaron left it was never the same again. Whenever I drive close to the church on 28th Street I feel a sharp pain in my stomach." (The report of a strong emotional and even physical reaction to the site of the early synagogue was not uncommon among CBST veterans.) But Edward, among Aaron's closest friends, was able to observe the changes at CBST more critically, as stages in an evolutionary process:

Aaron's appearance had perfectly suited the spirit of revivalism of those days. He was not a Hasid, but he was attuned to their spirit with the atmosphere of dance and music that he introduced. Everybody joined in and danced enthusiastically. Although efforts were made to keep it going after Aaron left, it couldn't really work any longer. The crowd was too big, the congregation became too bourgeois, and people were too embarrassed to join the circle of dancers. Many were just watching.

Edward believed, however, as do many others, that the synagogue still maintains much of the tradition, the customs, and the spirit Aaron implanted and nurtured.

Nevertheless, with Aaron's departure a new era began at CBST. As the newsletter announced, the board created a Religious Committee (as the Ritual Committee became known) composed of volunteers. The Religious Committee was responsible to the board and had limited autonomy. The committee chair, who was elected by its members, did not sit on the synagogue's board. Rather the board appointed one of its own as liaison to the Religious Committee. That arrangement demonstrated the board's intention to retain ultimate authority over religious matters and was a source of friction between the board and committee.

To my question of how he could envision the synagogue's functioning without Aaron, Leon told me triumphantly: "Larry was my hidden ace. He was already doing all the work for Aaron, and there were other active participants who could help him take over Aaron's job." The new Religious Committee was open to all who considered themselves able to serve, and of the initial fourteen members a few were Aaron's disciples. But Simon soon became a dominant force on the committee, conducting the Passover Seder and High Holiday services. His bid for religious leadership was helped by his close friendship with Gilbert, who was an expert in Jewish Studies and became a popular cantor and service leader. Simon described his own style as "humanistic-rationalistic" as opposed to Aaron's "mystical" one. But Simon, whose religious education was eclectic, lacked Aaron's yeshiva background and never achieved Aaron's spiritual authority or his uncontested monopoly in religious affairs. He shared, for instance,

43

▼

the role of drashah speaker at Friday services with other members of the committee. And his position could best be described as first among equals.

Before his departure Aaron had begun to compile a siddur, the basic prayer book for the Friday services. The need for an authoritative text that would express the congregants' special existential concerns yet preserve the crucial elements of a traditional prayer book now became particularly urgent. Simon's persuasiveness and ability to compile the vast materials involved are credited for the completion of this major text, which was introduced in May 1981, and continues to be in regular use.

Struggling with Growth: The Community Development Committee

By the end of the 1970s CBST was one of the strongest gay organizations in New York and a leading member in the expanding network of gay congregations in the United States. Its internal organization had undergone profound changes since its inception by the enigmatic Jacob Gubbay. Until Aaron's departure the synagogue functioned as a partnership between a charismatic spiritual leader and the skilled management of talented volunteers. The creation of the Religious Committee to replace Aaron's unique position marked a major step in the bureaucratization of the synagogue. However, the completion of this "routinization" process of the religious leadership at CBST occurred only after an additional stage of transformation carried out through what became known as the Community Development Committee.

Early in 1982 a few leading members initiated a program that was meant to change the character of the social relationships in the synagogue. To quote from a letter written in March 1982 by Joel, one of those involved:

An effort has to be made to create a dialogue with those who are called the synagogue family, all of them. A means should be created where everyone may be truly informed and truly have the opportunity to express the needs that they wish to have fulfilled from the synagogue. . . . As a teacher I have found that a class is more successful if the teacher listens, and we need to develop means of listening. I also know that many need to learn how to listen without becoming defensive.

This wish to change the style of communication among the congregants, to increase participation, to democratize decision making,
and to create a true communal family might not have become part of
official policy had it not been for one committee member's persistence. Though he never held an elected position, Harvey enjoyed the
congregation's respect for his eloquence and generosity. He suggested
employing a psychologist for the purpose of community development training, an idea prompted by his meeting a professional who
seemed particularly suited to that task. The candidate was a theologically trained, gay psychotherapist and a former Episcopal priest.

Writing to him on behalf of an ad hoc body, drawn principally
from the Religious Committee and formed to explore the idea of community development, Harvey set out the group's goals:

> To bring ourselves closer to each other. We understand that we
> cannot go back to an earlier stage of development as a commu-
> nity, though many of us actively wish we could go back to those
> warm days. However, we want: To explore the possibility and
> the ways of recapturing some of those desirable earlier qualities
> of warm fellowship. To reduce the gap—or the perception of a
> gap—between our formal and informal leaders, on the one
> hand, and on the other, our members and visitors who feel left
> out.

Harvey's long letter emphasized the need to develop a comfortable,
participatory, social environment; a more efficient organization was a
lesser concern.

In his response the candidate proposed that a consultation committee be appointed with members selected by the board and volunteers from the congregation. After working together intensively members of this core group could then branch out and organize discussion
groups among the wider congregation. With the strong support of the
ad hoc committee, this proposal was accepted by the board chaired
by Morris and the project begun.

Whatever its consequences, the community development project
formed a communal rite of passage. The core of active members, in
particular, went through an intensive period of self-searching, strip-
ping off their personal positions of leadership by revealing their inner
feelings in front of their fellow members and exposing their status in
the synagogue to challenge.

▼

For nearly a year the eleven-member Community Development Committee (composed of ten men and one woman), as it was finally called, met regularly at the synagogue or at members' homes for long and hectic sessions. Various communal and personal issues related to the synagogue's life were openly presented and analyzed. The majority of its members were from among the synagogue's "formal" and "informal" leaders. Among the first dramatic developments was a critical review of Morris's and Simon's leadership styles. An echo of these emotional discussions is found in a letter sent to Simon by another member:

> Yesterday, during the late afternoon, when the group's attention turned to your role on the Religious Committee, I, at one point, saw hurt in your eyes. . . . I guess I was upset because you, perhaps more than anyone else in the synagogue, have encouraged me to become involved and to participate. . . . I hope you won't, as Morris unfortunately has, let what others say bother you. . . . Finally, I just want you to know how happy I am that we are working together on so important a project as community development.

That encounter group self-examination was no doubt painful for some of the participants, but the feeling of intimacy that united them and the sense of urgency in their mission may have compensated for its discomfort. Both the effort and urgency can be sensed in the secretary's report to the committee in October 1982:

> By now, hopefully, you have recovered from Sunday's meeting. Out of that meeting came some very important insights, including the following:
>
> THE SYNAGOGUE ORGANIZATIONAL/COMMITTEE STRUCTURE DOES NOT WORK AS WELL AS IT COULD/SHOULD BE WORKING. . . . WE ARE SEARCHING FOR A BALANCE BETWEEN STRUCTURE AND CRE-ATIVITY.

In December 1982 the entire congregation was invited to attend a meeting at which they could choose from among ten sessions to be held at different locations. Each session was to be led by two members of the Community Development Committee. Its purpose was "gathering information about your perceptions and needs in order to help you, us (the Development Committee) and the Board of Trustees truly plan for the future."

The information gathered from the one hundred members—a third of the congregation—who participated in these discussion groups was compiled and reported to the board. The board subsequently made two concrete changes in the synagogue's organization: restructuring the Religious Committee and expanding the board itself.

47

Instead of being open to anyone who wanted to join, the Religious Committee was limited to five members (later expanded to seven) chosen for their expertise. This was less than half its then current number. Although smaller in number, the belief was that a group of experts could better respond to the congregants' religious needs. This view was reflected in a Community Development Committee flier proclaiming the change: "The Religious Committee is restructuring itself to make the religious life of CBST more responsive to our members and to actively increase our members' participation in the process."

The Board of Trustees was expanded from seven to ten members, each limited to two consecutive two-year terms. Each member was made responsible for a distinct area of the synagogue's affairs, corresponding to one of seven established standing committees: communication, education, events and activities, finance, house, membership, and ritual affairs. To the offices of chair and secretary were now added the vice-chair and treasurer. Reporting the congregation's adoption of its new bylaws, the Synagogue News of February 1984 commented: "These exciting changes are the direct result of your input to the Community Development Committee through a series of discussion groups last year."

These organizational changes were seen as opening up the synagogue to greater participation and instilling a feeling that the leadership should represent the wider constituency—despite the fact that most of CBST's leading figures continued to hold positions in the synagogue. Simon, who was among the initiators of the project, went so far as to declare that the old leadership was ousted: "It became clear that people wanted a new style with many participants!" One of these new participants was Joel, who was first recruited to the development committee from the general congregation and remained very active thereafter. He commented: "When I first joined the synagogue, a small group did everything. But since then, it was decided to expand the board to add officers and develop the functioning of committees."

▼

Larry corroborated this view of the congregants' wider involvement: "In any other synagogue you wouldn't find forty or fifty active members, including service leaders, cantors, and drashah speakers. In other synagogues they leave all this to the rabbi."

But if the Community Development Committee resulted in structural changes, it could not recapture the feelings of closeness and shared intimacy of the cherished founding days when, as Larry put it, "we were more social; we were close-knit."

Almost ten years after the synagogue's founding the leadership had been ready to evaluate its own performance and the quality of communal life at CBST. They had employed the techniques of modern behavioral sciences in an attempt to recreate the feeling of communitas experienced during the synagogue's first years, but, inevitably, the expansion the congregation had undergone precluded this return. By now there were over three hundred members. CBST was no longer a small intimate group of dedicated volunteers but a growing organization that had gained a considerable reputation in American gay life as well. Ironically, the most significant result of the Community Development Committee was the enhancement of the process of bureaucratization at CBST.

Reaching Out

Not only did the congregation expand from a few hundred in the early 1980s to over a thousand registered members by 1991—many of its most active members became involved in community affairs beyond the synagogue's confines. Most notably, Morris founded the Lesbian and Gay Community Services Center in New York, the first of its kind, and emerged as CBST's most prominent leader in the gay community. Though they had little relevance to the synagogue's daily life, Morris's activities were, nonetheless, a source of pride to the congregants, who believed the synagogue was the training ground for his later accomplishments. Other leading members received public notice, as well, for their contribution to various gay institutions.

CBST itself was instrumental in founding both national and international gay Jewish organizations. In December 1975, following the United Nations' declaration that Zionism was a form of racism, CBST hosted an emergency conference attended by representatives of other gay Jewish groups in North America. This was soon transformed into a permanent alliance. In February 1976 representatives of four congregations met in Washington. Leon, who represented CBST, became secretary of this growing organization of synagogues, whose gatherings were called the International Conference of Gay Jews, and was active in subsequent regional and world gay Jewish forums.   49

The International Conference of Gay Jews held in Washington in August 1976 was attended by nearly thirty representatives from six congregations in the United States, two in Canada, and one in London. CBST was represented by four delegates. The CBST newsletter commented:

Communication among all our groups has been limited in the four and a half years since the foundation of the L.A. temple. At this point in history, however, the scattered groups of gay Jews, determined to be positively Jewish and positively gay, have begun reaching out to each other for mutual encouragement and support.

The various congregations did not always take the same position on major issues. For example, the delegate from Chicago described his group's effort to write a new translation of the Sabbath liturgy with a view to embracing the concerns of gay people in each prayer. Other delegates felt they could easily relate to most of the traditional formulations and that fidelity to them served Jewish unity, a position representing that of CBST.

In April 1977 CBST itself hosted the International Conference of Gay Jews. In the newsletter that preceded the meeting Aaron described its significance in his characteristic style: "Despite our varying viewpoints on many matters, a very important and a united statement is being made just by our coming together. *We gay Jews are loyal to our ancient heritage.* This statement is a Kiddush Hashem, a sanctification of God's name."

Other congregants became active in this movement as well. One CBST leader became executive director of the World Congress of Gay and Lesbian Jewish Organizations in Washington, a permanent umbrella group, created in 1980, that grew out of these yearly conferences and alliances.

Reaching out to the nongay Jewish community became a major theme in the ideological and social agenda of CBST. Though often met with disappointment and frustration, these efforts were never abandoned. Representatives of CBST were always available for interviews in

▼

all channels of communication: radio, television, newspapers, symposiums, and lectures. In a 1979 radio program, for example, one congregant appealed for a return to "Ahavas Yisroel," love of one's fellow Jew, in place of the taboolike horror with which many traditional Jews regard Jewish homosexuals. A second speaker explained how the synagogue reinforced the attachment of many gay Jews to the Jewish community "in contrast to the misleading label of *outsider* that is sometimes attached to us." Although in later years the debate carried a more militant tone compared to these somewhat defensive pleas, the speakers were always anxious to preserve a dialogue rather than risk confrontation.

Over the years the synagogue has made significant contributions to various Jewish charities, the UJA in particular. Though its money was always accepted, its special identity was not openly acknowledged. Nevertheless, these contributions have been important to the congregation's sense of itself as a part of organized Jewry. That feeling was expressed by Martin in a 1989 interview with *Synagogue News*, following a provocative article he had written for the *Jewish Week* in which he attacked the Jewish establishment for its denial, indifference, and hypocrisy concerning AIDS and the suffering of homosexuals in contemporary society:

> We can't shut ourselves up in our own little gay and lesbian synagogue because the rest of the Jewish world feels uncomfortable with us. We're part of the Jewish world and should have a voice in it. After all, they accept our money when we give it, even if they find it difficult to acknowledge.

The International Conference of Gay Jews experienced this dual treatment as well when in 1979 the Jewish National Fund refused to mark the woodland the conference had underwritten in Israel with a plaque identifying the donors. The conference refused the offer of a plaque that concealed its identity but did not request its money back. CBST's delegates introduced a resolution, which the conference adopted, demanding that a blank plaque be installed in the woodland "until such time as the JNF (Israel) agrees to install the plaque with the inscription 'International Conference of Gay and Lesbian Jews.' " A plaque acknowledging the donors was finally installed thirteen years later, in 1992.

Despite this humiliation and the failure of gays in Israel generally to reap the rewards of gay liberation, identification with Israel has been a consistent element of CBST. The Zionist circle begun in late 1977 remained an active organ for many years, hosting speakers from the United States and Israel. Its major achievement, however, was in encouraging members to live for a while in Israel, or even emigrate. Among the latter was the editor of *Synagogue News*, who wrote of his and his lover's plans:

51

> Few people have gotten as much from the *shul* as I have. A lover, good friends, an introduction to Judaism in a serious way. . . . My entire life has been immeasurably enriched. And now it's being further changed, by our move to Israel, which would not be happening without the inspiration of five years of worship at the *shul*.

In addition to support for Israel the congregation participated in demonstrations initiated by major American Jewish organizations to secure the release of Jews in Russia and Ethiopia. In fact, there was no issue of Jewish public concern—unless initiated by the ultra-Orthodox—that was not supported by the synagogue's leadership. In participating in these events, for many years,[5] the congregants avoided antagonizing their mainstream brethren. The large banner that they carried identified the organization simply as "Congregation Beth Simchat Torah."

While it was reaching out to the nongay world of organized Judaism—and forming alliances with other gay Jewish institutions—CBST was also building ties to secular gay and straight society. Through the special contribution of Morris, in particular, the synagogue became closely associated with the network of gay organizations in New York. So much so that when in 1990 the synagogue received a Torah scroll that had survived the Holocaust, the dedication ceremony began in the Lesbian and Gay Community Services Center on West 13th Street. The speakers included representatives of both the governor and the mayor. From there the Torah procession moved on to the synagogue, where the dignitaries repeated their speeches.

The synagogue's participation in the annual Gay Pride Parade has vividly demonstrated its integration into New York's gay community. More than fifty members have regularly represented the synagogue each year, carrying a large banner and Israeli flags, dancing and

▼

singing along the parade route down Fifth Avenue and through the Village. In recent years the group was led by a van decorated with CBST and Jewish symbols and a tape cassette playing Israeli and Hasidic songs. The event has been preceded by a Gay Pride Dance at the synagogue, jointly sponsored by Dignity New York, a gay Catholic group.

The speakers who addressed the synagogue, particularly during the annual celebrations of its founding and during Gay Pride Week, have included Mayors Koch and Dinkins, congressmen, judges, and state and city officials. The synagogue has made its space available to community and neighborhood associations—gay and straight—as well as dinners and parties sponsored by SAGE (senior gays and lesbians). Its premises are an official polling place for city, state, and national elections. In recent years the synagogue has sponsored an antiques show, open to the public, with rent collected from participating dealers donated to people with AIDS. The synagogue was not a hidden space frequented by anonymous visitors but a visible establishment often open to the surrounding community.

From Voluntarism to Professionalism: The Search for an Ordained Rabbi

It was only five years after the reorganization resulting from the Community Development Committee that the leadership felt compelled to once again address the institutional needs of its growing congregation. In the *Synagogue News*'s Sixteenth Anniversary issue of February 1989, both Morris and Larry, past board chairs, expressed a similar wish for a more formalized and professional structure: "Our synagogue structure (all volunteer) was planned for a two hundred-member congregation. Our growth to nearly one thousand members is straining our original organized plan," were Morris's words.

Larry presented a much clearer position: "In many ways, we still operate the synagogue as it was in 1974 with a larger [and many times overworked and tired] volunteer staff. . . . We need to become more professional in our operations." By then there had been suggestions that the synagogue hire an executive director, a bookkeeper, and an accountant. A few months later Saul, the new chair, declared the board's wish to "take CBST into the nineties" and its decision to appoint a committee to study the pros and cons of hiring a full-time staff, in the interests of "professionalism."

In contrast with the original intention of the community development project, which was to increase volunteer participation and
revive the lost feeling of intimacy, new winds were driving CBST
toward greater efficiency. With membership close to the milestone of   53
one thousand, the desire for communitas could no longer be realisti-
cally entertained. The first years of the synagogue had ultimately
become a creation myth appropriate for theatrical presentation at the
anniversary celebration but no longer a model for synagogue life.
"We're no longer the shopping bag synagogue," was the way Saul,
board chair, put it in 1989, evoking the image of Jacob Gubbay with
his candlesticks, siddurs, and yarmulkes rushing to the synagogue.
During Saul's administration, he was able get approval for the hiring
of two part-time employees: an office administrator and a bookkeeper. Looking to the future, he suggested that his successor consider the possibility of hiring a rabbi and affiliating with a mainstream
movement.

The hiring of salaried personnel also reflected the growing affluence of the synagogue. For many years the annual dues had been
extremely modest in order to keep the synagogue's doors open to all
who wished to join. The low membership dues, which until 1991
were under $100, were a permanent source of pride to the congre-
gants and often compared with what they considered the exorbitant
fees at mainstream temples. The operation of the synagogue was
mainly dependent on the generous contributions made at the annual
appeal during the High Holidays. During the 1980s the annual appeal
goals became more ambitious, as first expressed in the *Synagogue
News* of March 1980: "Our budget grew quite a lot—from several
hundreds the first year to $34,000 this year. Those of you who were
here in the beginning will remember that we started with one coffee
urn and a metal storage cabinet on 28th Street."

The synagogue's assets also included the Premises Trust Fund,
which by 1982 totalled $42,000. While not giving up the dream of
one day purchasing their own building, the leadership began an
extensive renovation of the synagogue's space from 1989 to 1991.
During the High Holiday appeal the congregants were entitled to allocate a part of their pledge to the renovation. The synagogue's "face-
lift" was a visible sign of their communal success.

Martin, the next chair, personally had no doubt the congregation
needed a full-time rabbi. He bolstered this view with a report by the

▼

committee appointed by the previous chair that had come to the same conclusion. His position was supported by the board, which voted unanimously in May 1990 to hire a rabbi, pending congregational approval in open discussions. The decision to involve the congregation through public discussions but not a plebiscite, whether a calculated policy or not, actually left the board with the final authority. At the same meeting the board voted not to affiliate with any of the three movements conceivable (the Conservative, Reform, or Reconstructionist) at that time.

The decision to begin the process of hiring a rabbi was the most dramatic development since Aaron's departure. Aaron had been considered, for all practical purposes, "our rabbi." But he had voluntarily emerged from the congregation. Although he had exercised considerable authority in religious affairs and influence on the synagogue's social life, he was, nevertheless, part of a volunteer organization. The formal appointment of a rabbi meant a profound change in the character of CBST, not only from the days of Aaron's leadership but even more so from the many years of a lay-led congregation that followed Aaron's departure.

Martin explained a number of reasons why a rabbi was urgently needed. The AIDS crisis created a need for pastoral counseling, hospital visits, funerals, and shiva minyans (mourning services) that the Religious Committee could not adequately provide. There was also the growing demand for commitment ceremonies and the rituals for newborn children. Another important issue was the lack of direction in the synagogue's educational program and the troubling inconsistency in the style and quality of services. Martin declared: "The two words which answer the above unmet needs is spiritual leadership." Martin went on to say that another need that might be met was for a spokesperson for the synagogue: "Our rabbi will take his or her place among the rabbinic leadership of the city, thereby representing our viewpoint and needs to the larger lay and rabbinic Jewish community" (*Synagogue News*, July/August 1990).

I attended two of the three public meetings scheduled to discuss the hiring of a rabbi. The meetings that took place during the summer months attracted a small audience. Those who participated in the discussion were mostly critical of the prospect of change in the synagogue's management. Their doubts expressed a wide variety of concerns. People were worried about the loss of autonomy, the inevitable pressure to compromise with a rabbi's dictates, and the suppression of the diversity so prominent in their congregation. They questioned whether the rabbi would be male or female, straight or gay, Conservative, Reform, or Reconstructionist. Wouldn't a social worker better meet the congregants' counseling needs in the time of AIDS? Wouldn't a part-time rabbi be sufficient to fulfill pastoral requirements yet avoid a revision of the synagogue's style of voluntary participation?

55

The strongest opposition was voiced by Carol, who was known for the learned sermons she often presented from a powerful feminist perspective. She did not advocate the choice of a female rabbi, as had Sara, a frequent contributor to the *Synagogue News*, but resented the whole idea of hiring a rabbi. A rabbi would only create divisions in a synagogue as diverse as CBST. In other synagogues, she argued, people at least have some common expectations, because of their shared association with a particular theological movement, which was not the case at CBST: "What we really need is someone to lighten our administrative load and a part-time religious social worker to visit the sick. These we need right now, not in August, 1991. We have rabbis in the congregation. Why not a registry of rabbis who would officiate at ceremonies when one is desired?"

Joel, who was active in religious affairs and had served as chair of the Religious Committee, was opposed to hiring a rabbi, but believed the board would go ahead with its decision regardless of the opposition, hearing only the voices agreeing with their own position. He felt that those who wanted a rabbi were seeking legitimacy for the synagogue: "It looks good." In arguing against it, he emphasized the special loyalty of CBST congregants: "We don't need a spiritual leader. Our people are dedicated to the synagogue, to the organization. If we appoint a rabbi, they would be dedicated instead to the rabbi, as it happens in many synagogues." Joel, like Carol, was also concerned about the inevitability of conflict that would follow the appointment of a rabbi. As another member observed: "We manage to operate through a very delicate balance which preserves a consensus. A strong rabbi will break it; a weak rabbi, we'll eat him." Another member added: "A rabbi is the synagogue's leader. I have already left two synagogues because I couldn't stand the rabbi. Are we insured against a failure?"

Joel, Carol, and other opponents felt that CBST had broad appeal because new members were not scrutinized according to their adherence to a particular branch of Judaism and level of observance. They

▼

feared that, inevitably, a rabbi trained and affiliated with a particular movement would impose his or her definition on this open-ended congregation. The board's representatives during the discussions tried to convince the participants that this would not be so, nor would the rabbi interfere with the existing style of their lay-led organization, but would mainly help improve the service leaders' skills. The board's decision not to join a major movement from among the Jewish mainstream establishment was another ِuarantee promised during the discussions against a theological commitment on the part of the rabbi. It was an attempt to allay the fears expressed by one participant who warned that joining a movement "would narrow our focus and have a chilling effect."

The defensive arguments offered by the board, suggesting a limited rabbinical role, encouraged those who felt that a part-time rabbi would be sufficient. But Saul, the former chair, stood up against that idea and emphatically declared, "We have reached maturity, we need a full-time rabbi. A rabbi means structure!" Another trustee argued that a part-time rabbi was an impractical idea because no serious candidate would apply for that job, certainly not one that would fulfill their expectations.

The strongest defense of the board's plan was presented by Jack, chair of the Religious Committee. He detailed the great difficulties he faced responding to the growing demand for ritual services, which he tried to accommodate by calling on the good offices of ordained rabbis. It was only his favorable situation at work that allowed him the time involved in that endless search. His own lover, however, thought a part-time rabbi was sufficient.

At the second public meeting Joel, the previous chair of the Religious Committee, expressed his view that a "social worker who has compassion" would best assure the synagogue's needs. To the applause of his listeners, he exclaimed, "We need a rabbinic social worker!" The suggestion of one participant that a questionnaire be sent to all members to get their opinion was favorably received by the board's representative but was not later implemented. In any case, many participants assumed it would be a miracle if a candidate of ordinary human qualities could make it through the selection process.

The third meeting, which I did not attend, was conducted by Martin, the board's chair. By report, it was a quiet meeting and ended with the participants agreeing to the appointment of a selection committee for the hiring of a rabbi. The only issue apparently raised at that concluding meeting involved the expected deportment of the rabbi. Someone questioned what the synagogue's policy would be if the rabbi—assuming "he" was gay—was found to be a regular patron at gay bars. Although the participants had differing opinions, the issue was not viewed as a contentious one but rather offered a light-hearted coda to these public discussions. During its August meeting the board of Trustees unanimously voted to proceed with its decision to hire a full-time rabbi.

But Carol remained opposed to the idea, and was so angry with the board's decision to implement it before the majority of the congregants had a better opportunity to air their reservations that she prepared a petition. In it she argued that the synagogue was not a hierarchical organization; that the appointment of a male rabbi would offend women, while the appointment of a female rabbi might not accommodate the male congregants; and that the expenses of the new office would necessitate an increase in the annual dues, burdening the less affluent. The petition acknowledged an urgent need for administrative help in the synagogue's office and for a social worker to deal with the victims of AIDS. Finally, it argued, if there was a pressing need for religious authority, why not appoint a committee of rabbis from among the membership? To the surprise of many, Carol distributed her petition on Yom Kippur eve. Though her timing emphasized the gravity of her protest and gave it visibility, it was also considered an improper act for that most solemn day in the Jewish calendar. Despite her articulate presentation on that issue and as much as on other occasions, Carol was not popular at the synagogue. She was not publicly supported by women either, although few among them were enthusiastic about the board's initiative, assuming a man would eventually be elected to the position of rabbi. At the same time, however, most women empathized with the plight of the male victims of the epidemic, which was often suggested as the major impetus to the search for a rabbi.

Carol, and the few supporters who signed her petition requesting the congregation be polled by mail, did not sway the board. Martin presented its position to the congregation in an announcement in the *Synagogue News* of October 1990:

The most frequent issue expressed [during the three congregational meetings] was fear of change. This is a most natural feel-

▼

ing for a congregation that has done it on its own for the past 18 years. However, most people felt willing to put aside their fear and take the great leap.

Since no vote had been taken during the three public meetings, which in any case did not involve the majority of the congregants, the chair's statement could not be refuted.

In December the board appointed a Rabbi Search Committee consisting of five men and three women, cochaired by a man and a woman. But even members of the committee were skeptical about the prospects of their mission. The male cochair jokingly commented that only an androgynous and multimovement candidate would satisfy the synagogue's diverse expectations for a rabbi. Another committee member responded in a humorous vein to my question about the urgency of his task: "First, we'll spend three months deciding on the criteria which will guide our choice." The selection of a rabbi promised to be a long process, if it ever materialized. "It is a moot point," commented the Gentile lover of one committee member. At about this same time, I met a guest from the gay synagogue in Washington who described its three years of deliberation before finally deciding to hire a part-time rabbi, only to discover that not one serious candidate would reply to an ad for a position that offered so little opportunity to perform in a meaningful way.

Among those who supported the rabbi's appointment were the more traditional in their religious views, who complained of "Judaism bashing" by some service leaders in sermons and occasionally in the *Synagogue News*. They would have preferred a "pulpit rabbi," but were willing to accommodate other rabbinical styles. But it was the board chair, Martin, with the strong backing of his colleagues, who was the most powerful force energizing the complex process of hiring a rabbi. In December 1990 he told me: "If I survive, we shall appoint a rabbi by the end of next year." His affliction with AIDS, although it did not affect his robust appearance, made his appeals on various issues seem both urgent and disinterested. In order to avoid any appearance of a conflict of interest, he made it clear that he did not want his lover, a rabbi who might have been seriously considered, to be seen as a candidate for the job.

On December 21, 1990, the *Jewish Week* published an interview with Martin about the board's plan to hire a rabbi, including Martin's photograph against the background of the synagogue's banner. Mar-

tin elaborated on the inclusive nature of CBST and described the rabbinical position as open to all candidates, men or women, gay or
straight. This inclusiveness precluded the synagogue's affiliating with
one particular Jewish religious movement. (When the Reform movement demanded the synagogue join its ranks before advertising the
job in its newsletter, this complicated the search process.) As a
demonstration of the diversity of voices at CBST, the article quoted a
congregant who opposed the hiring of a rabbi.

The issue gained a much wider exposure when it reached the pages
of the New York Times (May 17, 1991:B1, B6). Martin and the search
committee's male cochair were quoted on the urgency of finding a
rabbi and the difficulties raised, particularly by the Conservative
movement. "We are in a Catch-22 situation, the place we probably
belong is the Conservative movement, but because they are still grap-
pling with the issue of homosexuality, we have to go to the Reform or
Reconstructionists for help," were the cochair's words. That position,
which contrasted with Martin's earlier statement in the Jewish Week,
emphasized CBST's affinity with the more traditional mainstream
movements. The article attributed the synagogue's urgency to the
challenge of AIDS, as Martin was quoted: "We're struggling to stay
afloat in the midst of an epidemic." The reporter, who began his piece
with reference to the many deaths in the synagogue, explained that
when someone died, friends and family members had to scurry
around to find a rabbi to conduct the funeral. The sympathetic article
ended with the search committee representative's emphatic plea: "If
only they [the Conservatives] would get to know us better they would
find that we are just a group of Jews who happen to be gay."

That message, addressed to the Conservative movement from the
pages of the New York Times, was a clear sign of CBST's gentrification
since the early days of Aaron charismatically enchanting new members with his inventive semi-Hasidic style.

The number of AIDS-related deaths did not figure significantly during the public debates over the hiring of a rabbi, but it became more
prominent in private discussions conducted later. Leon, for example,
according to his own story, had at first opposed the appointment of a
rabbi and, recalling the days when as chair he had eased Aaron out,
told me: "I am a pluralist; diversity and change are indispensable for
creativity. I was convinced a rabbi would implement a system in concrete." His change of heart occurred more recently. Leon's thoughts

were much concerned with the consequences of AIDS. He assumed that about 50 percent of the male congregants carried the virus. The frequency of funerals had taken the synagogue by surprise. In contrast to most mainstream congregations, CBST's membership was much younger, and until the early 1980s death was remote from its communal consciousness. Leon was very proud of the way the synagogue confronted the disaster and the sudden need to perform rituals so alien to the spirit and promise of gay liberation. But he realized it had become too difficult a burden to be carried by the synagogue's volunteer organization. A similar position was taken by Harvey, a member of the Search Committee, who dismissed Simon's argument about the reluctance prevalent in the synagogue concerning the appointment of a rabbi: "We need a rabbi particularly because of the death we must expect."

Morris, however, saw the hiring of a rabbi in terms of organizational growth and success. He told me a synagogue needs investment as much as any other business: "A rabbi is an investment; an executive officer is an investment." Though Morris was among those who had opposed Aaron, it was only when he moved toward increasing Orthodoxy. I assume he was thinking about Aaron, whom he described earlier in our interview as a man who "was part of a dream and whose spirit suited that dream," when he concluded that they would only be able to choose a candidate "whose character projects love, warmth, and feeling." He confidently believed, given that, the congregants would become reconciled to the choice in spite of their diversity of opinion and expectations. "There is a strong nationalistic feeling about the synagogue." They will never allow it to be destroyed, was his optimistic conclusion.

Morris was not impressed with Carol's Yom Kippur protest. If she wants to leave her mark here "let her put her money where her mouth is," was his indignant reaction. It was not enough to present learned sermons and protest without investing one's energy in the actual running of the synagogue by volunteering to work on its various committees. No doubt Morris could look back with satisfaction to his own work in two of the most successful gay organizations in New York: CBST and the Lesbian and Gay Community Services Center. He was able to retire from the latter when it reached a stage of maturity and stability that assured its survival for many years to come. The appointment of a rabbi at CBST would, for Morris, not only guarantee its efficient functioning but also symbolize its coming of age and equality with other synagogues. Morris shared Martin's desire to join the ranks of the Jewish establishment. A qualified rabbi, they assumed, would not be denied participation in the leading Jewish bodies.

In hindsight, Aaron's personal authority and magnetism had been a fortuitous gift for the synagogue's formative years in the 1970s; the egalitarian inclusiveness of a lay-led service suited the growing diversity and institution-building of the 1980s; the appointment of a salaried rabbi reflected the reality that volunteerism was overwhelmed in the face of new challenges in the 1990s.

The deliberations over the hiring of a rabbi also brought to the fore the growing visibility and influence of the lesbian constituency at CBST. A small number of women had been members since the synagogue's infancy—and greatly attached to Aaron. But on the whole, the position of women remained marginal until the early 1980s. In the *Synagogue News* of June 1989, Annette, a veteran member, gave testimony to that development. After years of "pounding the pavement" to attract more women, women's efforts finally began to pay off in 1982 with the first CBST activity especially for lesbians: a Sunday brunch. Since then it had become easier for women "to create their own space within a space." They remained a minority, Annette stated, but "a sturdy portion of the crowd." Women took an active role in the process of hiring a rabbi, both in the open discussions and on the committees that became involved in the issue. The best indication of their growing impact was the prevalent assumption that a woman, no less than a man, would be a successful candidate for the rabbi's position.

Postscript: The Search Concluded

In February 1992 after months of screening and interviews conducted in strict secrecy to avoid exposure that might compromise the candidates' future opportunities at mainstream synagogues, the Board of Trustees announced its selection: Rabbi Sharon Kleinbaum—a graduate of an Orthodox yeshiva high school and Barnard College, with ordination from the Reconstructionist Rabbinical College. She was also active in gay organizations and a member of the gay synagogue in Washington. A woman, a lesbian, and a graduate of the Reconstructionist school was not the accommodation to mainstream

▼

Judaism one might have expected from the image the synagogue's leadership projected in its public appeal.

The congregants were invited to approve a two-year contract. On March 25, 1992, the vote was taken, a last step in a long process that was due to introduce a dramatic change in the organizational and spiritual life of CBST. It had been nearly two years since the board first decided to hire a rabbi, but Martin and Morris could congratulate themselves on a formidable achievement; they had accomplished a dream considered by many impossible, if not absurd.

▼

CHAPTER FOUR

Why Join a Gay Synagogue?

Reflecting upon the synagogue he helped to build, Morris submitted that "gay Jews have not rejected the norms of community life." Drawing on the traditional New York City, and before that Eastern European, pattern of Jewish organization around shared association—often shared vocation—Morris suggested: "Synagogues are set up for their particular communities, and gay people need the same thing." He went on, "People need boundaries . . . and the synagogue is one of our parameters." In contrast, he pointed to the example of Israeli immigrants in New York who, he concluded, were paying a high price for not having established their own synagogues: their disappearance as a community.[1]

But Morris knew that this was not what first drew the majority of congregants to CBST. Instead, he posited four groups at the synagogue with their own reasons for joining: "those disenfranchised from Jewish life by their homosexuality, those individuals who found a supportive environment in which to develop their social skills, the unfortunate who had no opportunity for company elsewhere, and those who used to join their parents at synagogue, but whose death left them disconnected."

In my own observation of CBST I found a group of men and women, among whom were doctors, lawyers, computer programmers, academics, medical technicians, rabbis, teachers, social workers, administrators, librarians, business people, cab drivers, real estate

▼

investors, and artists. Not only were they varied professionally but they were diverse both in their Jewish experience and in their motivation for joining CBST. As I became better acquainted with them, and listened to their stories, patterns began to emerge—some more clearcut than others—in the paths that drew them to CBST, and motivated them to remain there.

A Return to Roots

I joined CBST in 1983 when I first moved to New York. I had minimized my connection with Judaism shortly after coming out; the term "lesbian Jew" felt like an oxymoron. The shul gave me back my Judaism and allowed me to integrate two very important parts of myself. Our *Brit Ahavah* [commitment ceremony], which occurred at CBST in 1988, completed this integration and allowed us to be out with family and co-workers as both lesbians and Jews. (Naomi, quoted in *Synagogue News*, February 1993.)

Naomi's succinct account outlines a pattern common to a number of CBST members. About two-thirds of those with whom I became acquainted had been involved in their youth in synagogue life. Many among them later went through an often painful stage of being unable to reconcile their sexual orientation with the Judaism of their parents' synagogue community. Dissociating themselves from that synagogue frequently constituted a major step in the complex social and psychological process of coming out.

Joseph's story of his sudden alienation from his family's synagogue is a dramatic example of that process. At fifteen Joseph already knew that he was different from other boys: "I kissed girls, but I wasn't into that. I felt I was misleading them. When I was called 'sissy' at school, I knew they were right."

On Yom Kippur, the day of fasting and atonement, he was reading the English translation of the confessional prayer Al Chet ("The sins we have committed") and was shocked: "I knew it was me the terrible words were condemning."[2] The next year he joined his family as usual for the Rosh Hashanah service at their Orthodox synagogue. But ten days later, when the family was ready to leave for the Kol Nidre service that begins Yom Kippur, Joseph refused to go, and despite his parents' anger and pleading, could not be budged from his sudden resistance. Nor would he explain his refusal—as he did years later: "I decided I couldn't be associated with a religion which defines me as a sinner!" From that day on, despite the gratifying experiences he had enjoyed for many years as a youth, he cut himself off from the synagogue entirely, except for a few visits on the festive holidays of Sukkot and Simchat Torah. 65

At twenty-nine, Joseph was still living at home with his parents. If the subject of homosexuality came up, during a television program, for example, he would leave the room feigning indifference. He was lonely, having avoided relationships, except for a few short sexual liaisons, mainly with non–Jews, and had discovered he was too inhibited by his Jewish upbringing to be comfortable with a Gentile mate.

He had heard about CBST when he attended college in the Village, and had been curious about it, but hesitated to go, expecting to find "a bunch of old gossips." Finally, in 1978, fourteen years after his break with his family's synagogue, he ventured there for the first time. Right away he felt comfortable. He recognized two young men he had seen at an Israeli folk dance class but never spoken to. He volunteered for one of the synagogue's committees and soon met someone with whom he established his first long–term relationship. Joseph then found the courage to come out to his parents. A few years later he was elected to the synagogue's Board of Trustees.

About ten years older than Joseph, Edward—the classicist and associate of Aaron—told a similar story. In his youth he had entertained the possibility of a rabbinical career, but later abruptly divorced himself from Judaism:

> Since I felt my gay identity and my Jewish identity to be antithetical, I stopped all my involvement in Jewish life; I simply did a flip–flop. Before that I had been practicing my Judaism and avoiding my sexuality; afterwards I began to practice my sexuality and to avoid my Jewish life. The choice seemed automatic at the time; I was only nineteen and I tended to see things in black and white.[3]

Edward told me it was five years before he realized how much he missed his Jewish heritage. During that period his friends were mainly non–Jews, and even his Jewish friends were not, in his words, "Jewish Jews." But in 1974, when he saw the advertisement for a gay synagogue, he was immediately intrigued—but hesitant: "I was afraid it would be a mockery of a synagogue." Edward continued: "After a month of wavering I finally went there one Friday night and was pleasantly surprised to find that the synagogue was not a farce but a group of men and women who were committed to Jewish life." He

soon became involved in CBST's religious affairs and was instrumental in moving it away from innovation and toward a more traditional style.

Leon, the board chair who ultimately nudged Aaron out, related a story almost identical to Edward's. Before college he had been very active in his synagogue's youth activities, but at age twenty-three he concluded he could not be anything but gay. He stopped the futile attempts to date women, left his parents' home, and went to find out what gay life in New York could offer. Being a joiner, he became active in gay organizations, which took the place of his synagogue participation. "This was now my life." In a Greenwich Village bar he met someone who told him about a gay synagogue that had been formed. He was amused: "A bunch of faggots, what do they know?"

Later that year, 1974, Leon felt a need to attend Yom Kippur services, a tradition he had stopped altogether since his parents' death a few years earlier. In the evening he went to Kol Nidre at a New York college but was not taken with the service. The next day he decided to attend Yizkor, the memorial service, at the gay synagogue and see what it was all about. He entered the church hall just as the Torah scroll was being carried among the congregants. "I kissed it with my *tallis* [prayer shawl] and felt immediately at home, as if I had gone there all my life." Leon attributed the warm atmosphere that engulfed him largely to Aaron: "He spoke English with a lilting Yiddish inflection. It was a familiar sort of yiddishkeit, and I felt so much at home. I was back at my father and grandfather's Orthodox synagogue." Leon soon joined a new committee, which enabled him to enter the synagogue's inner circle and ultimately become board chair of CBST.

Many, like Leon, who went on to become active in the synagogue's leadership described a similar experience of breaking away from a deep involvement with Jewish life and later returning to it through CBST. This separation typically followed an internal transformation that led them to feel an incongruity between their sexuality and the morality of their synagogue society. This process often occurred in their late teens or early twenties, before they actually experienced the social pressures that conflict was due to produce. But while the departure from their family's synagogue was a culmination of an emotional and intellectual crisis, joining CBST, many years later, seemed a most natural thing to them: they were connecting their present life with their past experience. The most difficult part of that step was, in fact, relieving their doubts about the likelihood of a gay synagogue being authentically "Jewish." Once they had done so they were not deterred by the synagogue's style, which was not necessarily the same as their parents' synagogue. Instead, they soon started to influence its workings, bringing it closer to what they had known. "I am going back to where I was always happy as a young boy," Nathan put it. For some that drive led them to ultimately seek a religious experience beyond that which could be satisfied at CBST.

Those whose path to CBST followed the pattern of religious alienation and return just described typically came from traditional—Orthodox, or at least Conservative—backgrounds, and an overwhelming number were male. Naomi's description of her journey, with which I introduced this section, was not common to the women I met. Women, by and large, did not report feeling a theological conflict between sexual identity and Judaism as many males had.[4]

A Search for Spirituality

Describing two new members of the board, Leon explained that their attraction to CBST was not for cultural reasons—as his own had been—or social, but "it is the spiritual experience which is important to them."

They were among a group of congregants for whom early memories were far less important in their attraction to the synagogue. While the "Jewishness" of CBST obviously facilitated their taking the initial step in joining, this seemed to be a secondary factor in its appeal. Rather, these women and men joined the synagogue because it offered them the spirituality they were looking for at a particular time in their lives. "I come here for the spiritual experience," "in order to cultivate my soul," "I am a spiritual person" were the explanations offered.

A CBST newcomer in his early thirties, a successful and sociable salesman, told me that until recently he had been busy accommodating his sexual identity, but now he felt a need to deal with his spiritual identity. Although he had not attended synagogue since his bar mitzvah twenty years before, for the last three months he felt an urge to recite the Shema prayer before going to bed. Another man in his

▼

early thirties explained that he had little previous experience in Jewish life and felt a need to make up for that gap: "The synagogue fulfills my spiritual needs."

When he joined the synagogue eight years ago, Arnold was at a time of emotional distress. He shared his feelings with an educated, gay Puerto Rican friend from work who, more deeply involved in New York gay life, knew of the synagogue. Recognizing Arnold's spiritual void, he took him to CBST for his first visit. A few months later Arnold came back on his own and fell in love with the place he often called "our home." He volunteered for the unenviable housekeeping chores and helped prepare the weekly Kiddush and holiday dinners. (Arnold was not the only one who discovered CBST, or was encouraged to join, through the information and advice of non–Jews.)

Ron, a social worker, told a similar story, but one that begins in Los Angeles. Coming from a nonaffiliated family, he had no religious education and no particular bonds with Jewish life. A friend at work, who was a member of L.A.'s gay synagogue, sensed a loneliness in him—in spite of Ron's involvement in many gay organizations—and thought he might find something at the synagogue that he lacked. Ron attended a service: "I was hooked." It started as a gratifying social experience, but Ron quickly developed a growing interest in Judaism. A few years later, on a visit to New York, he attended a service at CBST and struck up a friendship with Jack, one of the congregants most qualified in Jewish ritual and liturgy. After moving to New York Ron joined CBST and became active in its religious affairs. For members like Ron Jewishness was an acquired element in their life. As Jack put it: "Ron went to the synagogue without any intention of joining, but he discovered something he didn't know he was missing. Suddenly he felt good being Jewish, he felt that part which was hidden."

A Social Search

A very different group of congregants were drawn to the synagogue as a congenial place for sociability. They were neither nostalgic about their early religious experiences nor searching for spirituality. Many often confessed to being bored during the service and frequently arrived late, though in time for the "social hour" that followed. For them the synagogue ambience and membership compared favorably to bars and other gay meeting places. As one explained:

You have a comfortable opportunity to meet people and feel
safe. You know much more about what kind of people you associate with here. They look good. . . . The caliber of the people
you meet here is far superior to that in other places. In the community center, for example, you might meet a hundred unemployed artists.

Jay told me that having returned to the United States after ten years
in Israel, he joined CBST because it was a good place to renew his
social life in New York. In his mid–thirties, attractive, self–confident,
humorous, and affluent, he was very popular at the synagogue and
sometimes did volunteer work. "You know," he told me, "many people come not because they are religious; they show up in order to see
new faces and meet old friends." But he admitted the synagogue's
appeal had gradually diminished for him, as it often did for those
whose principal motivation was similarly social: "Somebody suggests
that we go out for dinner on Friday and end up at the synagogue. But
when it gets late, you think: why disrupt a pleasant evening if you
don't really want to go there?" On other occasions when he had no
other plans for a Friday evening, he went to CBST to take advantage of
the social hour. "I love the company of Jews." He went on to explain,
however, that he now knew other places that competed with CBST in
offering the opportunity to meet them.

For another congregant, a rabbi, the social attraction of CBST
evolved over time. After a few years of occasional visits to the synagogue, he developed a network of close friends, about ten men and
women who would meet after Friday services at a nearby restaurant.
His attendance became more regular in anticipation of these get-
togethers: "For the first time in my life I have a group of buddies. I
feel close to them and I can call on them when I am in need."
Although the majority of members drawn to CBST for social reasons
were not active in the synagogue and only attended irregularly, there
were a few notable exceptions who became an integral part of its
operation.

An unusual case was a man in his mid–fifties who had joined the
synagogue fifteen years prior, right after coming out. He saw it as a
natural place to start his social life, although he had been only "a
two–evening Jew," attending services solely on the High Holidays.
Since joining CBST, as he put it, "I have become a fifty–four evening
Jew." "I love that synagogue for its comfortable environment." But his

▼

involvement remained strictly social. He took upon himself the job of welcoming newcomers to the synagogue: every Friday evening he sat at a small table by the entrance, offering information, name tags and yarmulkes; remaining there through most of the service. And, though he subsequently expanded his involvement in the gay world and became active in other organizations, he has maintained his self-appointed role at CBST. He has obviously enjoyed meeting hesitant first-timers and helping them overcome their uneasiness, and although he has sometimes been accused of pestering the young and innocent, his dedicated attendance seemed indispensable to the smooth and safe running of the Friday night service.

Another veteran congregant, Harry, often repeated the story of his path to the synagogue. His Gentile lover used to express a preference for Jewish partners. When the two separated after a few years together, his lover's ideal of the perfect mate had fixed in *his* mind, and he too decided to look for a Jewish lover. Where better than at CBST? On his first Friday visit he met the man with whom he has shared his life for the last fourteen years. He joined the synagogue and has contributed his artistic talent to its decoration ever since. His continuing affection for CBST has also kept his lover there even though he would, otherwise, have preferred a more Orthodox environment.

A Late Step Toward "Self-Acceptance"

Another group of congregants were those for whom coming to terms with their homosexuality was a longer, more difficult, and more painful course. These men and women often described their joining CBST as the culmination of a process of personal reintegration, of merging their two identities—Jewish and gay. But unlike the first group with whom they bear some resemblance, they were alienated not so much from the religion of their childhood as from their sexual identity. Among them were those who both came out and joined CBST at an older age, who were married before they acknowledged their homosexuality, or were prevented by other emotional or social factors from a break with the norms and expectations of heterosexual society.

A man in his late forties who visited the synagogue irregularly told me his story:

I come from an Orthodox background. All my friends gradually married nice Jewish girls and had nice Jewish kids. I remained the only one unmarried, and I knew I could not marry: I hated women. But everybody was expecting me to get married. "A twenty-eight old boy and still single?" I felt I wasn't a mensch. They made me feel like some sort of fairy. So I left the syna-gogue. When I found CBST I felt immediately, "Here I belong!" Here I am a mensch, although I'll never marry and won't have any children. Here I don't need to pretend I am not what I am— although I leave the lipstick at home.

Isaac's road to the synagogue was more complicated. He had joined CBST at forty–eight, the year before I met him, right after coming out to his wife and their two teenage children. He had known at a young age that he was attracted to men, but when he confided this to his father at twenty-five, the reaction was devastating: "It is better to die than live the life of a homosexual!"

Chastised, Isaac suppressed his sexual inclination and got married. Professional success and child rearing covered over the unhappiness of his marriage. In an attempt to fill their spiritual void, his wife joined a secular Jewish circle while he joined a Reconstructionist syn-agogue. There he became friends with Ron and Jack, an obviously gay couple, and came out to them. He explained that for many years he had suppressed the urge for male company, except for a few fleeting experiences during troubled times in his life, but the need had become too difficult to deny any longer. Ron and Jack invited him to attend services at CBST, which he did occasionally when his wife was out of town. Finally, fearing that he might experience an emotional breakdown, he came out to his wife.

Although her shock and hurt made him sometimes regret his deci-sion, he explained that it was not an announcement about his sexual needs but a declaration "of my identity and that of my community." And in spite of the difficulties he experienced since coming out, Isaac was happy because, as he said, "I am now true to myself." For Isaac membership in CBST was a major symbol of his new existential posi-tion, a place to "validate my identity in the company of people who share it with me."

Bill first arrived in the synagogue shortly before I left New York in the winter of 1991. Now in his early thirties, he told me that as a teenager, without any family urging or even encouragement, he had chosen to enroll in a yeshiva, but when he discovered his "sinful" predilection, he distanced himself from his religion. At the same time, he could not reconcile with his homosexuality, however. He wanted

▼

to change, but could not, a predicament his family was unable to understand.

Bill went on to explain that for the last five years he had been closeted in cultural and social isolation. He was only involved with work and had no social life except for a lover with whom he had little in common, sharing neither education, religion, occupation, or cultural interests. He accepted this limiting arrangement because it conformed to his family's and his own expectations of the life of a stigmatized homosexual. Gradually, however, Bill came to realize that he need not stay in this self-inflicted isolation, and was in the process of separating from his lover when he first arrived at CBST. A few weeks after we met Bill officially joined the synagogue and volunteered to work in the kitchen. As another congregant observed, Bill's affiliating with CBST was part of a process of self-acceptance: not only did it mark a return to his love for Judaism but it was also a step toward his open participation in gay life. (When I returned to the synagogue on a visit nine months later, Bill was living with a young man he had met at CBST.)

Simon's story reflects the crucial role of the synagogue in the life history of a gay man who later greatly influenced its development. From a young age Simon was attracted to Judaism and Jewish life, but circumstances denied its expression. His parents were too busy and uninterested in Judaism; in later years his wife preferred a Christmas tree to synagogue life. His separation from his wife was part of a gradual process during which he acknowledged and reconciled with what he described as his homosexual "proclivity."

In May 1973 he cut out an ad for a gay synagogue from the *Village Voice* and kept it in his jacket pocket until October, when he finally decided to go and see. "It was wonderful," he discovered. For so many years he had hungered for a synagogue, and now at last it was waiting for him. What he called "my two fantasies" materialized at once: his attraction to Judaism and his attraction to men. Lacking a serious background in Judaism, he became a diligent student, gradually improving his command of Hebrew and his knowledge of Jewish ritual and liturgy. So much so, that when Aaron resigned as the synagogue's religious leader, Simon was appointed to the first Religious Committee that was established to replace him. He soon became a dominant figure in religious affairs, leading services during the High Holidays, and instrumental in compiling CBST's first full-fledged prayer book, which has served the synagogue for many years.

Social Comfort and Inclusion

For a number of congregants their motivation for joining CBST could be characterized as a desire for social comfort and inclusion. Many of the women were counted among this group. For those coming from Orthodox backgrounds, where women were seated in the synagogue balcony separate from men and denied any ritual role, or from some Conservative backgrounds, where until recently they were proscribed from rabbinical and cantorial roles and not counted in the minyan, full participation in ritual and leadership roles was liberating. Annette spoke of the women like herself who joined CBST in its early years:

> A large segment of women who were raised in traditional synagogues, and were given some education, soon discovered there was no place for them in the structure that existed. Once they matured there was no room for them to grow. They had to step back and leave it all to the men. These women, when they came to CBST, they were freed. Whatever happened, they learned to live with it, because there was room for them to participate. It was a great step!

Women found themselves included symbolically as well. Jill reminisced:

> I became a member of CBST in September 1979. I had attended services a few times prior to that date, but that night was the first time I had seen the new siddur, which had recently been degenderized. It was the first time I remember feeling totally a part of a Jewish worship service—there was not one jarring or exclusionary note that said I didn't belong. I remember how urgently I wanted to buy a copy of that prayer book, and how eventually I was directed to [Larry], who told me it wasn't for sale and then simply gave me a copy! That night I gave him a donation and filled out a membership form, and I've been an active member ever since. This is where I learned to pray, to lead services, and to integrate Judaism into all of my life. (*Synagogue News*, February 1993.)

CBST, of course, was not alone in offering these opportunities to women. The Reform movement first ordained female rabbis in 1972

73

▼

and various privileges in ritual were gradually allowed to women in many Conservative synagogues. Degenderized texts are not exclusive to CBST; the Havurah movement in particular was influential in that direction. Those from traditional backgrounds, however, may not have felt at home with these services. But more than that, there was a wider dimension to social comfort, one not unique to women.

Many left mainstream synagogues because they felt out of tune there, and could not fit into the social fabric. This is perhaps not surprising given the central position into which the traditional family has evolved in the American synagogue and given the synagogue's promotion of the ethos of marriage and procreation. In an Orthodox synagogue, for instance, an unmarried man is easily identified since he is not entitled to wear a tallith.

Women cited their discomfort among the sisterhood of the unmarried, with whom they did not share the same expectations for the future. Jill described her unease whenever she and her lover arrived at a mainstream synagogue. Invariably, someone would approach the young women and try to fix them up with "suitable" dates. After they showed no interest, they were then totally ignored. Naomi spoke of her unsuccessful search for a synagogue when her father passed away and, again, after she lost her mother. Only when she found CBST was she in a place in which she was comfortable enough to at last say Kaddish for her parents: "In order to be spiritual you have to lose yourself. And you can't do it if you are uncomfortable or afraid you might do something which would disturb other people."

Dov, a longtime member, argued that a gay couple would feel uncomfortable even in a Reform synagogue because "the fact that they have to state their tolerance is almost intolerant. Here at least they are not uncomfortable." Another congregant, whose declaration that CBST "fulfills my spiritual needs" was quoted above, added, "For that, I don't need a gay synagogue." He explained that it was only society's attitudes that made him prefer CBST, and reported having gone first to a Reform synagogue where he was not comfortable. Jane, a member who felt a social ease at CBST despite a lack of close friends there, concluded: "This is my identity, you are comfortable in the company of people who understand you."

Finally, one might also ascribe to inclusivity the, quite rare, service attendance of a CBST member I met. He knew no one in the synagogue and had no social expectations. He was also rather out of touch with it, inquiring: "Isn't this an Orthodox synagogue?" But CBST's open-door, no-questions-asked ethos allowed him to experience a Jewish environment whenever he felt the need, without having to explain himself.

75

Why Do They Stay On?

Up to this point I have described the various reasons offered by individual congregants for their initial attraction to CBST. A related but perhaps different question is, What is it that sustains their membership? What, if any, is its continuing meaning in their lives?

In my introduction, I quoted from Thumma's study of a gay Evangelical church, in which he observed that many sought out the church to resolve an identity crisis but "once the dissonance is resolved or reduced, they disappear" (1991:344). While the continuity of membership at CBST argues against the application of this principle, it is nevertheless true that just as their arrival at CBST often represented a personal evolution in religious and sexual identity, for many congregants this process did not cease at the door. For some, like former board chairs Morris and Norman, joining the synagogue and becoming active in its administration strengthened their gay identity and led them to become active in secular gay organizations. For others, like Simon and Ron, joining CBST encouraged them to a depth of religious education and synagogue involvement that they had not hitherto known and that they expressed through CBST. For still others, particularly those for whom joining CBST marked a return to synagogue life, a deepening religious commitment eventually—sometimes years later—led them to find expression for it in other synagogues. Aaron was the most notable case, although not the only one.

Nathan, one of the editors of the siddur and active for many years at CBST, went on to join a Modern Orthodox synagogue as well. He then attended services at CBST infrequently, mainly to be with his friends there. Nathan spoke of participation at CBST as a transitional stage during which people secure their Jewish and gay identities.

After returning from several years in Israel, Daniel, first editor of *Synagogue News*, and his lover became more observant and joined a Modern Orthodox synagogue. Although Daniel complained that the CBST service was "too loose, lacks structure and is too remote from tradition," they continued to attend occasionally: "It is still home; it feels

▼

like an old sweater." The couple later became active in promoting an alternative, once-monthly, traditional service at CBST.

Edward, whose return to synagogue life was chronicled earlier, became more Orthodox and in addition to CBST, joined a mainstream synagogue whose services he attended Saturday mornings. But though often sarcastic about CBST's religious style, he remained loyal to the place which first brought him back to Judaism. When the suggestion was made that CBST move its Yom Kippur service to a large hall in the Javits Center to accommodate all those wishing to attend, Edward vehemently objected: "Isn't this our home? You don't drive people out of their home on Yom Kippur."

Even among those for whom a search for greater orthodoxy was not a consideration, attitudes and practices evolved, and often so did the basis of their attachment to the synagogue. Over the years a number of active members joined other congregations, maintaining a dual affiliation with CBST: Martin, board chair, was an openly gay member of a Conservative synagogue, though his first loyalty was to CBST; Naomi and Simon both joined a Havurah group whose members were drawn mainly from CBST; others joined Reform congregations welcoming to gays and lesbians.

Though they explored other congregations such as the Reconstructionist one in which they met Isaac, Jack, the chair of the Religious Committee, and his lover Ron retained their allegiance to CBST, which had offered Ron an opportunity to discover his ethnic heritage and enabled Jack to return to a Judaism from which he had been alienated, in the typical pattern. But the "wonderful" feeling Jack experienced upon arriving at CBST, of being able to pray again and meet other gays with whom he could talk, had gradually eroded. Jack felt he could now separate the needs of his gay and Jewish identities. He explained that if he and Ron were to move to another city and find a congenial gay society there, they wouldn't need to look for a gay synagogue. Instead, Jack believed, they could satisfy their religious needs in a mainstream one.

Referring to CBST members whose attendance had become infrequent, Jack argued—echoing Thumma—that once they had become reconciled to their identity as gay Jews they could be content without regular attendance at a gay synagogue: "Then it is enough to visit CBST once a year and feel it is still there." Jack also felt that the rote nature of the service militated against regular attendance. He explained that this was not a problem for the Orthodox, for whom prayer was a way of life, but difficult for others to cope with. He concluded that though many leave, others stay on because it is a society they want to be close to. Among the latter was former board chair Leon, who declared of CBST: "We have the best combination of identities—Jewish and gay: Jewish for being smart; gay for being savvy."

77

A common thread running through all of these varied personal evolutions is a desire to maintain some connection with CBST, however attenuated. Even Aaron, whose break with the synagogue was its most dramatic, maintained a continuing tie to CBST through his leadership of the weekly Talmud class. Ben, whose reminiscence of Jacob Gubbay and CBST's beginnings was quoted earlier, likened this loyalty to that which he discovered on a trip CBST members made to the Spanish-Portuguese Synagogue in New York. Our tour was conducted by a member of the host congregation, who, to our surprise, identified himself as Ashkenazi. Ben was very moved by the affection the guide showed for his adopted synagogue and compared it to the love diverse CBST congregants have for their synagogue, a synagogue none grew up in that for all of whom is an adopted place. "It is wonderful there are these oases of Jewish space," Ben declared. On another occasion a CBST member observed: "We are more than accidental friends. We are . . . more than other congregations. There is something special to our connection."

Many explanations were given for this affective bond. Typically, members cited CBST as a place where Jewish and gay identities could be affirmed, and as a surrogate for family, home, and community. Membership in CBST as an affirmation of identity has already been explored and does not need elaboration at this juncture. Jack and Ron, appearing at a board meeting, declared: "Our synagogue is a strong statement of being gay and proud." Ron, though he complained of how undemanding and inexpensive it was for many congregants to do so, nevertheless agreed that being a member of CBST was a "statement of identity." Echoing Ron's complaint, Joel declared resentfully: "To register as members is a statement of identity which costs them only fifty dollars!"

Family, home, community—often used interchangeably—were frequently spoken of by congregants to explain their depth of feeling for the synagogue and often invoked by service leaders and drashah speakers, as will be seen in a later chapter. A woman who moved away

▼

from New York after a two–year membership sponsored a Kiddush, a postservice refreshment, to honor the synagogue that "was my family." Explaining the decision to renovate the sanctuary, a board member insisted: "This is our home!" Rebecca, a synagogue member for sixteen years, described the meaning of home:

> What CBST has become is my family—my home, a place where I will always be taken in. . . . My life continues to change, but the one thing I know in my heart is that regardless of what happens in my life, I can go to CBST any Friday night and find a group of gay and lesbian Jews with whom I can say Shema Yisrael (*Synagogue News*, February 1993).

Jill, a fourteen-year member, ended her comment, quoted earlier, about the feeling of inclusion she had experienced at CBST:

> CBST is more than my synagogue, its members more than friends—it is my home, my extended family. It is where I go to share my joys and where I turn for comfort and consolation in times of sadness.

There were others, however, for whom this metaphor was no longer valid. A congregant who only rarely came to the synagogue commented that when it was small there was a "family feeling," but when the synagogue expanded he "got lost." Another veteran member opined that it was relevant only for those actively involved in CBST committees and able to "transcend its many groups." Simon, on one occasion, complained that the idea of CBST as family was a "myth" held onto by lonely people separated from their families. He cited his own recent absence from services for several weeks due to illness: no one had called to find out what had happened to him.

If, for many, this analogy was a strongly held metaphor and, for others, a myth, in death it sometimes took on almost literal meaning. Simon himself related the story of an older, indigent, socially isolated man, a rather pathetic figure, who attended services at the synagogue. When he died it was learned that he had appointed Norman to see to his possessions and arrange his funeral. In fulfilling that request Norman stinted neither time nor money; members of the congregation offered donations to cover the expenses; and the isolated congregant was buried in a cemetery close to CBST's most beloved members. His request was deemed a test of CBST's ethos of family.

The synagogue increasingly faced these tests as AIDS introduced untimely death into its community. Martin, speaking of a congregant whose family refused to attend his funeral, declared that "we, his family, have been with him." When Lenny, who had described CBST as "my second family and home," died suddenly, his "first family" only begrudgingly attended his funeral. But as Martin observed: "Our extended family was all there. Lenny had been as lonely as the rest of us, but here in our synagogue we find our shared community."

However, death was not the only occasion for CBST to express its family ethos. Isaac, whose late self-acceptance was recounted above, voiced amazement at the Rosh Hashanah lunch he attended, which so contradicted the image he had held for many years of gays as lonely people. Other holiday dinners were often spoken of with enthusiasm—although the food was rarely more than barely edible. When Paul addressed a holiday dinner group of over a hundred congregants, he referred to them as "our extended family," and reported that other congregations, both gay and nongay, were now imitating CBST's model of communal meals.

Early in my stay at CBST two congregants proposed the initiation of a monthly Friday evening meal, a Shabbat dinner, before the service. One of them was a synagogue veteran who remembered the dinners Morris used to host at his apartment after the Friday night service. When the proposal was brought before the board Naomi expressed her hope that this might increase CBST's sense of community, and the project was unanimously approved. Jack, who subsequently made a report to the Religious Committee on one of these intimate dinners, commented: "This is not a CBST dinner, but a family affair."

Synagogue or Community Center?

In exploring the congregants' motives for joining CBST and CBST's evolving significance the reasons that emerge are, doubtless, not mutually exclusive. Naomi, for example, felt both theologically alienated from Judaism by her homosexuality as well as socially uncomfortable and unable to fulfill her quest for spirituality. Categorizing their motives risks not only making arbitrary distinctions but generalizing across what are significant differences. The imageries and constructs of a synagogue to which congregants sought to return, for instance, were frequently widely variant. A new arrival at CBST complained about the responsive readings—a staple at Reform and Con-

▼

servative but not Orthodox services—which reminded him of a church service. For him the individual praying alone, the "davenen experience," was the essence of a Jewish service. Not only did the congregants' experiences of Judaism differ in kind but also in amount. For many members regular attendance at only holiday services was the fulfillment of their religious commitment, a pattern common—if not thought exemplary—among Reform and Conservative congregations. Joel complained that on Passover and Kol Nidre "you suddenly discover a big crowd of strangers." The tensions engendered by these differences will be examined more fully in later chapters concerning the ritual and politics of CBST.

Thus far the varied reasons for joining CBST and the meaning that it has for its members—why join and why remain—have been explored principally in terms of their implications for the individual congregants themselves. But from the "institutional point of view" its members' motivations bear on the question of the kind of institution it is, and what it should be. In broadest form two institutional models of American Judaism seemed to emerge in the ongoing discourse at CBST: the synagogue (vaguely associated with Orthodox congregations and Conservative congregations of various shades) and the community center (associated mainly with the Reform, Conservative, and Reconstructionist movements). Veteran congregants, particularly those in leadership positions, tended to interpret CBST in terms of the first model. Larry, who Leon relied on as his hidden ace to help fill Aaron's void, commented:

We have a weak social program, no dances (except for Gay Pride and the annual dinner), no trips, etc. In New York there is no need for our synagogue to be a community center. People come here in order to daven. We are not a *beth knesset* ["assembly place," the standard Hebrew term for a synagogue] but a beth tefillah ["prayer place," a term mainly used in poetic presentations].

Larry admitted, however, that in the early days "we were more social, we were close-knit," although he didn't regret that loss. He assumed that the other gay synagogues, being smaller, were more socially active.

Leon himself traced CBST back to Jacob Gubbay's original aim: "He wanted a Jewish service, not a social group." Leon went on to argue that this was the wish of most of the early members as well:

We wanted a shul. We all came from a similar background and so it remained. It is still first a synagogue. Anything else, if it interferes with the service we say "No!" Those who leave CBST say that we are too traditional, which means that we are not a social center.

Leon buttressed his argument by pointing to the many visitors who overflowed the sanctuary for the High Holiday services: "They come for a religious experience; most of them have a rich [social] life." He also mentioned the regular participants whose needs were in his eyes evidently not social but for whom "the spiritual experience is very important." And he observed how few congregants remained in the community hall to chat while the services were going on. Another CBST regular pointed out, however, that while the board members were not engaged in the service they often found a remote corner *within* the sanctuary in which to gossip.

As Daniel, the first editor of *Synagogue News,* posed it: "The question is whom do we address first, a social or a religious community?" For others the answer was less monolithic than for Larry or Leon. "The synagogue provides for various needs of different people," a CBST regular declared, expressing a common view.

In a Yom Kippur talk to the congregation, Martin spoke to the issue of CBST's identity, seeing it as a combination of a community center and a *shtiebel.* He pointed to CBST's uniqueness: unlike other synagogues it is not organized according to a shared theology, class, or neighborhood. Considering the varied needs and metonymies of its diverse congregation, he declared: "The shared sexual orientation is the cement which unites us."

CHAPTER FIVE

The Ritual Process

American Judaism is uniquely diverse. Its diversity, however, is expressed through well-defined denominations: ultra-Orthodox, Modern Orthodox, Conservative, Reform, and Reconstructionist. One might similarly expect the gay phenomenon within Judaism to be defined by a movement as well, with its own theology, ritual, and central leadership. But, as will become apparent in this chapter, religious life at CBST was not fixed, but continuously negotiated and debated, often in terms drawn from mainstream Judaism. I try to encapsulate that complex realia of religious discourse in a few major topics: the services, the texts, continuity, change, and innovation in rituals and customs, the Religious Committee, and finally, theology.

The Services

The heart of the synagogue's life was the regular Friday evening service. Starting at 8:30 P.M., it ran from an hour to an hour and a half, and was followed by a coffee-and-cake kiddush and social hour in the community hall. By 11:00 P.M. the officers responsible for the premises would begin to try to move the crowd out. Two recent Friday innovations were a feminist service held once a month, which began at 6:30 P.M., and the monthly Orthodox-style service beginning before sundown.

Saturday mornings, once a month, there was a more traditional, egalitarian Sabbath service at 10 A.M. and a more recently established innovative Sabbath service as well. Both Sabbath services lasted for at least two hours and were followed by lunch prepared by one of the participants. Those who stayed to help clean up often didn't leave the synagogue before 2:00 P.M.

The service routine was broken by the holidays of Chanukah, Purim, Passover, Shavuot, with Rosh Hashanah and Yom Kippur—the highlight of the synagogue calendar—followed by Sukkot and Simchat Torah.

A typical Friday service would usually draw 100–120 congregants. On special occasions, such as Gay Pride Week or the outset of the gulf war, 200–250 congregants would attend. The Sabbath morning services were more sparsely attended, with no more than 20 men and women, and sometimes the service started with less than a minyan. On the High Holidays, Rosh Hashanah and Yom Kippur, CBST's sanctuary was too small to accommodate the 1,000 or more congregants wishing to take part in the climax to the annual ritual cycle. For the Kol Nidre service the synagogue rented another hall in the Westbeth complex to permit a second concurrent service. And in 1992 the two Yom Kippur services were consolidated to one for an estimated 2,000 people conducted at the Jacob Javits Convention Center, some distance from the synagogue.

There were, in addition, other services not included in the regular calendar, such as the ceremony for the reception of a Holocaust Torah scroll, memorial services, funerals, etc. CBST also took part in interfaith services, for example, the vigil commemorating the victims of AIDS held during Gay Pride Week. The synagogue sponsored a monthly Sabbath dinner as well as other holiday dinners, which preceded the evening service. These dinners seemed part and parcel of communal religious life.

1. The Friday Night Service

The regular Friday night service constituted the synagogue's main stage for religious and social affairs. Congregants would begin to filter in as early as 8 P.M., some still in business clothes, others dressed casually. Most walked to the community hall to greet friends. Others, the men immediately picking up yarmulkes (unless they had brought their own), while most women who wore a head covering brought their own, often decorated skullcaps or other types of unobtrusive headgear, took a prayer book (siddur) and joined friends already seated in the sanctuary or sat down alone. By 8:30 most arrivals had taken their seats, arranged in a U around the bimah (although men and women were integrated, most women concentrated in a few front rows). All looked up to the English service leader and the chazan, a cantor who could lead the congregation in participatory prayers, responsive readings, and Hebrew songs. Since most service leaders were well known, and the cantors, who were drawn from a smaller pool, even more so, one could usually predict the tone of the evening. Nevertheless, an experienced service leader would surprise the congregation occasionally with an unexpected innovation, or a chazan with a new musical rendition.

The services were coordinated by the chair of the Religious Committee. The service leader and cantor might have asked to perform together, but they might as often have been assigned to a particular Friday evening without prior consultation, except for confirming the date. The service leader and the cantor were expected to meet before the event to work out the selection and order of the discretionary prayers and the members they wished to call to the bimah to read from the siddur or other sources. The service leader might prepare a special handout or read a meditation or poem written or selected for the occasion. The particular darshan (drashah speaker) appointed to present the sermon later during the service also affected the quality of that week's assembly. The darshan, however, was under no obligation to coordinate with the service leader and cantor.

Any congregant could ask to lead a service or present a drashah. Until they had demonstrated their ability to perform these roles alone, they were supervised by a skilled congregant appointed by the Religious Committee. Those whose performance was obviously unsatisfactory were given a more infrequent slot. But only in extreme cases of incompetence or egregious performance were congregants completely denied the opportunity. The right to lead a service seemed an essential element in CBST's egalitarian ethos. That policy sometimes caused grumbling among the congregants, but it was not openly challenged. At the time of this study about thirty congregants were qualified to lead services for the congregation.

Leading a service or presenting a drashah for the first time was usually an occasion for celebration, and the performers were clearly elated as friends and other congregants came up to congratulate them. Both acts represented a coming of age and a deeper integration into the congregation. Performing them publicly marked one's commitment to the synagogue's affairs and goals. However, they were not, in and of themselves, seen as signs of Jewish scholarship, nor was leadership in the synagogue dependent on assuming these tasks. Only late in his presidency did Saul lead a service for the first time. He was excited and anxious beforehand and overjoyed at the end of his maiden service. Sheila led a service for the first time only after she came onto the board and had become a member of the Religious Committee.

All services were reviewed at the monthly meeting of the Religious Committee. Service leaders were often informed about the reviews, particularly when these were critical. The Religious Committee had prepared a detailed ten-page manual to guide the service leaders "to help you make intelligent decisions about your options." The manual suggests that service leaders invite at least three congregants to the bimah to lead responsive readings, giving preference to those who "have never or rarely read before the congregation."

The manual also stated: "Music (instrumental or recorded) is totally acceptable throughout the service; dancing . . . may also be incorporated anywhere in the service." However, on the few occasions that music was actually incorporated in the service, it raised complaints on the part of the synagogue's "traditionalists." Even those among the supporters of music were often dissatisfied with its specific application. Though many congregants probably enjoyed the controversial events, their reactions were not recorded.

The service leader's guide was prepared in response to a board decision that services should be conducted according to the synagogue's "tradition." Joel, who told me about that decision and the incident that had provoked it, exclaimed: "What is the tradition they are talking about? Our services have always been eclectic; that is what characterizes our synagogue." The service leaders could augment the basic list of prayers customary in most synagogues (which included Lecha Dodi, the Shema, the Amidah, the Aleinu, and the Kaddish) from a vast collection of traditional and modern sources, or create their own. The controversial event was the New Year's service of 1989 when the Amidah[1] was deleted, Christmas melodies were incorporated, and a few dozen congregants walked out in protest.

"The word *siddur* means order or arrangement, and the Friday evening service provides an order, a framework, on which to build a

85

▼

structure." The Religious Committee tried to develop some clear standards for performance without dictating the style and details. Naomi, who could not be accused of conservatism, suggested introducing a feedback form in order to improve the performance of the three major participants in the service. Among the criteria she included was "*kavanah*—the heart and spirituality that you bring to the service."

On the Friday evening of Gay Pride Week, June 1990, the service leader and cantor were a man and woman recently ordained as Reform rabbis. Both wearing sixties-style clothing, they conducted a sing–along accompanied by guitar for about twenty minutes, which allowed those who participated in the AIDS vigil to join the service they might otherwise have missed. To my comment on the size of the crowd, which was considerably larger than usual, I was told: "Of course. It's a *yontef* (holiday)!" As befitting a holiday and an event of great significance, the Hallel[2] prayer of thanksgiving was proudly recited.

When we had lunch the next day, after the traditional Sabbath morning service, the previous night's service was a major topic of conversation. When the morning's cantor commented on how moved he had been by the service, Henry, a board member and liaison to the Religious Committee, who had walked out, reacted angrily: "I was also moved, moved out twice." Not only had the leaders tired him with songs unknown to most of the congregants, but he claimed the woman rabbi committed the gross error of announcing that this was the first Sabbath of the month. An announcement already made the prior week! Simon was amused by Henry's reaction and jokingly said it showed clear signs of early aging. Simon added that he himself had no problems with innovation. The traditional Sabbath morning service itself had not been untouched by the innovative spirit of Gay Pride Week. The Hallel had also been recited that morning, and the congregants greeted each other warmly with the holiday felicitation Good Yontef. The special feeling of the day had obviously affected the most traditional service at CBST.

The Gay Pride Friday night service was also reviewed at the Religious Committee's next meeting. Opinions differed sharply among its members. When Henry exclaimed, "It disturbed me!" a congregant in his late sixties attending the meeting replied: "It thrilled me!" Henry explained his position: "Our people forgot it was a service and applauded! They overstepped the boundary between a service and a

Gay Pride celebration." Sheila agreed, "I was shocked, I lost the service, it was a song fest!" Henry went on: "When they played the guitar again at the end of the Amidah I felt 'No way!' " But Ze'ev defended the service, arguing that it was infused with the spirit of the external world: "True, the Sabbath had lost its centrality, but that happens only once a year, and on a day which is so important to our people." Larry joined those in support, describing the joy he felt during the service and his intention to encourage the use of music again. Yes, there are people—he mentioned two past presidents—who hate the guitar, but the only mistake had been in a selection of songs unfamiliar to the congregation.

The committee was called upon to come to a decision for its final report. Henry, the liaison, wanted to inform the two rabbis they would not be allowed to lead services if they repeated their last performance. Simon opposed Henry and characterized the issue as one of "conservatism versus innovation." "You can't legislate taste," he added. Larry, in a conciliatory tone, expressed the view that the resentment felt toward the service was not so much against the innovation per se, but its rather artless introduction. The congregants would accept a poor traditional service but resent a poorly prepared innovative one. "You can't insult people twice," was his conclusion. Without dissent, the final decision was made to withhold any formal criticism.

The content of the Friday night service was never fully formalized. Even the most popular part of the service that became almost a symbol of CBST, the Shalom Aleichem, was not compulsory. That song, taken from the repertoire of traditional Sabbath hymns, was performed at CBST in a communal fashion. Standing side by side with arms around each others' shoulders, the long rows of men and women would slowly sway from left to right as they sang the poetic and melodic hymn. I was very impressed by that evocative scene as I first described it in my notes: "The synagogue crowd was moving together like a boat making its way between the waves." The service leaders could include that song anywhere during the service or drop it altogether.

During one of the first services I attended the leader, a woman, introduced a meditation she had written a few years earlier: "To the synagogue which is our home and our family. Here I can express my intellectuality, my Jewishness, my sexuality, my spirituality, and my

87

humanity." She also used a new translation to a basic prayer because she thought it more poetic. The new version was distributed before the service under the title "An Interpretation of *Ma–riv Aravim*, to be read responsively." Active service leaders often prepared handouts to be used during the service, some of which have been added to the permanent repertoire available for service leaders. Ron frequently prepared special contributions for his services, often about the love of Sabbath and the synagogue. And his evocative piece "We Are a Community of Strength," subtitled "A Prayer in the Age of HIV Disease," was frequently included by other service leaders.

The services rarely satisfied all congregants. I was told by a few members that they stopped attending the Friday service because the atmosphere was not religious enough for their taste. One of these regularly attended the traditional Sabbath morning service instead. But others complained that the Friday service was too traditional. Two women who voiced this complaint chose to attend the innovative Sabbath morning service instead.

At one Friday service the cantor used an unknown melody for Lecha Dodi. The frustrated congregation, which attempted to sing along with that popular prayer, was literally stuck by the middle of the last stanza. In the restroom afterward I overheard a conversation between two men who had abandoned the service: "I couldn't stand the service," one complained. On another occasion, during a particularly long and dreary service, Jeff, who was seated next to me, commented that it reminded him of an Off-Off-Broadway play doomed to see its final curtain after the first performance.

Bob, who had completed a graduate degree in Jewish studies and was on the board, introduced an innovation in a service he led. He digressed for about five minutes with an interpretative discourse on a particular section of the prayer book. This explication was apart from the usual drashah. He later asked the Religious Committee to allow him to repeat these educational talks during services he was not leading, promising to restrict them, implausibly, to two minutes. The Religious Committee's response was based on the assumption that service leaders were at liberty to introduce minor innovations but that, at the same time, these changes were not to be considered formally established for future services. Granting Bob the committee's approval to present his lectures in services led by others would have conferred institutional authority upon his project. It would also have infringed on the autonomy of other leaders to prepare a service of their own choosing. The committee decided to inform Bob that it did not object to those talks during services he led, but that he could not present them in other services without the prior approval of the leader involved. Even Simon, who complained about the "concretization" of the synagogue's tradition and saw himself a champion of innovation, was upset by Bob's request. (I shall later discuss another issue related to this same request.) When Bob made his next presentation, he smilingly informed the congregation he was not speaking on behalf of the Religious Committee, a comment that provoked much laughter.

89

Aaron told me he would not go to the synagogue because "they are always changing, always arguing about the order of prayers, and are far removed from the Jewish sources." A close friend of his added that he wouldn't attend CBST's Purim service, though it was a chance for him to see friends on a holiday without Sabbath travel restrictions, because the megillah is read in both Hebrew and English. Another member of Aaron's circle, Nathan, was able to gain a particular accommodation to his Orthodox requirements. When leading the Friday night service he was allowed to light the Sabbath candles before dark (as Aaron had unsuccessfully insisted). He was given this permission even though it deprived the congregants of a popular service ritual and an honor for the participants.

Debbie, a heterosexual woman in her late thirties who discovered the synagogue through a gay male friend, told me she preferred CBST to other synagogues because the congregants were more seriously engaged in prayer. She found she could daven at CBST. A somewhat similar reaction was expressed when a few congregants attended a service at Temple B'nai Jeshurun, the elegant Upper West Side synagogue. In spite of the impressive service led by Rabbi Marshall Meyer, Paul said he preferred the services at CBST because they have "more spirit"—the congregants take an active part in reading and singing. In particular, he compared their respective kiddush rituals. At B'nai Jeshurun only the service leaders drank from the cup of wine, while at CBST the entire congregation took part: during a break for announcements wine was distributed in small cups to all participants; they would then all raise their cups and recite the blessing over the wine together. So ingrained was this tradition that once when there was an unexpected delay in distributing the cups, the service came to a halt. Edward turned to me and indignantly commented on CBST's

▼

priorities: "Here, first comes the local [CBST] tradition; next comes *minhag Yisrael* [traditions of later generations]; and only last, Halakhah!"

In contrast, an aggressive attack on what he saw as the synagogue's fealty to traditional Judaism was voiced by a young Reform rabbi in an article in the December 1990 CBST newsletter. He related his experiences as an openly gay man in a rabbinical school and his ultimate disappointment with his cherished gay synagogue. "For me it was wonderful to have a 'safe space' in which I did not have to justify myself," he wrote, but his major message to the synagogue was his indignation with "a pervasive attitude of nostalgia for traditional Judaism, and for the notion that the more traditional a service is, the more authentic it is." His article provoked resentment from "traditionalists," who complained of "Judaism bashing," and support from proponents of innovation who were involved in organizing a new feminist service.

2. The Traditional Sabbath Morning Service

Until the introduction in 1991 of the Orthodox-style early Friday evening service, the more traditional Saturday morning service was the most standardized in liturgy and ritual. Its liturgy consisted of those parts of CBST's Sabbath text that came closest to the mainstream Conservative style. Moreover, its ritual fully conformed with traditional practice in Orthodox and many Conservative synagogues when it came to the Torah reading: a complete reading of the parashah, the maftir, and the haftarah. This service actually came closest to that which Aaron attempted, unsuccessfully, to introduce a decade earlier.

The service was led by a core group of ten men and three women who attended most monthly meetings. That group was drawn heavily from the Religious Committee, with a few coming from the Talmud class. But while these members were closest in their theological orientation to the Talmud class, most were, nevertheless, not fully observant. The service was also regularly attended by a few eccentric members among whom Tom was the most ostentatious.

Tom was a regular at CBST's services. Though not Jewish, he considered himself a partner to the Jewish experience through mystical association and personal choice. He was a huge man whose size was accentuated by fantastic robes and headgear he made himself. He was an artist, and although he never took an active part in the Sabbath ritual, he was treated in a friendly manner and became an integral participant in the meal that followed. In fact, in the Sabbath service, more than in others, the leaders were careful about the participation of non–Jews, who were not counted in the minyan. Jewish women as ⁹¹ well as men were counted, but another regular attendee in the process of conversion was not, despite his familiarity with the ritual.

The atmosphere of the service was noticeably more intimate. The participants were individually given portions of the responsive reading and honors during the Torah reading. The subsequent meal offered a special opportunity for friendly conversation and joking. Once when this Sabbath service was being discussed in the Religious Committee, Sheila, a newcomer to the service, posed a question: "I ask myself, why did I enjoy that service so much?" Other service attendees on the committee answered: "It is more intimate." "Everyone participates; no one is invisible." "It is more traditional." Sheila concluded with emotion: "It is heimish!"

3. The Innovative Sabbath Morning Service

The very opposite of the traditional in its liturgy and ritual was the innovative service. It was conceived by Simon, a member of the Religious Committee who often participated in the traditional Sabbath morning service as well. Simon thought there were people who could not adequately satisfy their spiritual needs within the regular framework of CBST's services, or like himself, needed an additional vehicle for their expression. But without a specific constituency, the service drew only an erratic attendance, beyond a loyal few.

The prayers were selected without a strict adherence to the regular Sabbath text. Participants were invited to read or sing prayers or Israeli songs they particularly loved. Both Simon and Naomi, occasional leaders of this service, agreed that those who have a stronger background in Judaism are less reluctant to introduce or experience innovations, "but those who have learned their Judaism at CBST are scared of any change."

No doubt, Naomi, who served on the Religious Committee and was the leading female cantor at CBST, was ready to experiment with new ideas. I attended an innovative service she and Susan, her lover, presented. We were seated in a circle close to the bimah, at the center of which they had laid out a vase with flowers, colored stones, colored ribbons and glasses with plants of various scents. We tied the

▼

ribbons together and held this new thread connecting the congregants, enhancing the feeling of intimacy between us. The stones and the fragrant plants were circulated among us to touch and smell.

Simon, who arrived somewhat later, couldn't contain his amazement. Looking at the stones, the ribbons, and the glasses, he jokingly referred to them as *avoda zara* (idol worship). But his amusement was not criticism, and he himself sometimes invented rituals like the "Jewish tea ceremony" he celebrated on his birthday. After its novel introduction, Naomi and Susan's service followed the standard Sabbath text for the selection of prayers, but the Torah reading was done partly in English. When Naomi commented she had no alternative to offer for the Amidah, Simon immediately offered an alternate version he had prepared for the coming holidays. On another occasion, the Amidah was read aloud responsively with a moment of silence between the stanzas.

In contrast to the traditional Sabbath morning service, the issue of homosexuality was frequently raised at the innovative service. For a Hebrew prayer whose English translation would literally be "Blessed are you God, King of the universe, who tears away the bonds of the jailed," the CBST siddur had substituted the ending "who brings liberation to the oppressed." Simon drew the congregants' attention to this prayer and its special relevance for the congregation. When in history had a despised and ostracized minority been as liberated as they were? Moreover, that liberation was spreading to other parts of the world. In the innovative service the selections typically made from the siddur were those with suggestive gay implications. In sharp contrast the only reference to gay identity in the traditional Sabbath service was during the reading of the prayer for recovery of those ill with AIDS.

What to call the new alternative Sabbath morning service—and how to distinguish it from the older one—remained unresolved until the service itself was abandoned for lack of leadership. Although they used them among themselves, the Religious Committee members refused the formal use of the terms *innovative* or *alternative*, versus *traditional*, as disparaging to the regular service. The committee minutes of February 1989 report: "The Sabbath Morning minyans should have names without negative connotations. Committee members should think of some alternatives and be able to discuss this at the next meeting." The suggestion of "Contemporary" versus "Custom-

ary" was also rejected. Another idea was to name the innovative service the "Havurah Minyan." But the issue became moot. Those who
were best suited to lead it, including Simon and Naomi, were already
involved in Havurah groups outside the synagogue and unable to take   93
responsibility for its operation beyond a meeting or two. Without any
official announcement the "innovative service" ceased to meet again,
six months after its initiation.

4. The Feminist Service

In December 1990 when Naomi first presented the Religious Committee with the plan of a number of congregants to start a new Friday
night service, she did not characterize it as a "feminist" service. She
called it a "different service." She did not ask for financial support but
only for use of the space. When Henry, the board's liaison, asked
about the committee's role in supervision, Jack, its chair, replied that
they would not control the new service since they had not done so
with the Sabbath morning services. Henry responded that this was
different: Friday was the major day of prayer at CBST. Jack argued,
however, that the committee wanted to make the synagogue a "space"
that answers to the needs of more people. Naomi concurred: "We
want to accommodate the growing diversity in our shul." Naomi, who
along with others had been energized by a lecture at CBST given by the
Jewish feminist theologian Judith Plaskow,[3] told me that the regular
service did not fulfill her spiritual needs: "It is true the women are less
satisfied with the service, but not mainly because of the issue of degenderization. It is the nature of God as formulated in the CBST service which is the most disturbing. For me, God is not so distant." The
God presented in the synagogue's siddur, although not referred to as
"King" or "Lord," remained a dominant, patriarchal figure—"Creator"
and "Ruler." Not loving and supportive as she conceived the deity.
Susan, Naomi's lover, was also very active in promoting this new service. She was disappointed when only women showed up at the first
meeting called to discuss the new service. Susan believed that the service would resemble a Havurah, with more singing, music, and dancing.

A year later, in December 1991, I attended a feminist service, as it
was now known. About forty women and ten men were present. We
were seated in a circle toward the rear of the community hall, which
was lit only by candles. Except for a few basic prayers, the service

▼

leader made exclusive use of handouts prepared for the occasion. An
alternate prayer was substituted for the Amidah. Many female congregants took an active part in reading prayers. Jean presented a lec-
94   ture on the position of women in Jewish history and Judy gave a
drashah on the role of women in Moses's life—his sister, his wife, and
his adoptive mother, Pharaoh's daughter. She argued that they all performed an important role, but one defined for them by destiny. Judy
was unhappy with the position of women in the Jewish texts as much
as in Jewish history, but expressed her belief that they were now
building a new future. Her lover read a poem she had written and
another couple celebrated their second anniversary by reading a piece
they wrote for the occasion entitled "Why Are We Here Today?" Their
answer was that at home their families expected them to marry; in
college they sensed they were different, being lesbians—all this
because society rejects the bonds between women. But in the synagogue they could express their feelings freely and be themselves as
Jewish lesbians.

I was told the crowd was smaller than usual because of winter
vacations. The men who attended did not take an active role in the
service. Except for the usual CBST Shalom Aleichem hymn, there was
none of the singing, dancing, and music I expected. The service was
rather somber and reflective. In contrast with earlier failed attempts
at innovative services, the feminist service appeared to draw a large
and loyal constituency that included some who had not attended regular services at CBST before.

5. The Early Minyan

During 1991 another monthly Friday service was initiated to satisfy those congregants who wished to experience a more stable, traditional Orthodox-style service, one not subject to the personal intru-
sion of the service leader. It was also designed to bring back to the
synagogue members whose search for a more authentic Judaism had
led them to join other synagogues despite the need to conceal their
gay identity. The service, which was at first named "Orthopractice" to
avoid a direct association with an Orthodox service, was later called
by the less peculiar name "Early Minyan," and finally was advertised
in the 1993 newsletters as the "Traditional Minyan."

I attended a service in December 1991. Because of the winter's
shorter days it started very early, at 4:15 P.M. The group of twenty men

and five women included the core members of the Talmud class and the traditional Sabbath morning service as well as a few, such as Simon and Arnold, who had attended the innovative service. In contrast to the casual dress at all other weekly services, the men wore jackets or suits. "It's a service for the middle-aged," was Daniel's humorous reply to my comment about the small number of young attendees.

95

Aaron, both cantor and service leader, inspired the group with his enthusiasm. He and his friend wore the traditional Jewish black caftan. Annette lit the Sabbath candles in the community hall without any special attention paid. The drashah was presented between the close-of-day Minkhah and evening Ma'ariv services by a young woman, a student at a rabbinical school, who introduced the sages' interpretation of the weekly Torah portion. It dealt with Joseph's emotional outburst at his second meeting with his brothers. Joseph, who could foresee the future, knew that the tabernacle and temple to be build on territory allotted to his and his brother Benjamin's tribes would eventually be destroyed. Joseph also realized that his brothers' arrival in Egypt was the first step in the long history of Jewish exile. The sermon made no reference to any contemporary issue.

After the service the congregants assembled for dinner. Aaron led the Sabbath songs, but his nostalgic audience insisted on a song of which his lover of many years ago had been fond. "This was the rebbetzin's *niggun* [song or wordless melody]," they murmured good-heartedly. The meal and the benediction ended just before the congregation began streaming in for the regular Friday night service.

The continued operation of the feminist and early minyan services reflected a desire to allow "room for diversity" at CBST, a position shared by both Martin and Paul on the board, and Jack on the Religious Committee.

Holiday Services

The High Holiday—Rosh Hashanah and Yom Kippur—services were the least controversial, and no suggestions were offered for alternatives. They were well-rehearsed events, completely controlled by the High Holidays Committee, which was composed of past and present chairs of both the board and the Religious Committee, with the help of other committees appointed for specific tasks. All details of ritual, texts, service leaders, cantors, drashah speakers, honors, sho-

▼

far blowers, seating arrangements, sound systems, breaks, and food were meticulously prepared far in advance. Accommodating hundreds of visitors on Rosh Hashanah and more than a thousand on Yom Kippur could not be left to last-minute improvisation. Even innovations such as handouts for an alternative Amidah with references to the AIDS crisis for those who might prefer it were prepared and carefully vetted well in advance.

There were decisions to be made about specific rituals. For example, in 1988 it was decided to completely eliminate that of *dukhanin*, calling to the bimah the Cohanim, male descendants of the ancient priestly clan, to bless the congregation. This practice had been criticized, especially among women. "It was against our ideology of equality between men, and between men and women," I was told. Until 1988, since there were also those who supported that ancient tradition, it had not been entirely eliminated, but only practiced on Yom Kippur. In 1989 its supporters attempted to reinstitute it for Yom Kippur, but after an open congregational meeting its elimination was confirmed.

Another important decision involved the location of the Yom Kippur service. Two Kol Nidre services had been conducted simultaneously, one at CBST and another, mainly for nonmembers, at a rented theater in the same Wesbeth complex. Although the idea of renting one large hall to accommodate the entire congregation had been raised more than once in recent years, it was repeatedly rejected because of the congregants' refusal to go elsewhere. Eventually, in 1992, the decision was made to consolidate Yom Kippur services in the Jacob Javits Convention Center.

The congregants attending the High Holiday services were elegantly dressed, in contrast to their usual casual attire. This formality also extended to their demeanor, which included less of the usual wandering in and out. The synagogue itself "dressed for the occasion," employing its most skilled service leaders, cantors, and speakers. The cantors did their best to emotionally involve the congregants with traditional melodies familiar to most. And the congregation was moved to tears during the Yizkor (memorial) section. The congregation joined in powerfully for the Avinu Malkenu ("Our father, our king have mercy on us") and Hashivenu ("Take us back and renew our days"). And the concluding Ne'ilah prayers were sung with the enthusiasm of a Red Army chorus.

The High Holiday season also included Selichot, Sukkot, and Simchat Torah services. Here the field was more open to innovation and
spontaneity. The Selichot service, which preceded Rosh Hashanah,
was attended by a small group of about thirty men and women. The
service was led by Alice, a Reform rabbi, who used both the synagogue's text and one she had prepared for the occasion. The sanctuary was dark except for a dim light over the bimah and six candles on
a table in front of it. At one point during the service, only the candles
remained to light the dark sanctuary. Six congregants then proceeded
to each extinguish one candle representing a negative human trait—
jealousy, greed, cynicism, etc. The candles were then relit to celebrate
positive qualities—charity, honesty, belief, etc. Some thought the candles represented the six days of creation; others assumed they also
represented the six million Jews destroyed in the Holocaust.

For Sukkot the synagogue was thoroughly decorated with flowers
and leafy branches. But its most extravagant feature was one that Tom
had planned and executed. Over the pulpit he erected a canopy, a
chuppah, to represent this holiday's sukkah, a small open-air pavilion
covered with branches. He painted a silken material with various
symbols, some Jewish and others known only to himself. They represented, according to Tom, the Hebrew letters, Jerusalem, and the
unity of male and female. Edward, who was less than impressed by
the imaginative construction by a non–Jew in the heart of the synagogue, commented, smiling: "I've never understood the meaning of a
'symbolic sukkah.' "

During one Sukkot service the prayers were led by a member who
was rarely given this role because of the resentment his kabbalistic
ideas had generated in the past. He wrote a song to add to the prayer
for rain that highlighted biblical figures whose actions involved
water—Rachel and Hannah who had shed tears for their children. He
also prepared a new English version of the Shema that lamented the
destruction of God's creation, the environment, with explicit reference to deforestation in Brazil. His performance received mixed
reviews.

On Simchat Torah of 1990 the evening service was convivial, but
quite chaotic. Its leaders made serious mistakes in the choice of
prayers. Magen Avot, for instance, a Sabbath prayer, was included
even though it was Thursday. These mistakes were soon identified by
the cognoscenti, who expressed their dismay. In traditional fashion

the congregants paraded the Torah around the synagogue, but they were also called up to the bimah a number of times for a group aliyah. Among them was Tom, in a colorful garment with a big astrological ornament on his chest, who would ordinarily not have been called to the Torah.

The chaos reached a climax when Dov, serving as gabbai, called individual congregants to the bimah for the Torah blessing. Carried away by his enthusiasm for Jewish tradition, he announced these roles with the terms *khatan Torah*, ("bridegroom of the Torah") and *khatan Bereshit* ("bridegroom of Genesis"). Angry women shouted back *kalat Torah* ("bride of the Torah") and *kalat Bereshit* ("bride of Genesis"). Faced with this commotion, the bewildered Dov finally got the message. But his dismissive response only compounded his offense to degenderization and other acute sensitivities at CBST: "Okay, Okay, let it be *khatan Torah—kalat Torah*."

As I later learned, the custom at CBST was to eliminate these specifically male honors in the Simchat Torah evening service but retain them for the much less well-attended service the next morning. In their place, past presidents—men and women—were called to the bimah without the traditional khatan Torah announcement; present board members were given the unstated khatan Bereshit honor. But Dov decided to reinstate the traditional ritual because of its ancient–exotic attraction. Unfortunately, his enthusiasm made him forget the constraints and the ethos of a CBST service.

Dov created an even greater disturbance when he corrected what he insisted was an error in Ron's Torah reading. The interruption threw Ron off, and in his confusion he could hardly complete his portion. Ron's lover Jack, an expert in Torah cantillation, was outraged by Dov's intervention to correct a minor mistake, and an unpleasant exchange of words ensued. Dov angrily left the bimah and had to be persuaded not to go home immediately.

Commenting on these outbursts, Naomi exclaimed in exasperation, "I come here for a spiritual experience; is this my spiritual experience?" These incidents brought to the fore personal and ideological conflicts within the congregation. Such conflicts were never allowed to surface, however, during Rosh Hashanah and Yom Kippur services, when CBST was on stage to "the world" as a showcase gay synagogue.

When the Religious Committee met after the High Holidays, Larry, who had taken a leading role in the Rosh Hashanah service, praised

it for having been "as old-fashioned a service as you can get at CBST."
But he termed the Simchat Torah service an "orphan," without
parental control. The committee concluded a stronger service leader
was needed next year. Sheila felt that the lack of any protest over the   99
elimination of the dukhanin augured well for the future relations
between men and women in the synagogue.

Holiday services were often accompanied by a congregational dinner. On the second night of Passover, 1989, almost 250 members participated in a service followed by a seder meal. Many were not regular
service-goers, and women comprised half the group, a much larger
proportion than usual. The seder was led by Larry and Naomi, who
added a reading of her own to the Hagaddah. In order to enhance the
feeling of intimacy, she suggested that each table share Passover memories. The board chair gave a short talk associating the freedom of the
ancient Israelites from the yoke of Pharaoh with his hopes for a more
complete gay liberation. Rose, who regularly attended services, told
me: "The food was poor, but the company was good."

Ad Hoc Services

In addition to the regular weekly and holiday services CBST periodically sponsored or took part in services surrounding special events
such as the installation of the Holocaust Torah scroll and the AIDS
Vigil held during Gay Pride Week, 1989.

Carrying an American flag, a gay rainbow flag, and the Israeli flag,
CBST led a solemn procession of gay organizations and individuals
along Christopher Street to an interfaith assembly. The second speaker,
Norman, introduced himself as the first openly gay president of the
local community board, made a short speech, and read a hymn from
Psalms. After a Catholic priest spoke, David, as CBST's representative,
invited Gilbert to lead the evocative El Maleh Rakhamim prayer for the
repose of the dead. Then, to the growing uneasiness of the congregants
next to me, David invited another CBST member to read the mourner's
Kaddish and asked the seated dignitaries and orchestra to all rise. It
appeared as if CBST had taken over the event with David as master of
ceremonies and the Israeli flag in the background. "This is how
anti–Semitism is promoted," I heard one CBST member complain.

When the synagogue's participation in the vigil was discussed at the
next Religious Committee's meeting, Sheila expressed her dismay at
seeing the Israeli flag during the ceremony. Simon commented that the

▼

Star of David has become a CBST symbol, but Henry expressed his uneasiness with the synagogue's adoption of the Israeli flag, which has no religious meaning, as its symbol. There were complaints that David, who had organized CBST's participation in the event, had made the vigil his own business and a show of strength against the original planning, which gave twenty minutes to the Catholic Dignity New York and only three minutes to CBST. "He is an independent operator," Larry observed and he agreed with the chair's conclusion that all activities that involve a service be reviewed by the committee in advance.

David, a board member who often attended Religious Committee meetings, also had elaborate plans for the coming adoption of a Holocaust Torah from a synagogue in Czechoslovakia—one of more than a thousand scrolls expropriated by the Nazis for a planned ethnographic museum of a soon-to-be extinct race. These scrolls, now back in Jewish hands, were gradually being given on permanent loan to interested congregations. CBST's request for one of the scrolls had been accepted by their custodians, and two congregants traveled to England to collect this remnant of a lost community. David wanted to invite Governor Cuomo as well as the Gay Men's Chorus and carry the scroll in a grand procession through the major streets of the Village, stopping at the site of the Stonewall Bar. "David wants to make a political statement" was the unhappy reaction of the committee. This time the committee was careful to make its own arrangements for a more intimate event, "to bring a family member back home," as one of them characterized it. "It has to be our ceremony and avoid unnecessary street violence and anti–Semitism." Instead of a big chorus, one clarinet (from a Jewish klezmer group) was decided on. Instead of the Stonewall Bar site alongside Sheridan Square, the ceremony would begin at the Lesbian and Gay Community Services Center and continue through the quiet streets leading to the synagogue. Instead of Governor Cuomo, it was suggested that Elie Weisel be invited. Religious Committee members Larry and Simon were given responsibility for the installation ceremony at the synagogue following the procession. David, who attended the meeting, was persuaded to support that plan.

Texts and Subtexts

A Siddur for CBST

A frequent question raised at Religious Committee meetings, and elsewhere, was the status of the "new siddur," intended to replace that used by CBST for nearly a decade. Had it been adopted, it would have been the third major text for the Friday night service.

The first prayer book had been prepared by Aaron, assisted by Larry, Edward, Gilbert, and Dov, and was remembered as the "blue thing," the "blue bound book," or the "blue *shmateh* [rag]." Bound together within blue covers, it was a small collection of the major prayers, hymns, psalms, and folk songs, in Hebrew and English, used at CBST. Included were Lecha Dodi, Ma Tovu, Ahavat Olam, both a concise Shema and the Amidah, the Aleinu, the kiddush, Adon Olam and Yigdal, and modern versions of traditional prayers. (It also contained the Agnon eulogy as an additional mourner's prayer, which in later years became the synagogue's standard commemoration for its dead.) But that first thirty-five page siddur made no reference whatsoever to the gay identity of the worshippers. In addition, the English translation remained close to the original Hebrew, without degenderization. For example, the Amidah, begins as it does in the Hebrew: "Blessed art Thou, Lord our God and God of our fathers, God of Abraham, God of Isaac and God of Jacob." That style would have been considered a gross offense soon after its compilation. The second siddur traduced this passage—both in Hebrew and English—into: "Praised are You Adonai our God, and God of our fathers and mothers, God of Abraham and Sarah, God of Isaac and Rebecca, God of Jacob, Rachel and Leah." Recognizing its limitations, Aaron himself had planned to rework this first attempt to standardize the liturgy at CBST.

After Aaron's departure, the Religious Committee appointed Larry, Simon, and Nathan to prepare a revised siddur suitable for a congregation no longer led by one individual and reflecting the growing sensitivity to gender. The Siddur Committee consulted the prayer books used by the Reform and Conservative movements and made selections suitable for the congregation. Particular prayers, hymns, and songs were chosen because of their closeness to gay themes such as love and pain.

The result was a 250-page siddur titled in English and Hebrew "With All Your Heart," which was officially introduced in May 1981. It opens with an editors' preface:

> This Siddur reflects the tradition of blending the familiar with the interpretive, the old with the new. It is as heterogeneous as is our Congregation. . . . The Infinite God has no gender. Our Siddur

▼

reflects this fact through its translations and readings. . . . This Siddur stands as an open statement of who we are as an integral part of the Gay and Lesbian community, as proud Gay and Lesbian Jews, as members of *K'lal Yisrael*, the Community of Israel.

The siddur begins with the traditional Ma Tovu praising the children of Jacob and their love of God. But its second prayer opens with the line "We, gay Jews, have come together to strengthen our bonds with our people, Israel." Soon afterward comes Yedid Nefesh ("Soul mate"), which a footnote describes as a passionate and sensual plea for the fulfillment of love between God and Israel written by a seventeenth-century kabbalist. Larry explained its inclusion in terms of gay yearning for the love of God: "A Jew comes to the synagogue. He feels 'I am gay, I am rejected; my parents don't know about it, I can't tell my boss; but coming to this place I have no secrets; You, God, know it.' " I was also told that because this passionate love poem casts the love of God not in terms of a powerful ruler and his subject but in terms of the warmth of friendship, the bonds of "soul mates," it resonates to a gay audience.

In the English translation of the traditional R'etze prayer, a few pages later, a direct reference to homosexual identity is interpolated into the text: "May we, the gay daughters and sons of your people Israel find rest on this day." Later, comes the hymn Vetaher Libenu ("Purify our hearts"), dedicated to the Sabbath, which contains the line: "Help us to make our shul a true sanctuary." The term *shul*, I was told, was not found in the sources but added deliberately to make the text sound heimish. Three poems that Aaron had used to stimulate a feeling of intimate community among the congregants were included for their evocative, nostalgic value. Aaron's English translation of one made a gay connection:

Give us now as much joy as the sadness
You gave us during our years of misery.

Though two of these have since fallen out of use, the third one, Shalom Aleichem ("Peace with you"), sung arm-in-arm, has become a popular CBST tradition as described above.

An emphatic reference to gay identity appears in the introduction to a later psalm:

As gays, we often feel forced to pretend to be that which we are not . . . and sometimes with outright lies. . . . We do not have to tell untruths to You as we are often forced to do in the straight world. . . . Eternal God, purify our heart to serve You in truth.

The same committee that compiled the siddur, assisted by a few other members, produced a High Holiday machzor, prayer book and, sometime later, a siddur for the Sabbath morning service to complement that of Friday night.

Yedid Nefesh also appears among the first pages of the High Holiday machzor. "Because it is love oriented, we thought it would have deeper significance for our people," I was told by one of the editors. Prayers were selected from other mainstream machzorim because they "spoke directly to our condition [although not written for gays]—about gratitude and joy, sorrow and bitterness, hunger for friendship." The machzor also includes a special prayer addressing the condition of homosexuals written by a CBST congregant:

> As gay and lesbian Jews we are aware of the loss of integrity we suffer under the pressure of the larger society. We often feel forced into a dishonest presentation of ourselves—to ourselves and others. . . . We are the new Marranos—the modern counterparts of the Jews of early Spain who were forced to pretend to have converted and who could only retain their true identity in secret. With the chanting of Kol Nidrey we ask that our enforced hiding draw to an end . . . that our fullest creative expression as Jews, as gays, as human beings, be among the blessings in store for the coming year.

Another meditation, before the Aleinu ("Our duty to praise") later in the service, was also written by a congregant. But it referred more subtly to the congregants' identity:

> How can we do other than praise the God of all? . . . For we especially have been blessed by God with a rare appreciation of our own uniqueness, without which any creative sense of our own purpose and meaning is all but impossible.

Gay references were also interpolated into traditional prayers with an added stanza in the style of the original. For example: "[God] Be with our brothers and sisters whose lives are made difficult because they are gay. Give them strength to endure, and lead them soon from their bondage to freedom, from darkness to light."

▼

The editors assumed the siddur would "not be set in stone, but be very open to change, reform and reconstruction." To accommodate it, at intervals, they skipped numbers to allow pages to be added later. But as Simon, among the proponents of change, soon learned, this was not the case: "What we thought would be open to change was concretized." Not only had none of the editors the energy to go on changing the text, but they didn't want their work subject to review. Once the siddur was accepted any change had to be refereed and then approved by the Religious Committee. Instead of adding prayers or changing those in the siddur, service leaders prepared handouts to supplement the text. The proliferation of handouts, however, often caused confusion during services.

Within a few years the mood of the synagogue was pressing for a new siddur to better express the changes that had taken place at CBST and reduce the use of handouts. A committee was appointed for the task, consisting of Larry and Simon, among the editors of the siddur in use, and three new members, including Linda, a rabbi. But that group was unable to work together. Larry and Simon dropped out of it, and Linda—highly regarded by all—left New York. The project was carried on by the remaining members: Dov, and his close friend, Gershon, with Jill newly appointed.

In April 1989 the Religious Committee met to consider their work. The consensus among the committee members was unfavorable. A third of the new siddur was thought good, a third totally unacceptable, and the remainder, tolerable at best. Despite its use of prayers written by congregants and its reliance on translations made by the editors themselves, in its tone it represented a more traditional style of liturgy than the committee was looking for. It was not the contemporary text they were looking for.

A rabbi in the congregation who had been shown the proposed siddur was invited to give a critique. His report was highly critical. He thought the editors had made a poor selection of prayers, and the English translations were too literal and lacked poetic power. He was particularly annoyed with their method of degenderization. For instance, they retained the inclusive phraseology of the current siddur, which was now seen as patriarchal: "The God of Abraham and Sarah, the God of Isaac and Rebecca, the God of Jacob, Rachel and Leah." Not only were the men named first, but the women were related to God only through the men as intermediaries. Moreover,

Rachel who was Jacob's second wife was named ahead of Leah, who though less favored by her husband was the mother of many tribes. Was it her lesser looks that made her second in the liturgy? The referee had, at least, expected the editors to have substituted: "The God of Abraham and the God of Sarah, the God of Isaac and the God of Rebecca." As a final blow to the new siddur, the reviewer argued that the editors had not directly addressed the issue of homosexuality. Rather they had hidden it under vague references to "our identity and our problems." Naomi, who fully agreed with the criticism raised, argued that the Religious Committee had never actually discussed the ideological issues that should have guided the editors of the siddur. For example, what is the nature of God in CBST's doctrine? Assuming the truth of her argument, the Religious Committee wondered how it could find a consensus on these issues. Call a public meeting? Could one decide matters of theology in a big crowd? In the meantime, how could they adopt a new siddur that might be used for many years to come?

Henry was not impressed with the reviewer's complaint about the order of Jacob's wives. In defense of the editors, he argued that it is easier for cantors to end the sentence with the open vowel of "Leah" rather than the closed consonant of "Rachel." Nevertheless, he agreed that the editors "do not have a sense of the pervasive ideology of the synagogue."

The committee was not alone in its rejection of the new siddur. That position was shared by those close to the synagogue's religious affairs. Leon expressed his disdain for the editors' selection and style: "They tried to go back to traditional readings. It is cold. Their God is a fearful being, not a loving one. I couldn't see the joy of praying with that siddur."

But if the decision was clear, delivering the message to the editors was difficult. Simon, who agreed with all the criticism raised, worried that the editors would blame him for the rejection of their work. He hoped the bad news would be delivered by prominent synagogue leaders and palliated by casting it not in terms of a poor effort but in terms of one that was different from the committee's expectations. "We were waiting for a Picasso, but we got a Rembrandt instead," was his conciliatory suggestion. In the end, the board chair Saul was given the unenviable task. He found the editors to be hurt and angry. They complained of a biased reviewing process but offered to make

changes to the siddur if specifically advised. Unable to deliver the final verdict, Saul told them he would invite ten more congregants to read their siddur before the board made a final decision. The Reli-
gious Committee was unhappy with that concession, which some thought made the selection of a siddur a "political" issue. The committee felt the siddur's editors only had themselves to blame for refusing to show their work before it was finished. Eventually, Saul gave up the idea of a wider refereeing process, and the siddur was rejected without a formal decision.

Dov and his coeditors held the Religious Committee responsible for denying their wish to let the congregation see their work and judge it favorably. They felt Simon and a few others on the committee had a vested interest in retaining the current siddur, which they had produced. The editors defended their English translations. They had consciously sought a "simple" style close to the austere Hebrew original, even at the expense of "poetry." To the ideological criticism Dov explained their orientation: "Our God is not merciful. For each blessing, you find twenty threats and curses. But the Americans need a lyrical style." They ridiculed the rabbi's critique of their degenderization as "superfeminism." One of their supporters resented what he saw as the self-indulgent practice of service leader handouts that the committee allowed. He called these literary creations "liturgical masturbation." "It's okay to masturbate in private, but not in public," he exclaimed.

Dov viewed the rejection of his siddur in a wider context, one that included his clash with Jack over the correction of Ron's Torah reading:

> I told him we have to do it right! We live outside the ordinary rules. But we must follow some rules. If we have to create our own rules, then we should at least abide by them. But as I see it, the rules are being adjusted to the convenience of particular individuals.

He saw the Religious Committee's criticism of the siddur for being too close to the Hebrew original as yet another breach of the obligation "to do it right," this in a world beset by doubt and insecurity.

The rejection of the proposed siddur continued to foster ill feelings and occasional emotional outbursts. Gershon, outraged with both the Religious Committee and the board, threatened to resign from his position as a cantor of the 1990 High Holiday services, but was dissuaded. The goal of a revised siddur remained unfulfilled by the time a permanent rabbi was appointed two years later. It remained for her to guide this effort in the synagogue's third decade.

Degenderized Texts

Gender neutrality became a yardstick for judging a text appropriate for CBST. "God has no gender here," Joel declared. Since the siddur in use was not always satisfactory, careful service leaders would correct it spontaneously to accommodate the emergent sensitivity. When I questioned Simon about the inevitable poetic loss involved in naming seven matriarchs and patriarchs, each preceded by "God of," he answered that it was not just a concession to gender equality, but that God is not the same for everyone, "Each one has his or her own God." But not everyone greeted this practice so equably. Edward was annoyed with that degenderized litany during a Sukkot morning service and was seen to close his siddur and continue to pray in silence. Degenderization was sometimes a source of amusement. Simon, reading a prayer thanking God for the covenant he had made through circumcision with Abraham, automatically added—as he always did—"and Sarah." On another occasion a woman new to the synagogue came to the bimah to read a passage that contained the word *brotherhood*. Her substitution of the term *filialship* prompted laughs from attentive listeners.

CBST's facility with degenderization was revealed at an annual convention of gay synagogues that a number of CBST members attended. As the assembled were reading the grace after meals from a text provided by the host synagogue, they were stopped by the implicit slight to women in the crude English translation: "We thank you for the covenant you made with Abraham through circumcision." (In contrast to CBST's own less literal "We thank you for the covenant sealed with Abraham.") Larry saved the situation by skillfully guiding the prayer around these shoals. When the story was repeated at a meeting of the Religious Committee, Simon suggested that in future events of congregational meals the Hebrew text itself be changed to read: "The covenant that you sealed in our heart" (rather than "in our flesh").

At the same convention Larry gave a lecture on his strategy for degenderization. He gave the example of using the English "ruler of the universe" for the Hebrew "king of the universe." When he came, as CBST service leader, to the reading in Hebrew of the prayer Magen

▼

Avot ("Shield of our fathers"), he would substitute Magen Dorot ("Shield of our generations"). In the CBST siddur, of which he had been an editor, the English translation of the Shema contains the injunction "Teach them to the generations to come," rather than "Teach them to your sons." And in a gay reference, "liberation" is often used instead of "redemption" or "salvation."

Actually, the editors of CBST's siddur had compromised between those who wished to see the Hebrew text, like the English, thoroughly degenderized and those who objected to manipulation of the Hebrew original. The result was only modest changes to the Hebrew. Consequently, it remained to the more radical service leaders to introduce additional changes to the Hebrew text spontaneously, some of which became part of a CBST oral tradition. To a number of members it was a failure of the new siddur that it did not incorporate this oral tradition in its written text.

Aaron was less impressed with all these efforts at selecting and rewriting texts. He thought the ordinary siddur used in many Orthodox synagogues was wonderful, and that the enthusiasm for degenderization was producing grotesque results. He pointed to the Purim megillah reading at CBST, when, he felt, for the sake of equality the humor and fun of the text were lost. Instead of the megillah's light-hearted conclusion reassuring each man's dominant position in his home, the following was interpolated: "Each man and woman would be master of their home." Aaron also considered it ludicrous to add the matriarchs to all references to the covenant. Women play an important role in the Bible, he argued, but not in that particular event.

Ephemera

For the 1990 Purim festival Simon prepared an invitation to be mailed to all CBST members and included in the newsletter. He submitted it to the Religious Committee for approval. It opened with the announcement: "The Queens invite you to a Purim celebration," and ended with a reference to a *faygeleh* (literally "little bird," the Yiddish euphemism for *homosexual*) performance. Larry immediately expressed his reservations about using those terms in the synagogue's official publication: "It is not appropriate for our newsletter, but I wouldn't mind it for a flier." Jack shared his feeling and suggested instead, "The queen of Persia invites" or "The king and queen." Simon rejected these alternatives, which eliminated the humor as well as the nostalgia *faygeleh* might prompt among those who remembered a CBST Purim play under that name performed years before. Sheila supported Simon and questioned the rationale for tolerating those terms in a flier but not in the newsletter. She declared she wouldn't mind the use of the term *dykes*. Larry responded: "The newsletter represents our congregation to the world, and *queens* is a degrading term." Ron agreed: "We are better off without these terms. Psychologically it is not healthy to put ourselves down." In the end Simon gave up his plan for a provocatively worded invitation. This incident, although not an issue of degenderization, equally reflected the textual sensitivities at CBST.

Ritual Innovation Versus Tradition

Ashes in the Synagogue?

The first debate I attended over a controversial practice involved a request made by the family of a CBST member—practically unknown to the Religious Committee—to allow his funeral service in the presence of the deceased's ashes. Jack, who received the request, was very uncomfortable making the decision alone about a practice that conflicts with the Jewish requirement that the body be buried in its entirety. He was spared, however, by a delay in the cremation, allowing the service to proceed without the problematic substance in the sanctuary. Nevertheless, Jack raised the issue at the next meeting of the Religious Committee so as to determine future policy. David, a board member, suggested the issue be left to individual cases, but Jack objected and asked for a clear vote on the matter. One committee member argued he himself wished to be cremated and could not see the difference between the body and ashes in the synagogue. He also thought cremation avoided the problems of burial when non-Jewish partners were involved. Simon was hesitant and thought they needed more time for deliberation. But Jack pressed for a decision despite the late hour. Finally, four voted against allowing ashes in a synagogue service, one voted for, and one abstained.

The Elimination of Dukhanin

I have already written about the elimination of the dukhanin. That important ritual of Orthodox holiday services, connecting the modern synagogue with the ancient Temple, was completely discarded despite strong protest, mainly by descendants of the Cohanim clan.

▼

When I met Sam during the AIDS Vigil, he asked me if I had heard about the dukhanin issue. Obviously angry, he pointed to one of CBST's active members and exclaimed, "These women are sometimes so radical!" He continued, "I told her, 'You deny me my heritage as much as Arafat does.' " According to Sam, the women had refused a compromise letting them participate in the ritual. They felt it was a male chauvinist tradition. "But this is also true for the rabbi's role [which women have taken]!" he ended with indignation.

But not all so-called traditionalists supported the dukhanin. Dov, himself a Cohen, told me he didn't care about that ritual since his own father hadn't. "It is not my tradition," he concluded. But, he continued to explain, he was ready to condone change in ritual "only if there is a reason to do that, not because it is convenient or pleasing." Too many rituals and traditions are changed in the synagogue without an appreciation of the meaning behind them, he claimed.

Aliyah for a Non-Jew?

Dov carried on a long battle with Aaron against allowing non–Jews to bless God for the gift of Torah (the privilege of aliyah). Aaron had himself given that honor to his Gentile partner, who repeated in English Aaron's Hebrew blessing. Dov used to argue with him: "How could a non–Jew read a blessing that states, 'You have chosen us from among all nations?' " (In the English version Aaron prepared the phrase was somewhat less explicit.) Dov thought Gentiles could participate in the service, but should refrain from that particular part. He himself had begun a relationship with a non-Jew during my stay in New York.

Soon after Aaron's departure Dov pressed the issue with the Religious Committee, and a debate that, in Dov's words, threatened to "split the synagogue" raged for some time. Sam, who years later was so enraged at the elimination of the dukhanin, was deeply offended by the proposed rule change that would deprive his lover of the honor of blessing God for the Torah. He thought it was an ungrateful act considering his Gentile lover's special contribution to CBST. But Dov succeeded in persuading the committee to discontinue Aaron's custom, a custom he felt Aaron himself would eventually have abandoned. "Even here there are some limits," Dov observed, years later. There were, nevertheless, occasions when that rule was breached, more often without complaint, but sometimes with angry complaints to the Religious Committee.

Inventing a New Ritual

The enthusiasm that greeted the synagogue's installation of the Holocaust Torah and the special service Simon had led in its honor prompted him to suggest incorporating it as a regular feature of CBST ritual. He proposed to the Religious Committee that they recommend service leaders read a portion from that Torah during the Friday night Service. While Torah reading, in general, is customary on Friday nights among Reform congregations, it is not so among Conservative or Orthodox ones, and neither is it at CBST. As there was no specific ritual surrounding a Holocaust Torah, Simon saw an opportunity: "We as a gay synagogue are going to invent one: we will read from it, and sing and dance around it." Henry, the board's liaison to the committee, wasn't enthusiastic. He questioned the need for a new ritual, and why one only for the Holocaust scroll while another scroll was unused. Larry, with whom Simon had already discussed the matter and who had advised him to first get the committee's approval, tried to mediate. He drew a distinction between the ritual Torah reading of the Sabbath morning service with blessings preceding and following, and the darshan's quoting passages from the text: "It's not going to be a Torah reading, but scripture reading." Simon tried to placate Henry by suggesting they try it once at the next service, which was being led by Saul, known to have been instrumental in getting the Holocaust Torah. When Henry seemed, or pretended, not to understand why it should be at Saul's service in particular, Simon lost his composure and exclaimed angrily, "We have a real need for something more than the tradition concretized for eleven years." He expressed his frustration at trying to introduce innovations in the past and threatened to resign from the Religious Committee if his proposal was rejected.

Other members tried to appease both sides. Ze'ev reminded his colleagues of CBST's tradition of flexibility in ritual, and recommended that Simon's invention be left only as an option, not a requirement, for service leaders. Jack reminded the members that many elements of the Friday service are adapted from that of the Sabbath morning, so that reading from the Torah without blessings would not be so unusual. To my naive suggestion that the innovation had a precedent in Reform practice, both Larry and Simon himself demurred that CBST had a policy not to imitate the Reform service. Larry confessed that he had recently been hurt by a piece in the newsletter that claimed that the committee was not open to change and that the services were not responsive to the congregants' needs. Responding to a desire to prove they welcomed creativity and change in ritual, despite their reservations about Simon's invention, the majority finally acquiesced.

112

With only Henry remaining in opposition, the last issue was how to word the committee's recommendation to Saul. Simon suggested that Saul be told, "The committee decided it is appropriate that you . . . " Henry objected and demanded a more neutral recommendation: "It is okay that you . . . " Ultimately, Saul had his own idea for his service, which involved telling the congregation about his family's roots in Europe. The Holocaust Torah itself was soon moved from the ark and installed in its own wood and glass case—"vitrified"—and Simon's ritual invention was never enacted.

The acceptance of innovation, the discarding of old traditions, and the reinstatement of traditional practices were a continuing source of discussion and sometimes conflict at CBST. The service leader's elimination of the Amidah from a New Year's Friday night service was often remembered as breaching the bounds of propriety. When the story was recalled during a Sabbath lunch, Ze'ev commented: "Innovations are not so bad, but they must be applied with moderation." He thought the substitution of a meditation for the Amidah would have been tolerated were it not for the "many other things they did" (Christmas melodies, etc.) at that unprecedented service.

When Larry, as service leader, was upset because Bob, his cantor, included a prayer that Larry had decided to eliminate and, to add to his annoyance, used an unknown melody, he was told at the Religious Committee: "We can't do anything about people's style. We are a diverse congregation and we have to live with it." A Rosh Hashanah service was reviewed at the same committee meeting. Members were annoyed with Edward and Saul, who, instead of reading part of the haftarah in Hebrew and part in English, read the full text in both languages. Clearly, Edward's "traditionalist" preferences led him to override the committee's wishes, telling Saul: "You do what you want, I know what I'm going to do!" The issue was put to rest after some discussion with the conclusion that it was a personal problem. A committee member added, referring to Edward's behavior, "If you're not a team player it doesn't work." Ultimately, Edward was tolerated on the grounds of CBST's diversity.

For the 1989 High Holidays it was suggested that video cameras and monitors be used to enable those seated in remote spots to observe the bimah. Larry explained that the innovation had a "religious aspect and a sociological aspect." Sociologically, "it will inte- grate and include more people." Religiously, "it's O.K. with me; but like the loudspeakers, we won't repair them during the service."

Was there any consistency in the cases above? I have describeded the committee's refusal to allow ashes in the synagogue or Torah blessings by non-Jews, despite their visibility as partners of influential members. On the other hand, the committee discarded the dukhanin ritual over the vocal protest of an interested group, but accepted an inventive Holocaust Torah ritual in spite of serious reservations among its own ranks, dismissing several minor instances of discontent. One might recruit some variables from the social and religious domain to reveal a "pattern" in the decision making of the Religious Committee. But I think that professional revelation of a concealed order would actually detract from an understanding of CBST's ongoing negotiation along a path of undefined but continuously contested theological space.

"What Is Our Theology?"

The congregants often commented on the character of their services by comparing them with those of mainstream Jewish movements as well as other gay synagogues. Members who were pleased with CBST often described their synagogue to newcomers as being on a path of its own between the Conservative and Reform movements. They would point out that there is more Hebrew than in a typical Reform service, and that the congregation takes a more active role in reading and singing. They were also obviously proud of CBST's egalitarian tradition of lay-led services, of its sensitivity to degenderization, and of its inclusion of special prayers touching on gay identity. Those congregants would also favorably compare CBST to other gay congregations, which they considered less proficient in Judaism but compensating with music, singing, and dancing.

On the whole other gay synagogues did not, however, play an important role in the religious and social discourse at CBST. No one on the Religious Committee, or in synagogue leadership generally, promoted the idea of a united front with other gay synagogues, nor did the synagogue approach the outer world as representing a nationwide

▼

movement. The leadership thought of CBST as a unique institution, by virtue of its size, its success, the diversity of its membership, its lay-leadership, and its independence from mainstream movements. Membership at CBST was a unique mark of Gay-Jewish identity as much as being a New Yorker was to being American.

But there were those who considered CBST too traditional, so much so that they attended services only rarely. They complained in particular about the extensive use of Hebrew. Old-timers in that group claimed that had not been the case in earlier years, and they also missed that period's more intimate atmosphere. A serious assault on the synagogue's style was made by a member who happened to be a rabbi, quoted earlier, in the newsletter: "I do not understand why we vest so much authority in a system that has denied us so long?" Instead, he wished to see a practice of Judaism that drew its inspiration as much from gay life: "We must make our experience as gays and lesbians an integral, not incidental, component of our Judaism." His criticism appeared to coincide with that of Jewish intellectuals at the forefront of secular gay culture. Seymour Kleinberg, author of *Alienated Affections*, who was invited to address the congregation, described it to me as not radical enough, and too sentimentally engaged in the typical Jewish concerns of Israel and the Holocaust. He thought the congregation was too anxious to resemble a mainstream straight synagogue and concluded sarcastically: "They would prefer the company of a straight Jew to that of a gay Gentile!"

On the other hand, there were those who were equally unhappy with the synagogue's "radicalism," its "Judaism bashing," as they termed it. They disliked the extensive use of English and sought a more traditional expression of their faith. Some found their way to Orthodox synagogues who tolerated their inconspicuous presence. But they preserved their bonds with the congregation through the Talmud class, the new early minyan service, and occasional attendance at regular services and social events. Except for Aaron and his closest friends, the decision to join a mainstream synagogue was rarely a permanent act. Nathan, among the editors of the 1981 siddur, became active in a modern Orthodox synagogue, but had the humiliating experience of standing next to its rabbi on the bimah when he ridiculed the Reform movement's announcement of its acceptance of gay rabbis. In spite of Nathan's complaints about the ignorance of Judaism at CBST, his attendance at services became more frequent.

Setting aside the presence of gay-related prayers, visitors, usually straight, who attended CBST services differed in how to characterize them. A student at the Reform rabbinical school felt the Friday night service was somewhere between Conservative and Reform in style. Compared to Reform, there was more Hebrew, but no Torah reading. However, the Sabbath morning service was, he thought, even more traditional than that of a Conservative synagogue. A student at the Conservative rabbinical school agreed there was more Hebrew in the Friday service than in Reform, but argued it also contained some "unacceptable" parts for a Conservative service. Another visitor commented that he could not see any important differences between CBST's and a Reform or Conservative service except for same-sex couples blessing the Torah together and the absence of a benediction at the end of service. But a gay visitor claimed the service at CBST was essentially different from Reform, Conservative, and even other gay services, which he thought were closer to Reform.

The diversity of opinions and preferences concerning synagogue ritual, and the agitation for change from "right" and "left," became part of CBST's official rhetoric. While welcoming the congregation to the 1990 Kol Nidre service, Jack, service leader and Religious Committee chair, pointed out that the synagogue brought together people of "various theologies." Later that same night Paul read Martin's speech, which contained his favorite comment about the diversity at CBST: "Opinions in our synagogue run the gamut from Orthodoxy to Reform Judaism, and people always complain, 'The service is too Orthodox. . . . The service is too Reform.'" In an interview in the *Jewish Week*, Martin described the heterogeneity of the population at CBST as ranging from Orthodox to secular and all shades in between. He claimed they were closer in their practice to Conservatives, but ideologically closer to Reconstructionists. This diversity was the reason the synagogue did not affiliate with one of the more tolerant mainstream movements as Martin and other members would have wished. Martin refrained from advocating that course because he believed it might split the congregation, an outcome he as board chair sought to avoid. (Though he had, in the past, entertained that possibility as a way of dealing with the synagogue's diversity and internal dissent.)

The invocation "We are a diverse congregation" also became a vehicle for accepting—as well as rejecting—any claim made on the synagogue's ritual, either for its retention or its alteration. It provided

▼

an immediate answer to a pressing dilemma and probably a substitute for the search for CBST's theology.

That the synagogue had an ethos, "unity within diversity," but not a clearly defined theology was most evident in the deliberations over the proposed siddur. The editors were criticized for missing the synagogue's ideology. "They lack the vision and the spirit needed; it was a mistake to let them start with it," was one comment. But Naomi, who along with Henry had tried to explain to the editors that their work was flawed in more than details, felt the fault was partly with the committee: "We are looking for a vision we haven't yet articulated." As Sheila asked her colleagues on the Religious Committee, "What is our theology?"

This dilemma also arose when Bob asked permission to give short interpretive talks at the services. His request was rejected in part because of fear that it would bestow on him a formal theological position, and one usurping the multiplicity—the diversity—of service leaders. Simon complained that Bob had been with the synagogue for less than a year and "is not familiar enough with our ideology." Another committee member responded, rhetorically: "Do we have a theological perspective; do we have a theology?" In chapter 8 I explore the organizational weakness of the Religious Committee. Although it carried enormous burdens and was responsible for the running of most services, it lacked the authority and institutional autonomy to codify the principles of a "CBST theology."

Amid the Religious Committee's wrestling with issues of theology and ideology, discussions sometimes took a lighter tone. Sheila jocularly observed that individuals themselves could be inconsistent in their ideology. She poked fun at those who raised theological arguments against the inclusion of the matriarchs in the text and then retired to a corner to smoke on the Sabbath. She defined that apparent inconsistency as "Smoking and Ima'ot [mothers]." These were men who were adamantly Orthodox on the issue of changing the text but careless with the rules of the Sabbath. She pointed out that the Torah does not forbid the elevation of women in ritual but does command the sanctity of the Sabbath and proscribe lighting a fire on that day. Women were far less represented than men in religious affairs, but they were more often engaged in discussions about CBST's theological orientation. That observation of women's greater proficiency in theological discourse seemed to reflect the impact of the feminist critique of Judaism.[4]

Jeff, who visited the synagogue only irregularly, nonetheless told me he loved the place because it offered various things to different people: Judaism, congenial company, and emotional support. He objected to the idea of splitting the services because he declared: "The synagogue is more than its parts." Joel, a former Religious Committee chair, commenting on the synagogue's heterogeneous congregation, observed "We are not a neighborhood synagogue." He went on to explain that the loyalty of the congregants was not to a particular religious movement or to the personality of a rabbi, but to their organization, despite the diversity of their religious and social backgrounds.

The idea that diversity was both a unique and essential dimension of the synagogue's persona was not a slogan, employed by shrewd politicians or incompetent spiritual leaders, but a pervasive feeling experienced by the majority of congregants.

▼

CHAPTER SIX

The Drashah: Negotiating Multiple Realities

The most anticipated point of the service at CBST was the presentation of the sermon or drashah. This interpretation of the week's—or
holiday's—Torah reading was the most personalized, least formula-
rized part of the service, and allowed the speaker to express his or her
feelings and attitudes toward God, Judaism, the synagogue, family
and friends, homosexuality, and other shared experiences. Both the
content and presentation of the drashah became a major topic of conversation among the congregants as well as a source of personal pride
for the presenter.

The drashah's historical roots lie in the Jewish culture of the Middle Ages and a homiletic literature of moral and ethical instruction in
which ancient texts are points of departure for a discussion of everyday life. Appealing directly to its audience, it was an artistic achievement in which seemingly unconnected ideas were suddenly shown to
be related and, it has been suggested, a means of introducing new
ideas into traditional Judaism.[1] Adapted in the nineteenth century by
the Reform movement as the rabbi's sermon, in most synagogues in
the Jewish world today it is an essential element of the service, and
one of the rabbi's major tasks. In the role of darshan, the rabbi has the
opportunity to demonstrate his or her scholastic skills, eloquence,
and compassion as teacher and moral guide.

During CBST's early years Aaron, Edward, and Gilbert rotated the
role of darshan weekly. Aaron's presentations, though sometimes mys-

tical, generally followed the normative, traditional style. Edward's *drashot* (pl.) reflected his interest at that time in kabbalistic ideas and spiritual meanings "not apparent to the senses or obvious to the mind." Gilbert's were more psychological and literary, and often 119 referred to gay experience in the context of the biblical text. Commenting on its first *darshanim* (pl.), Simon observed: "It was certainly another example of the shul's unity within its diversity to be morally taught and intellectually stimulated by three such eloquent and varied teachers." After Aaron departed, however, Gilbert ultimately became less active in the synagogue, and Edward's style less popular with the congregation.

In time the Religious Committee instituted a new policy, which opened the role of darshan, like that of service leader, to the entire congregation—a highly valued tradition that continues to the present day. Any congregant in good standing could ask to deliver a drashah. The congregant was then placed under the supervision of a Religious Committee member and given a manual outlining the rules to be followed. Among them were that the address must be no longer than fifteen minutes, have a beginning, middle, and end, be relevant to the weekly parashah (portion of the Torah), not be "political," and be gender–neutral in reference to God. Congregants who had satisfactorily gone through the process several times, demonstrating their ability to perform this role, were confirmed as qualified darshanim and exempt from further supervision—as were ordained rabbis. The Religious Committee then had little influence on their presentations except for limiting the number of their talks. (In one case the committee was unhappy with a rabbi whose presentation had not been gender–neutral and offended many in the congregation. He was approached by the committee's chair, and promised to be more careful in future appearances. After delivering another drashah that was still not fully satisfactory, it was decided to limit his talks to no more than two per annual cycle.)

The tradition that entitled any member to deliver a drashah was considered an important and unique facet of CBST and a major component of the congregation's self–perception as an egalitarian, lay–led organization. (The fact that only two of the twenty–four darshanim I heard were women did not seem to diminish that idea.) So well ingrained was it that despite wide discontent with certain presentations and resentment, in some quarters, of specific darshanim, rarely if ever was anyone denied another opportunity to deliver a drashah. And during the long deliberations over whether to hire a rabbi, proponents of the idea made clear that CBST's tradition of lay service leaders and drashah speakers would not be affected. Only occasionally would the rabbi lead the service or present the drashah. More often, he or she would coach the congregants, improving their skills as service leaders and darshanim.

The drashah speaker had the ear of the congregation. On the High Holidays and other special occasions, such as the Gay Pride Friday evening service, this honor was usually given to a leader of the synagogue, and for some it became a personal privilege traditionally granted. But at other services those who might not be prominent in the synagogue had the opportunity to address the membership at "prime time" on the "main stage." If they performed ably their standing was enhanced, and they might aspire to a greater role in the synagogue's affairs. This avenue of advancement was particularly open to those who brought with them prior experience in Jewish scholarship or public speaking, but there were a few proficient darshanim whose skill was acquired at CBST. Dov, who was remembered as a poor speaker, had grown into a powerful orator whose narrative was interesting, learned, and dignified. He was often pointed out as an example of the synagogue's success in educating and promoting its own spiritual leaders from within. Demonstrating ability as a darshan, however, was not the only road to leadership at CBST, and a number of those involved in running the synagogue avoided the role because they lacked the confidence required to address the congregation as religious, intellectual, and moral guides.

They were not alone. While open to all congregants, in practice a limited number actually undertook the role of darshan. During my stay I counted twenty–four men and women who addressed the congregation as darshanim. Among them twelve spoke only once, four twice, four three times, two gave a drashah on four occasions, and two on five occasions—those appearing more frequently becoming known for their own styles and major themes.

Altogether they presented fifty drashot that I attended. Of these nine were exclusively concerned with the biblical text, with no digression to unrelated issues. Eighteen presentations made a detour, using the story of the ancient Israelites or God's claims and demands on his people to comment on the present situation of lesbians and gay men in America and elsewhere. Fourteen drashot—often described as "political"—contained comments about the synagogue and its leadership. Six offered a platform for comment on public issues not involving the audience as gay congregants. In the smallest category were three homilies that were unrelated to a Biblical text but poetic in style and intended to stimulate a soothing, spiritual atmosphere. (This grouping is somewhat arbitrary since a number of presentations overlapped several categories.)   121

The discussion that follows is based on notes I wrote immediately after returning from services as well as on the text of fourteen drashot I received from their presenters. In addition, I draw upon fifteen drashot from earlier years that were published in the synagogue's newsletter. Collectively they offer a window on the thinking of the congregation.

Addressing the Biblical Text

A minority of the drashot were confined, canonically, to an interpretation of the Torah text in terms of its historical and religious sources. They were typically presented by congregants thought of— by themselves and others—as "traditional." Edward and Dov, members of the Talmud class and among Aaron's closest associates, were particularly eloquent in that style. But while Edward hewed to it exclusively, except for pointing out the shortcomings of innovative Judaism, Dov was equally forceful and eloquent when presenting a drashah relevant to gay issues such as at the Gay Pride Friday evening service.

Edward's homily on Yom Kippur, although analytical, was typical of the traditional drashah. He addressed himself to the meaning of that solemn day of atonement and its uniqueness among Jewish holidays. He argued that Yom Kippur is Judaism distilled, since it is not a reenactment of seasonal or historical events, or of Temple ritual, but instead the reenactment of Judaism itself, through the process of purification that we experience as individuals and as a community. In his scholarly and reserved presentation Edward made no reference to any other issue related to the congregants' life and social identity as gay people, as Jews, or as American citizens. Nor did he attempt to poetically evoke an emotional state of mind.

Apart from traditionalists like Edward, there were a few other congregants who, while not traditional themselves in their religious out-

look, presented what might be termed classic drashot. They refrained from injecting contemporary matters into their talks, and considered the reference to gay issues, in particular, a cliché that violated the dig-
nity of the form. "I am not going to talk about the problems of gay Jews," one congregant announced as he prepared for his first drashah—to be delivered on his fortieth birthday and based on the same portion that was read during his bar mitzvah twenty–seven years before. An educator in his professional life, he also enjoyed the discipline and restraint in avoiding the temptation to speak from his own private agenda. Having discovered CBST only two years earlier and joined together with his Gentile lover of many years, he was over-whelmed by the opportunity of presenting a drashah, an experience he could never have had at his parents' synagogue.

Addressing General Issues

Another small group of drashot, though outside the bounds of the traditional homily as a pious lesson for living, did not make reference to CBST or gay identity but spoke to a broader contemporaneity. Carol, a strong opponent of the idea of hiring a rabbi, eschewed the oppor-tunity to argue her case from the pulpit in her two drashot. Instead, she chose two biblical chapters related to women.

In her first talk Carol discussed the parashah (Leviticus 12:1–8) concerning purity rites women perform after giving birth and posed the question: Why is it that the period of impurity is doubled after the birth of an infant girl? Her answer was that in a society that preferred male infants the longer period of impurity and the avoidance of sex with the husband promoted a strong bond between mother and daughter, countering the natural inclination to treat girls negligently. Carol saw a humane and advanced attitude toward women in the Torah as opposed to the discriminatory patriarchal attitudes of the ancient Israelites.

In her second drashah Carol discussed the composition of the household as described in Genesis, focusing on the position of Jacob's concubines, Bilhah and Zilpah, who were given to him by his legal wives Leah and Rachel (Genesis 30:1–13). She demonstrated that the concubines' offspring were not discriminated against, although born of slaves, and along with their half-brothers founded tribes of Israel.

In both presentations Carol spoke dispassionately in a restrained tone, employing a disinterested scientific–anthropological reasoning.

She did not use the drashah as a platform for commentary about the position of women at CBST, but wove her feminist convictions into the discourse as an integral part of the text's logic. Carol's scholastic ability and forceful presentation surprised many congregants who had stereotyped her on the basis of her occupation as a limousine driver. Having gained visibility with her drashah presentations, Carol ran for the board in 1992, though unsuccessfully. 123

Abe, a lawyer in his mid-thirties with no special standing in the congregation, also ran for the board in 1992 unsuccessfully. In the Candidate's Information Form he described his current CBST participation as "*darshan*, concerned member." I attended two drashot he presented.

His first dealt with the parashah detailing the laws of shemittah—the sabbatical year forbidden for farming—and the release of slaves (Leviticus 25:1–22, 39–55). Abe focused on the Torah's determination to let the land rest periodically and thus enable nature to rejuvenate itself, guaranteeing its preservation. Not so today, he argued. We ruin our planet by over exploitation and the use of toxic pesticides. We make more money but destroy the world. We do the same in our own lives through the restless pursuit of worldly achievements, was his final point.

Abe delivered another drashah on the second afternoon of Rosh Hashanah, 1990. The subject of its parashah was the *akeida* (Genesis 22:1–19), the binding of Isaac by his father Abraham for sacrifice. Departing from the conventional interpretation of the text as an example of the ultimate devotion of Abraham to God, Abe emphasized an aspect suggested by some commentators: the intended sacrifice of Isaac was no less Abraham's ultimate test of God. He ended his talk, "We are not begging God for whatever God might decide to give us, we are asking God to fulfill the promise which had been made to us!"

If there was any subtextual reference at all to gay experience, it was extremely subtle in comparison to a drashah given earlier in the day by Alan, which addressed the same startling test in the book of Genesis. A respected law professor and among the most influential congregants, Alan delivered a learned talk that demonstrated his scholarship but concluded by giving evidence of his position as a gay rights activist: "Like Abraham, we trust that God would not command something that is impossible. We trust, for example, that a Creation

▼

which includes diversity in sexual orientation provides an appropriate place and function for those of us who are lesbian, gay or bisexual. " And ended: "It is our task to find in each of the mitzvot a central kernel of principle upon which to construct an interpretation suitable for our circumstances, without losing sight of the broad principles suggested by the original text."

On the last Friday evening of January 1991, coinciding with the first days of the gulf war, Ze'ev gave a long homily on the story of the Israelites' victorious departure from Egypt. In his drashah he also referred to the haftarah of the same Sabbath that told the story of another famous victory led by the heroes Deborah and Barak against Sisera. The ancient struggles against tyrants and other adversaries on the battlefields of the Middle East were given a contemporary meaning, with the Iraqi dictator and his army compared to Amalek, the prototypical enemy of the Jewish nation. Speaking for the congregation, Ze'ev declared, "For most of us here, as Jews, Israel is an extension of ourselves; we are together part of the Jewish people." He went on to observe that when the Israelites, in need, appealed to God, God listened and gave them miracles, and Ze'ev concluded: "We are a mixed crew here this evening [a much larger crowd than usual] . . . but I believe that if a poll were taken right now, just about all of us would be pulling for something miraculous."

A college professor, Ze'ev believed that the Religious Committee of which he was a member had an educational role in the synagogue and should tutor and closely supervise the drashah speakers. When we met a few weeks before his own drashah, Ze'ev was uneasy about his talk. He rejected the idea of revenge and the celebration of the bloodshed of one's enemy, but asked himself how he could take a pacifist position when Israel's safety was on the line.

Sometime after his presentation I came upon a drashah he had given on Rosh Hashanah, 1989, which was published in the *Synagogue News*. In it, Ze'ev discussed his special fondness for the shofar and the moving power of its sounding on Rosh Hashanah. He recounted a suggestion he had heard that the staccato, frantic nine notes of teru'ah[2] echo Sisera's mother lamenting the killing of her son. He concluded that "if we forget the humanity of our enemies, we will fail our moral tests and never be able to make peace; this being currently the great moral test of the Jewish people, both in Israel and wherever else we are." (After six years on the Religious Committee, and active in many other areas, Ze'ev ran for the board in 1992 as well; he alone among the darshanim was successful.)

The last drashah in this group was delivered by an older congregant, an accountant who was respected for his efforts on behalf of the synagogue's financial affairs. He spoke on the Torah portion (Leviticus 19:1–20:27) that relates God's expectation that the Israelites demonstrate honesty, justice, and charity toward both strangers and converts. The parashah opens with the demand that the Israelites prove themselves holy—*kedoshim*, a divine attribute. The speaker associated that moral injunction with the liberal tradition in Judaism, citing two recent articles in the *New York Times* discussing American Jews' historic involvement in issues of social justice in the United States. Like the darshanim preceding him, he spoke on contemporary themes without reference to CBST or homosexuality—Carol, who considered the fate of women in Jewish scripture, Abe, the environment, and Ze'ev, the problem of reconciling a concern for the safety of Israel with abhorrence of the bloody consequences of victory.

Addressing the Synagogue's Congregation

1. "We Are a Family . . . We Are a Community"

A great number of drashot addressed themselves to the synagogue, its leadership, and occasionally to specific debates that had erupted during meetings of the board. About half of these extolled CBST as the embodiment of a model community and a substitute for the family from which many had been rejected. A few speakers made this point regardless of the content of the parashah and the occasion of its presentation. Lenny, who took charge of the CBST kitchen and, with little help, did all the work for the parties, synagogue dinners, and the weekly kiddush, presented two drashot I attended, which were said to represent his usual style and theme. At a Friday service on *Yom Yerushalaim*, which commemorates the return of Jews to Jerusalem after the Six Day War, Lenny used the occasion to assert that just as the Israelites are seen in the Torah as a moral community, so it is with CBST. "We are a community!" he emotionally declared more than once. At the same time, he saw the synagogue within the larger gay community, pointing to the city's renaming of a street in honor of the Stonewall Bar as an action he felt reflected honor to the synagogue as well. From behind me I could hear Joel comment sarcastically: "Of course, Lenny must end up with 'We are a community,' "—later

▼

explaining that it was not the idea he resented but the arbitrary line of reasoning that always led to the same conclusion.

A few weeks later Joel himself gave a drashah on the story of Abraham's departure to Egypt (Genesis 12:1–12). He traced the roots of the idealized Jewish family to the close bond between Abraham and his nephew Lot. The two left for Egypt together, they returned together, and Abraham remained interested in Lot's fortunes even after they split up and Lot went to live in Sodom. "Even our synagogue is considered a family," Joel commented in an ironic tone, leaving a hint of skepticism about the stereotypical Jewish family and CBST's embodiment of it.

A few months later Lenny, who had a doctorate in Jewish studies, presented a poetic homily that included a Yiddish song. He repeated the phrase "we are an extended family" a few times and called on the congregants to renew the familial and communal relationships that are expressed in the synagogue. It was not easy to follow Lenny's train of thought, but Isaac—the academic whose recent reconciliation with his gay identity was portrayed earlier—told me the drashah had been inspiring because it offered the warmth that he was looking for. Leon, former board chair, although unimpressed by the scholastic quality of the speech, commented that Lenny made him feel guilty he was not kinder to many fellow congregants.

The theme of family also figured in two sermons that Bob—a newcomer who became among the most prolific darshanim—delivered. One Friday evening he was both service leader and darshan. Again discussing the story of the binding of Isaac, he suggested that Abraham actually wished to get rid of Isaac because the son did not fulfill the father's expectations. As evidence, Bob reminded the congregation of the meaning of the name Isaac—"a source of laughter"—and of the disrespect later demonstrated by Isaac's wife Rebecca and son Jacob in taking advantage of his blindness to steal the blessing intended for his beloved eldest son Esau. Giving additional examples of Isaac's misfortune, Bob postulated that Abraham was disappointed with him and wished to eliminate his source of embarrassment. Bob then drew a moral lesson from the story, concluding that the akeida reflects the situation of many parents who are disappointed with their children. He cited a former lover, a Catholic, who told Bob his father would have killed him had he known his son was gay.

In another drashah Bob spoke about his own brother "the doctor," who asked him not to visit his home because Bob's nephews loved him too much; that "educated brother" was worried the children might get too positive a view of homosexuality once they discovered 127 their beloved uncle was gay. Bob concluded: "We are the family of those whose own families have rejected them."

Right after Bob completed his drashah Martin, the board chair, came up to the bimah wearing a black ribbon on his sleeve and gave a eulogy for a congregant who had died of AIDS a few days earlier. It was after telling the congregation that the deceased's family had not shown up for the funeral that Martin declared—as quoted earlier— "but we, his family, were there."

Norman, a former board chair increasingly involved in local politics, was a frequent darshan whose talks usually led to a moral conclusion related to synagogue life. At a CBST dinner for members and their families he spoke of the synagogue's first congregational dinner, which was meant to offer an alternative for those who had been severed from their families. He commemorated those who had suffered, and even committed suicide, because of their rejection by flesh and blood, explaining: "We *are* the family for many in our congregation." Norman complimented CBST's guests as outstanding individuals who might help lessen the prevalence of homophobia. Recalling the parashah story of the agents sent by Moses to report on the prospects of the promised land, Norman hoped that, like Joshua and his companion Caleb who brought back good news from their mission, CBST's guests would spread the word of their experiences at the synagogue.

On the High Holidays, when the most prominent congregants presented drashot, the special nature of CBST was often invoked. In his talk Morris reviewed the many changes that had taken the world by surprise during the concluding year—the dialogue between East and West, the impending war with Iraq, the continuing exodus of one million Jews from Russia to an embattled Israel, the reemergence of the ugly face of anti–Semitism, and the continuing toll of the AIDS disaster. In the face of all these upheavals Morris felt CBST's congregants could enjoy the shield of "a safe space"—to whose preservation they must actively contribute time and money.

Harvey—whose promotion ten years earlier of the community development project as a means "to bring ourselves closer to each other" was reported in chapter 3—delivered a very moving drashah

▼

on the bond that united his huge High Holiday audience: "We travel through life. We are all here together tonight because we all choose to travel together. We aim for a state of perfection, but that is merely a concept in the kingdom below. For traveling companions we have each other, and that is no small thing."

2. The Discourse of "Politicians"

The congregants, however, were not always as affectionately bonded as Harvey portrayed them, nor, seemingly, always traveling in the same direction. And despite the injunction against "political" drashot, intramural tensions and disagreements frequently found expression in this forum. I first witnessed this when Norman discussed the parashah dealing with the high priest's garments (Exodus 39:1–31). He confessed that the only thing he could relate to in this difficult and technical text was the absence of Moses from its pages. Norman adopted an interpretation suggesting that Moses made an effort to minimize his own presence in order to promote the position of his brother Aaron. He concluded:

> We have to take a lesson here at CBST that the *vatikim* [colloquial for "veterans," from the first waves of Ashkenazi settlers in modern Israel who have monopolized power], the older generation, must give up power and allow the younger members to take over. Like Moses and Aaron, we must act together for the benefit of our community.

Since Norman himself was then considered a "politician"—a former board chair and active in the wider secular community—who preserved his influence in the synagogue, his homily was received with amusement.

Another more veiled reference to CBST's leadership was made by Joel, who discussed the story of the golden calf (Exodus 32:1–35). He blamed both Moses and Aaron for the sad events that took place while Moses was on Mount Sinai receiving the tablets of the law. Moses had been so busy with his mission that he had not properly taught his people their new faith nor considered what might happen in his absence; Aaron was too soft with his people, believing that Moses would easily correct any temporary lapse. Joel concluded his drashah warning of the consequences of a leadership whose members assume they know a tradition with which they are, in fact, not sufficiently familiar. And he beamed with satisfaction, having no doubt his message was understood by the *machers* (big shots) for whom it was intended. As Joel told me later, his comments were prompted by a board meeting where, following some dissatisfaction with a particu- lar service leader, it was declared that service leaders should carry out their task "according to the synagogue's tradition." "What is the tradition they speak of?" Joel exclaimed, indignant at the pretension of those he considered amateurs in Judaism canonizing ritual.

Joel, a past chair of the Religious Committee, was less concerned about the rightness and wrongness of ritual than he was that CBST be a place where congregants could meaningfully express their religious needs and feelings. He gave voice to this view in another drashah— one that reported a curious incident. Joel related the story of a phone call he answered at the synagogue. The caller, a student on vacation from his yeshiva in Monsey, asked whether he could be put in touch with someone with whom he could have sex. This led to a more serious discussion with the anonymous caller about the importance of ritual and the relationship between the congregation and God. Unlike his caller, Joel argued, "God doesn't care what ritual we use, but God does care that we pray and how we live our lives." Relating more specifically to the parashah, Joel expressed his displeasure with the text, which banned disabled men from performing in the priesthood.

Martin, then a board member, was another darshan who commented directly on synagogue affairs. He saw his parashah (*Pekudei*, Exodus 38), detailing the structure and furnishing of the tabernacle, as relevant to the synagogue and, by extension, to education, because the former was always a place where Jews came to "pray, to learn and argue." Becoming more specific, he asserted:

> Our synagogue takes a role in education, and as such we offer courses which last season drew forty participants. Is this a success or a failure? We show movies which attract an audience of forty, some of whom are not synagogue members. Is this a success or failure? We have an obligation to preserve our role in education.

Had I not attended a recent board meeting at which Martin, as liaison to the Education Committee, clashed with Norman over the issue of funding programs only modestly attended, I might not have fully understood Martin's point.

▼

One Friday night Simon took the novel approach of not preparing his own drashah, but reading one from a book of Torah interpretations. His text suggested fourteen explanations for God's refusing Moses and Aaron entrance to the promised land, the final one being that Moses was out of touch with the process of change among the Israelites: he was angry with his people and neglected his role as educator. Here Simon added a comment of his own: "There is a message in the parashah to the leaders of Israel who are not sensitive to changes and new needs among their people and are not reacting to them adequately!"

Though ostensibly directed to the leaders of Israel, two board members sitting next to me did not miss the point. They winked at each other and, smiling, waited for me to ask, "Wasn't it 'political?' "

On another occasion Simon predicted we might both hear a controversial drashah, as Bob walked to the bimah. Since Bob had recently resigned from the board, Simon assumed he would not let things rest without sharing his views with the congregation. Simon proved right. Bob's parashah (*Toledot*, Genesis 25) told the story of Jacob's manipulation of his brother Esau, who sold him his birthright for a pot of lentils. An experienced darshan, Bob began with a quotation from the book of Ecclesiastes, "there is a time for joy and a time for sorrow," and posed the question, Should Rebecca rejoice that one of her sons received his father's blessing by tricking his brother? Should we be happy with Jacob our ancestor whose conduct was less than exemplary? Bob then moved to the introduction of a more contemporary issue, one of immediacy for the synagogue: the Holocaust Torah.

The congregation was about to hold an elaborate celebration the next week in honor of the adoption of a Holocaust Torah scroll (the politics of whose reception have been briefly described in chapters 3 and 5). A CBST committee appointed to plan the affair announced, after much deliberation, a day–long program of public events to welcome the Holocaust Torah—altogether promising a joyous day. Finally, the Torah scroll would come to rest in its newly constructed glass and wood case as a reminder of the horrors of the Holocaust and a memorial to its victims.

However, there were contrary opinions at CBST about how the scroll should be welcomed and displayed. There were those who wished to see a solemn religious service without public extravagance and, in particular, the traditionalists, preferred to see the Holocaust scroll placed together with the congregation's other Torahs in the synagogue's ark.

Bob, whose resignation from the board had been prompted in part by this issue, rejected the whole idea of publicly adopting the tragic remnant. He told the congregation he was not sure whether the next Sunday's event was an occasion for joy or grief. For him the Holocaust was a disaster beyond redemption. He described the pain and horror he felt, five years before, visiting the elegant Reform synagogue in Prague now devoid of its congregation, empty of its treasures and Torah scrolls. He dramatically recounted the experience of visiting a concentration camp. Should he celebrate the adoption of a Torah scroll that was desecrated, whose legal owners could never reclaim it? A tense silence followed Bob's last words. Jane, the service leader, obviously upset by the drashah, made an unusual reply upon her return to the bimah. She commented that the adoption of the Holocaust Torah scroll is, in fact, a joyful event for her and the rest of the congregation.Bob's homily and Jane's response were received uneasily, both having breached rules of decorum. Bob had used the drashah as a platform to dispute a settled decision by the board, virtually on the eve of its implementation. Jane had commented on—in effect, corrected—the darshan, assuming the prerogative of a rabbi, which in CBST's egalitarian, nonhierarchical ethos the service leader was not.

Almost a year later, however, Bob again addressed the same issue in a drashah. Having returned to Prague, and having had enough time to observe the Holocaust Torah prominently displayed in a memorial case in the sanctuary, he admitted that he had changed his mind. He now associated the Jewish Holocaust with the AIDS holocaust and expressed his belief that insofar as the Jews survived there is hope for the gay community as well. From this new vantage he saw the Torah scroll as a symbol of victory and survival.

The drashot described in this section addressed themselves to the synagogue. Those in the first group associated it with the lost family and community not only metaphorically, but by investing CBST with the actual attributes of family and community. Here was the place and here were the people who resembled home and close relatives. The second group of drashot also demonstrated that here, as well, was the stage for acting out the conflicts between close partners. The messages were not disguised. On the contrary, the darshanim often

▼

looked directly at their antagonists. But these were safe confrontations played by the rules of a supportive environment—it was all in
the family.

Addressing Homosexuality

More frequently than anything else, the drashah at CBST was
addressed to the congregants' major existential concern—homosexuality. Dov, prominent among the synagogue's traditionalists and
known, along with Edward, as well for his "classic" drashot, approached homosexuality from a moral–religious viewpoint in dealing
with the most difficult parashah for a gay congregation, chapter 20 in
Leviticus. Enumerated here are the rules of sexuality and the punishment for their violation, including death for "a man who lies with
another man as though he were a woman" (20:13). Dov began by
asserting that a believing Jew cannot pick and choose from the Torah
those portions that suit him and discard the others, remarking: "The
Torah may be compared to a seamless garment woven from a single
thread; it is impossible to unravel even the smallest length of that
thread without destroying the entire cloth." Dov then soberly stated
the problem: "The necessity of maintaining this wholeness creates a
dilemma for the gay Jew who wishes to be observant in the traditional
sense."

Seeking to resolve the contradiction between the words of the text
and the sexual orientation of the congregation, Dov employed ratio-
nalistic historical reasoning. He argued, first, that the Leviticus text
was, in fact, a prohibition against temple prostitution as practiced in
Canaanite times. He had a good basis for that thesis, he maintained,
since the rule against homosexuality is found in the middle of a list of
prohibited cultic practices. Second, he assumed the rule was intended
to support marriage, the major bond and institution in ancient society, explaining, "To these generations, then, *mishkav zakhar* [sex
between males] was a prohibition against disturbing the relationship
between husband and wife . . . whether as an adulterer with the wife
or as *mishkav zakhar* with the husband."

Finally, what the injunction prohibited was engaging in what Dov
defined as "situational homosexuality" that might occur, for example,
in prison or at sea: "To do so would be to use men as though they were
women." This became the central point in Dov's presentation, and,
relying on the words of the text but adding a new perspective, he

asserted: "To our modern understanding, this means that you should not sleep with men if your preference is for women. But it is equally valid to say that *mishkav zakhar* means that you should not sleep with women if your preference is for men."

Dov then elaborated on what he saw as the moral implications of the text—the protection of human dignity and the integrity of relationships. Thus, a gay lover is not a substitute wife, nor is he a substitute husband to whom you must submit. Dov concluded that we can both maintain Jewish tradition and, by reinterpreting it, accommodate the personal needs of the worshiper, ending with the triumphant promise: "We can continue to be governed by Judaism, which is the wellspring of our belief, and still remain faithful to the core of our inmost souls."

Dov presented several other drashot on the subject of homosexuality. The one he delivered on Gay Pride Week in 1989 celebrated the twentieth anniversary of the riots at the Stonewall Bar that sparked the gay liberation movement. He spoke on the values and basic principles that transform a group of people of shared sexuality into a mass movement. Dov distinguished between homosexuality and gayness, which he saw as a distinction between physical attraction and the "gayness principle" that "demands nothing less than a restructuring of our society." The gayness principle, he argued, requires the gay community to establish a new set of rules for valid behavior, and it is the function of religious institutions to provide moral guidance for this task. Dov himself suggested a few rules for this moral code. It is wrong to have sex with someone for whom a person is responsible, such as a student or employee. It is immoral to interfere with the relationships between lovers. It is right to have sex with a "significant other" with whom one is bound. Although it was a secular drashah, Dov, nevertheless, invested it with an aura of spirituality.

In another drashah Dov offered an innovative interpretation of the fascinating story of Balak, King of Moab (Numbers 22–24) who hired Balaam to use his oracles to curse Israel after its victory over the Amorites. Dov explained Balak's refusal to allow the Israelites to go through his land despite their promise to cause no harm: Balak assumed they would do what he himself would under similar circumstances. "He projected from his own mode of behavior and understanding." Caught in his "projection," Balak was unable to lis-

▼

ten to Balaam, who under God's command refused to curse the Israelites. This is the same sort of projection that people employ about Jews or homosexuals, Dov concluded. "People are unable to listen to or discuss the lifestyle of others. They assume there is only one right way, that of the mainstream."

On Passover 1989 Larry, among the most dedicated congregants, compared the fate of the Israelites in Egypt under the yoke of Pharaoh to that of homosexuals in contemporary society. Pharaoh was suspicious of that foreign nation not only because of their growing number but also because he was not acquainted with the Israelites' history in his land. "We are all afraid of what and who we don't know," Larry declared, and went on to elaborate:

> The religious right, from all religions, including many Orthodox Jews, looks upon us homosexual men and women as an abomination, a plague. They don't know us and they don't try to know us. . . . They have not learned the lessons from history that lesbians and gays have always been integral and productive members of society!

Larry's personal warmth and his simple arguments, which associated the liberation of the Israelites with the promise of liberation for gays and lesbians, seemed appropriate for the occasion and earned him wide approval. Larry was more combative in another drashah, which told the story of the daughters of Zelophehad (Numbers 27:1–11) who, having no brothers, claimed their share of their father's estate even though only male offspring were given inheritance rights. Larry saw that parashah as the first text in history that offered equal rights to women. The daughters' successful appeal, he declared, demonstrated the importance of determination in the battle for justice and human rights.

Bob's drashah on Gay Pride Week, 1990, was taken from the story of Korah, the central figure of the revolt against Moses during the forty years of wandering in the wilderness (Numbers 16). Taking a radical position, Bob claimed that Korah had a legitimate complaint but was a poor politician. He argued that Korah's position was like the congregation's, since he too had asked for equality:

> Korah was a rebel, and today on the anniversary of our rebellion we should be proud to be twice blessed with the good for-

tune of being both Jews and gays. On this day we are obliged to join the parade, advertise our identity, and inform friends and close relatives about our true selves.

Bob, who was a prolific darshan and controversial on occasion— as his Holocaust Torah drashah attested—received mixed reviews on this sermon, particularly for its conclusion. His revisionist view of Korah as rebel appealed to many in the congregation. But Gilbert, a Biblical studies scholar, who was seated next to me, could hardly contain his amusement at the peroration. He swore he was not going to perform the mitzvah tonight of revealing to his eighty-seven-year-old father his only son's homosexuality.

A similar approach to Bob's was taken by a rabbi in the congregation who delivered a drashah on Hagar, Sarah's handmaid and mother of Abraham's son Ishmael, who fled to the desert from Sarah's contempt (Genesis 16:1–16). He saw Hagar as a symbol for an abused and oppressed people. "We can identify with her," he claimed. "We have to choose between Hagar and her masters Abraham and Sarah." This radical suggestion was shadowed, however, by what was seen as his condescending style and, in particular, his insensitive use of masculine references. It was on this basis that the Religious Committee—as mentioned earlier—decided to reduce the number of his future drashot.

The issue of coming out was not an infrequent theme in the drashot I attended. In one of them a new darshan, who appeared to be an experienced speaker, discussed the emergence of Moses as leader of his people. He was particularly fascinated with the process by which Moses revealed his true identity, declaring: "He came out of the closet as a Jew." The speaker considered this an important lesson "for us gays and lesbians," a lesson already learned and adopted by CBST in openly acknowledging itself as a congregation of gay and lesbian Jews. His presentation was well received by many congregants. Arnold—whose discovery of CBST at a time of emotional distress was recounted earlier—appreciated the idea of the double coming out as lesbians and gays and as Jews. He told me it was a very good drashah, particularly for the newcomers who might learn the meaning and contribution of the synagogue. When I complimented the speaker on his performance, he told me he had been a rabbinical student but dropped out after a few years when he discovered that the rabbis preferred the word of the text to the feelings and needs of human beings.

▼

A number of drashot dealt specifically with the health crisis challenging the congregation. One of the most powerful was delivered by Morris on the solemn occasion of the Yom Kippur Yizkor (memorial) service in 1990. In a dramatic appeal Morris pleaded with the congregants to take the HIV test. And he surprised them by revealing that the severe illness that had brought him near death, and from which he had made a miraculous recovery, was AIDS-related. As described in preceding chapters, Morris, a leader respected both in CBST and in the wider New York lesbian and gay community, opened the door to a bold discussion of the AIDS epidemic by those who lived with it. The subject was no longer confined to a eulogy for an unfortunate individual, remote from the public arena, who was rediscovered and lamented only at his funeral.

Norman's appeal on the same subject one year later was less effective, however. Addressing the large crowd, which packed the sanctuary for the Yizkor service, he began with a cry: "Why? Why is the world silent when so many people are dying of AIDS? Isn't it because they want to get rid of gays as much as they want to get rid of drug addicts? Isn't it the same story with the Jews and the Blacks? Why did the world keep silent during the Holocaust?"

In the face of this indifference, however, Norman found a note of consolation, "We are an extended family, and we take care of each other," and transformed this thought into a practical message, pleading with his listeners to take the HIV test and save their lives. He went on to describe a reconciliation with his ailing father, who even came to visit him and his lover, and ended the drashah with a call for generous contributions to support CBST. Later I met a few congregants who asked my opinion of Norman's presentation. I responded, diplomatically, that for every drashah there is a receptive audience. They were less charitable. One, a physician, was irritated by Norman's introduction of too many issues of disparate significance. He thought he should not have manipulated the Yizkor drashah. The other questioned Norman's sensitivity as darshan. We asked a few other acquaintances what they thought of the drashah and received varying opinions.

Very different in its rhetoric was the drashah that Ted presented dealing with AIDS. When he first asked to deliver a drashah, no one expected that Ted, whose muscular appearance concealed his gentleness and yeshiva education, would display such skills of learned ora-tory. Interpreting the parashah that tells the story of God's command to Abraham to leave his birthplace for the land chosen for him and his offspring (Genesis 14), Ted concentrated his discussion on Abraham's two major characteristics. The first was his ability to carry on a dialogue with God and even challenge him when confronted with an issue of justice. This was evidenced in his challenge to God's plan for the destruction of the evil cities of Sodom and Gomorrah: "Would you destroy the just together with the wicked?" (Genesis 18:23). The second was Abraham's great kindness, which Ted felt the term *charity* did not adequately convey. 137

Ted invoked Elie Wiesel's claim that God can be questioned and called to account for having hidden himself from the world, most notably from the Jewish people during the Holocaust. He asked, "In these days of the AIDS plague, many of us have wondered, how could God allow such suffering—the devastating illness and deaths of so many vibrant, vital, and good people? How could God so prematurely take away so many of our friends and lovers?" Ted's theological complaint differed from the usual protest against the malice and indifference displayed by outsiders and the withdrawal and denial evidenced by insiders toward the AIDS epidemic. And while charging God with responsibility for the worst calamity ever to have stricken homosexuals, which presented a serious dilemma for believers, it presumed an intimate discourse with God.

As his drashah continued Ted found that from the story of Abraham a brighter meaning could also be deduced. Abraham's kindness, generosity, and charity teach us about the essence of Judaism as a practical philosophy of life that is more concerned with behavior, human action and interaction, than it is with belief systems. Therefore, regardless of the troubled dialogue with God, each time we comfort, visit, and care for those very many who are sick, we are realizing the essential message of the Torah. Then, in Ted's final words, "we can again begin to hear more clearly the ongoing dialogue between God and humankind."

Invoking a Spiritual Mood

On three occasions during the High Holidays I attended drashot that did not relate to the Torah text or to a specific issue involving a moral or intellectual lesson for practical consideration. In this they were unlike most other homilies presented on the Days of Awe that

▼

carried clear messages concerning the congregants' lives and their duties. Dov presented one of these, on Rosh Hashanah morning, 1990. When he and I spoke afterward it was clear that I couldn't reconstruct the details of his presentation, which, nonetheless, had left a strong impression of solemnity. Dov explained that he had prepared his drashah when he was out of town and away from the books he needed for a more scholastic talk. "I wanted to create a mood," he told me.

Alice, a rabbi in the congregation, gave a drashah on the second day of Rosh Hashanah that took a lyrical tone. Rather than relate to the Torah text, she spoke of the longing for nature, for God, and for a happy year. Alice pointed to the ability of children to experience concepts and feelings that are lost on adults, such as the idea of the word *norah*, "awesome." But even adults can sometimes be carried away by the wonders of nature, as when, fascinated by the beauty of a butterfly, for example, we miss an appointment. Simon, responding to my ambivalence, told me that the drashah was intended to stimulate a mellow and grateful atmosphere, adding he overheard a congregant declare it the most wonderful drashah he had ever attended.

The third of these mood pieces—and the last drashah to be presented in this chapter—was delivered by Gilbert, the congregant who with Edward and Aaron had rotated the role of darshan in the synagogue's early years. It was given during the final Ne'ilah service on Yom Kippur, 1990, only hours after Edward's drashah—the first of this chapter—interpreting the Day of Atonement as a reenactment of Judaism itself. A gifted speaker and singer, with a joyful personality, Gilbert was a good choice for that late hour on a day of fasting. His eloquent and carefully styled drashah, though no less analytical than Edward's, was delivered in a manner that made it more emotionally effective. Gilbert opened by explaining that the name Ne'ilah, " 'the locking of the gates'—suggests rather ominously that time is running out for us." He went on to explicate the meaning of the day and its component parts:

> The drama of Ne'ilah, like that of the rest of Yom Kippur, is an internal drama—it is played out on no physical stage before a seated audience. . . . We see before us massive gates, half–open, but cannot quite see to what greater structure these gates are attached . . . : the Temple of Jerusalem? The heavenly abode of

God? As the act begins, the light reflected off the gates is unmistakably the light of twilight.

Though he was probably not acquainted with Victor Turner's (1967) exploration of the liminal stage in the rites of passage, Gilbert's narrative was evocative of it—anthropological, albeit with a dash of humor. He concluded: [139]

> Ne'ilah not only signals the end of our role in the spiritual drama of these Days of Awe, it likewise signals the beginning of a new role for us in living the drama of our everyday lives. Ne'ilah is one last act after which the curtain does not fall; it goes up!—to which one hardly knows whether to say 'Amen,' or 'Break a leg!'

"This Is Not What the Synagogue Is For"

When the Religious Committee sat down to review the first drashah a leading congregant—not considered particularly well versed in Judaism—had delivered, his supervisor, being generous, explained that it was not so much a drashah as a combination of two pleasant lectures on separate issues. Sheila, a committee member, responded that she had enjoyed the drashah, prompting another to observe: "We have different darshanim and an audience with varied tastes." The chair echoed this sentiment, citing the rabbi whose presentations were generally criticized for being sexist but whose last drashah had nonetheless been praised by some.

Rarely were the congregants unanimous in their view of the performance of individual darshanim. with opinions often varying according to which constituency was being polled. One of the most colorful descriptions I heard of a drashah was "kasha and borsht" (barley and beet soup)—a Yiddish expression for a mixed-up, incoherent talk. But on the whole the congregants were very tolerant of their darshanim, and I know of no one who was denied a request to present a drashah, as long as they accepted the supervision of a guide appointed by the Religious Committee. Even when confronted with complaints about poor performance or the introduction of a controversial subject, the response by many congregants, including the chair of the Religious Committee, was generally along the lines of "We are unique in our diversity; otherwise it would be boring" or "Our unity is in our diversity." Moreover, in most cases the evidence of failure was not clear-cut.

▼

In one instance, however, near unanimity was achieved. This was in response to Simon's attempt to experiment with the CBST drashah tradition. When Simon presented that drashah, on God's refusal to allow Moses to enter the promised land—to which he added his "political" message—his sermon was not one he had prepared himself, but, as I have mentioned, taken from a book of Torah interpretations. Simon was a qualified darshan, but he hoped that by introducing this innovation more congregants would become familiar with the variety of sources available on Jewish subjects, the quality of sermons would improve, and more would be able to undertake the role of darshan.

An opportunity to give this a fuller test arose in December 1990, when an upcoming darshan was unable to fulfill his obligation. Simon offered to choose a suitable text from a published source, but insisted that someone else read it—a proposal the Religious Committee accepted. When I saw Ze'ev, a committee member, a few days later, he was already regretting his unequivocal support for the idea. "It is going to be a sort of a cassette production instead of an original drashah," he complained. Meanwhile, Simon found an article in the *Jewish Week* dealing with Chanukah and asked David, a CBST board member but one not knowledgeable in Judaism, if he would present it at the Friday service. Although it would have been his first opportunity to act as darshan, David immediately rejected the suggestion. Simon then approached Barry, an older congregant who had given just one, not particularly impressive, drashah and was not a confirmed darshan. Barry, pleased with the opportunity to address the congregation, accepted the offer.

Barry's presentation of Simon's text, however, was not well received, with criticism coming from many quarters. Edward complained that the drashah hadn't related to that sabbath's Torah reading, but instead to the parashah for Chanukah one week before. The same point was made at the next Religious Committee meeting. The chair quoted a congregant who, complaining about the tardy drashah, had declared: "We Christianize Chanukah [by confusing it with the Christmas season]!" A committee member reported that David had been outraged by Simon's suggestion that he read someone else's drashah and that it had taken ten minutes to placate him. Another member declared, "I was appalled. The concept doesn't work." Simon's defense that it was mainly the fault of his having chosen the wrong speaker, who hadn't adequately prepared for the task, couldn't save his idea. David's angry outcry, "this is not what the synagogue is for," reported to the committee, seemed a powerful claim against Simon's experiment in drashah presentation. Only one congregant attending the meeting suggested giving it another try. The verdict was clear.

In accounting for the rejection of Simon's idea, it was not the content of the drashah or Barry's poor delivery that harmed it so. There had been weak presentations before—some by leading members—as well as divergence from the Torah reading, as Simon pointed out. However, it was the breach of the tradition that privileged—but also committed—the darshan to leave a personal mark on the event with a display of "original" commentary that caused deep displeasure among many, both traditionalists and reformists.

The congregants were fully aware of the discursive, extratextual, nature of the CBST drashah. Dov and Abe, for example, eschewed the role of service leader, preferring to present drashot because they "offered an opportunity to educate." Ze'ev told me he gave a drashah just before the last annual congregational meeting and used the opportunity "to tweak the nose of a few *machers*." When Larry's drashah compared the Israelites' suffering under the yoke of Pharaoh to homosexuals in contemporary society, Simon, wondering if I wasn't surprised by this, explained that in prior years homosexuality had been the theme most frequently raised. A few weeks later, when Edward presented one of his learned drashot, Simon commented that it might have better suited an Orthodox synagogue, adding that Edward was completely indifferent to the audience he was addressing. It was with this quality, by which he judged Edward's drashah wanting, that his own experiment failed. Simon's innovation deprived the drashah of its unique discursive element: the engagement, the personal communication of a perspective on the text or on social relationships that became an important part of the ritual and social negotiation at CBST.

If the drashot I have presented offer a window on the congregation, the view is a kaleidoscopic one, changing with the rotation of each darshan. We have witnessed Edward's traditional–analytical exegesis, Carol's learned feminist reading of the text, Abe's restrained commentary on both human beings' and God's priorities, Ze'ev's disdain of war and violence but commitment to Israel's security, Lenny, Bob, Martin,

▼

Norman, and Harvey's manifestations of love for the congregation, and Joel's skepticism. We have heard various interpretations of the akeida, Martin's bitter argument with Norman over the synagogue's educational responsibility, Bob's dispute with the board over the Holocaust Torah and his call for coming out. We have seen Morris's and Norman's emotional pleas to take the HIV test; Dov's analytical search for a new understanding of the Levitican condemnation of homosexuality and his psychological exposition of King Balak's projection; Bob's radical identification with Korah's rebellion against the authority of Moses; and Larry's more conciliatory association with the daughters of Zelophehad. We have witnessed Ted's remonstrance with God for deserting the victims of AIDS; Alice's lyrical paean to spirituality in nature; and, last, Gilbert's poetic drama at the close of Yom Kippur.

No doubt the congregants at CBST expected the darshan to offer a critique of both the Torah text and the shared experiences that brought them together. This was a major part of the service, one open to individual interpretation. It was an honor and a privilege to have the congregation's attention; in return the darshan's responsibility was to offer listeners meaningful insight and an emotional experience, elevating their feelings of spirituality and enhancing their sense of communitas. It was the personal viewpoint and sagacity rather than the superior scholastic or literary achievement that endeared the darshan to the listeners through the egalitarian system that developed at CBST.

The drashah, presented essentially by lay congregants, became a quintessential mark of CBST. It seemed to endow both the individual darshan and his audience with the sense of having come of age, performing a role reserved in most other synagogues for the rabbi. The return of the congregants at CBST to Judaism was not in conformity with the style of mainstream synagogue life, nor was it an open rebellion bent on developing an alternative pattern of Jewish ritual and belief. The drashah became the stage for their ongoing negotiation, both with the outside world and among themselves, about the definition of their identity as lesbian and gay Jews and their special role in both communities.

▼

CHAPTER SEVEN

The Talmud Circle: Identities in Conflict

Like the last column of some ruined temple, he
remained standing mute and solitary in the middle
of the otherwise deserted room.
HERMAN MELVILLE, *BARTLEBY*

If a gay synagogue seems a paradox to the traditionalist, a gay Talmud class (*shiur*) can appear completely surreal. I remember the
bewildered reaction of my colleague and Orthodox friend Shlomo
Deshen who joined me for a lecture at CBST. He noticed a group of
somber–looking men seated around a large table at the center of the
community hall. When I told him they were studying the Talmud, he
didn't believe me. "They can't be using a real Talmud text!" he
exclaimed. "Go and see for yourself," I answered. "But how do they
resolve the theological problem? How can people who consider themselves Orthodox be gay at the same time?" This dilemma, introduced
by a casual visitor, sets out the major issues of this chapter: Why do
people whose behavior is considered abhorrent in the words of the
Torah and the eyes of traditional Jews, enthusiastically endorse the
text that is considered among the highest symbols of Jewish religious
engagements and participate in a style typical of traditional Orthodox
synagogues (Heilman 1983)? And why are they tolerated by their fellow "sinners," who openly challenge the upholders of their shared
stigma?

The Talmud class I observed was started in 1975, and consisted of
a core of ten men in their late thirties to early fifties, most of whom
had attended for many years. There were other men—and a few
women—who were related to the group through their loyalty to and
affection for its leader, Aaron. They rarely attended weekly classes but

often participated in holiday parties. Both core and peripheral members were mostly professionals (computer programmers, educators, lawyers, etc.), with a few engaged in business. In contrast to the majority of CBST members, the behavior and attire of the group resembled more traditional elements in Jewish society. Several wore black suits and hats, tzitzit,[1] and yarmulkes. And they eschewed the hugging and kissing typical of CBST.

I was told that there had been a woman in the class, for nearly a year, who had learned Talmud from her father. A few other women joined briefly but, lacking her exposure, dropped out. Younger women who in recent years have gained a better Talmud education did not seem attracted to this traditional group of middle–aged males. I managed to keep up with the class, though with some difficulty, because of my elementary religious school training and knowledge of Hebrew.

The sexual orientation of the participants was not inquired into. During my time with the class an Orthodox man joined the group and was assumed to be gay. Later it was learned that he was not, but simply felt more comfortable there than in mainstream Orthodox society, from which he was alienated. He ultimately dropped out, for unrelated reasons, but remained on friendly terms with the members.

The class followed an unvarying routine: it met every Tuesday evening at 7:30 and ended at 9:30 after a short break for Ma'ariv prayers. The first ten or fifteen minutes were usually devoted to "schmoozing" about work, relatives, the health status of friends with AIDS, and political developments, particularly in the Middle East. With most of the members assembled, the class resumed the reading and discussion of the Talmud. In March 1989, for instance, several meetings were devoted to the issues of tithing (ma'asrot); a series in June 1990 probed the practice of shofar blowing; September 1990 was taken up with a discussion of whether an egg laid on the Sabbath could be consumed on the next day if it were a holiday.

These esoteric legal issues of ritual and practice were meticulously poured over until all the participants felt satisfied with the interpretation reached. The reading of the text was shared by most of the class including one Gentile who had learned Hebrew under the guidance of a knowledgeable member. Most also did homework to familiarize themselves with the text. The analysis often prompted far–reaching discussions related both to biblical and modern times. Aaron compared tithing to income tax and inferred that not all Israelites were scrupulous in their observance of ma'asrot. Why else would Boaz's permitting Naomi and Ruth to glean be seen as an act of generosity to kin, when the law conferred this as a right? Another suggested that religious conflicts between the Pharisee and Sadducee sects might be comparable to the assault of the Reform and Conservative movements on the hegemony of one halakhic interpretation. A week later, still focusing on ma'asrot, an animated discussion of the Messiah ensued. Would the Jews rebuild the Temple and resume all rituals including animal sacrifice?

Linguistic queries often set off lively discussions. Edward, with his Ph.D. in classics, was particularly instrumental in revealing the philological and phonetic sources of the Hebrew and Aramaic Talmud. Wasn't the Hebrew term *yovel* (a cycle of fifty years) associated with the Latin *jubilee*? What was the source of the Hebrew term for rice, *orez*? Edward assumed a Greek origin. After the Talmud class conversation continued as the members walked together to the subway or apartments in the neighborhood.

A different atmosphere dominated the Talmud class holiday parties, which were celebrated in the homes of the inner and outer circle. The Purim party of 1989 was given by a member who rarely attended regular meetings. His elegant East Side apartment offered a sharp contrast to the barren community room, notable for its lack of intimacy. Aaron brought a cassette of Hasidic songs to guide a sing–along. Its highlight was a Yiddish melody with the stanza "The rabbi commanded that one must be *freilach* [gay] every day until the last white day [the day one is buried in white shrouds]." The association of the rabbi's command for happiness with the term for *homosexual* caused much delight.

Joseph suggested that a man who is gay every day keeps the angel of death away. Someone invented another line adding to the amusement: "A gay every day keeps the doctor away." In the spirit of Purim Aaron offered an interpretation for the popular belief that King Akhashverosh invited Queen Vashti to attend a party dressed only in her crown. Apparently the king and his guests were completely drunk when someone in the crowd claimed the king was homosexual. He immediately challenged his accuser: "I'll call for Queen Vashti and you'll see for yourself if I am homosexual!" Such direct and humorous references to the sexual orientation of the participants were very rare in other meetings of the Talmud circle.

▼

More typically, the following Passover the group was seated around a large table in Aaron's modest Upper West Side apartment for the final holiday meal. The participants were called on to discover new theological ideas in the Haggadah text. It was nearly dusk when Aaron expressed his deep feeling for this holiday of freedom and the rebirth of nature. He pointed to the trees outside with their new–green leaves, a beautiful color unique to spring. Now, nearly dark, the Sabbath clock switched on the lights. All were intensely looking at Aaron as if by some magic he could prolong the last day of the holiday. The spell was only broken as Aaron bid the group join him for evening prayers at the nearby Spanish and Portuguese Synagogue. Gay identity had hardly been referred to in this celebration, which had lasted many hours.

The core of the Talmud class consisted of men who had been exposed in their youth to some form of Jewish life. Most had been raised in families affiliated with the Conservative movement, but others had come from Orthodox and even ultra-Orthodox backgrounds. A few had attended yeshiva. But at a later stage they had all abandoned Jewish life, unable to accommodate their sexual identity to Jewish dogma on homosexuality. Joining CBST was the first step they had taken toward reconciling their gay and Jewish identities.

Though differing in specifics, Ralph exemplified this pattern of Jewish departure and return. Described by Aaron as a "sixties leftist," Ralph told me that his return to New York from California was much influenced by his discovery of the Talmud class. He first heard about it from another member who was visiting San Francisco. Ralph thought how wonderful it must be to experience something more authentically Jewish. He was tired of the atmosphere in California and wished to return to something older and more stable. Ralph believed that Jewish identity could offer much more than gay identity: "What is gay identity—gay bars, Bette Davis movies, and a few other things of that sort?" When he came to New York, he immediately joined the Talmud class, which was his first introduction to that scholastic tradition. By the time I met him he attended services at CBST only occasionally, regretting that the synagogue wasn't more traditional and therefore, in his words, "more authentic." This differed from his initial assessment upon arrival in New York in 1983: "I was surprised that unlike the San Francisco gay shul, which was Reform or 'creative' in style, CBST was traditional, with lots of singing and a surprisingly large weekly turnout."[2]

In spite of Ralph's commitment to the Talmud class, he did not excel. He usually looked tired, and had to make an effort to concentrate. He admitted he sometimes had second thoughts about his participation, but he did not give it up. Ralph's attraction to Talmud learning, despite his difficulties with the Gemara text, was eloquently expressed in the following: "It's like listening in on a long-distance telephone line to hundreds of Jewish conversations over the centuries. You feel as though you are suddenly connected to an uninterrupted Jewish channel of debate and discourse that goes back to Mount Sinai." 147

Ralph's disaffection with the CBST service—despite his commitment to the Talmud class—reflected the history and evolution of these two respective bodies and the individual who at one time united them. When Aaron began the Talmud class the synagogue itself was only two years old and Aaron was its spiritual leader. Reminiscing about that time, Aaron told me he wanted to develop a community of people who would share major Jewish values. It was part of his perception of Judaism as a religion and a way of life that had to be practiced in community. He did not wish to see a synagogue that was essentially a cruising place where people showed up until they found a partner and disappeared.

This vision attracted a number of adherents who, along with Aaron, followed a path of increasing traditionalism. As expressed by one of his disciples: "Aaron hoped to develop full Jewish life. He wanted a place where gay Jews would feel comfortable at fulfilling Jewish life. He was ready to compromise for an interim period—he considered *yerida* for the sake of aliyah [a kabbalistic phrase meaning going down for the sake of going up]." But this traditionalism, as already described in an earlier chapter, was ultimately out of step with a congregation growing in number and diversity. As a result, Aaron left the congregation, which took its own direction, but remained with the Talmud class on the periphery of CBST.

Since then, Aaron discovered he could fulfill his spiritual needs within the social context he had escaped many years before. He joined an Orthodox shul in Manhattan. "It is my community; I pray with them; we talk and gossip together. True, I am somewhat peculiar because I am not married, but I don't advertise my sexual identity." Aaron went on to assert that most congregants in regular synagogues also have their own peculiarities: "It is foolish to assume that the so-called Orthodox are 100 percent Orthodox!"

▼

This nonconfrontational strategy was also employed by a few others among the Talmud circle who joined Orthodox synagogues in Manhattan and Brooklyn. They claimed that the situation for gays had improved immensely in recent years. Nachman, a strictly observant *ba'al tshuvah* (one who turns from secular life to Orthodox Judaism), argued that as long as gays don't make a fuss, they can enjoy a tolerant atmosphere in many synagogues. Ten years ago gays were ostracized, and therefore CBST was very important. But now, he went on, "there are many CBST graduates in other synagogues."

Although Aaron described the Orthodox synagogue he adopted when he left CBST ten years earlier as "my community," he did not give up his deep involvement with the Talmud class. "It is a primary group," Aaron explained, defining the Talmud circle in sociological terms, "but this activity also carries some *kedushah* [holiness]." He went on to say that the members were close friends, often speaking to one another. He knew how important the meetings were to its members, for whom this was a very meaningful community. "When men are young the search for sex is their major goal; but when they reach the age of forty that drive declines, and then they discover loneliness." Aaron further observed that "homosexuals don't constitute a community any more than the people on my block do." As Edward, another class member observed: "Someone who has never studied Gemara can't really understand the bond that is created among those who study together." Thus, in their religious life Aaron and the rest of the Talmud class belonged, in fact, to two, if not three, communities: the Talmud circle, and their primary synagogue—CBST for a minority, an Orthodox shul for the majority. But even among the latter a few remained associated with CBST through occasional attendance at religious and social events.

Tuesday evening was often a time for many busy activities at CBST. While the Talmud class met at the center of the community hall, other meetings might take place in the sanctuary, the library, the office, or in another part of the community hall. On June 26, 1990, for example, the Talmud circle prepared for the *siyum* celebration marking the completion of a volume of the Gemara. The big table was covered with a lavender tablecloth (a delicate reminder of gay identity) and loaded with a variety of salamis, salads, drinks, etc. In the sanctuary the trustees met for an executive board meeting. In the library the former presidents and a few other influential members were planning the inauguration ceremony of the Holocaust Torah scroll. At a later hour a few participants at the library meeting joined the celebrants at the Talmud table and were invited to partake of the food. Once the group was short two men for a minyan for the Ma'ariv service. Aaron went to the office and brought along the synagogue's secretary and another active member. On another Tuesday evening a large crowd attended a film in the sanctuary and a noisy meeting of the High Holiday Committee went on in the library. Morris, one of the committee's members, who years ago could not accommodate Aaron's growing orthodoxy, spent some time before the Talmud participants showed up chatting with Aaron about mutual friends and family affairs. Once the class began there were no further interruptions. The class carried on its business as usual, in spite of the noise of arguments heard from the library and the constant movement of people coming and going to the film, the rest rooms, and the kitchen adjacent to the Talmud "corner."

After one Friday service I unexpectedly met an Orthodox Talmud class regular. He humorously derided the service and added that to his astonishment an earlier Gay Pride Week service he attended had introduced a Christian melody [in a bid for universality] and deleted the Amidah! This skepticism about the quality of Jewishness at CBST formed one side of a smoked glass through which each group reflexively viewed the other. An incident on a busy Tuesday evening offered an observation from the other side: Leon, leaving a board meeting (he attended for a special report) to make a phone call, paused on his way to the office when he heard voices coming from the library, through which he had to pass. Suspecting the Talmud class in an unaccustomed location, he asked in a timid, yet sarcastic voice—to the amusement of the other trustees—"Are the *Jews* there?"

This ambivalence, if not resentment, toward the Talmud class membership was not uncommon among the congregation. Simon, who still fondly remembered the first years with Aaron, nevertheless believed that he and his group were too ethnocentric: "They believe the Jews are better than anyone else. . . . They are too traditional; too confined to the words of the text." Simon was puzzled by the Talmud circle's growing Orthodoxy, a tendency no less evident among those with Gentile lovers. He saw Aaron's departure from CBST as proof of his failure to convert the congregation to his style of increasing Orthodoxy. He didn't see it as a conflict between leading members but as an

149

▼

ideological and social split that left Aaron in the minority. Another former admirer of Aaron summed him up in a metaphor of Jewish New York geography: "Aaron first left Brooklyn for Manhattan, but then he made it all the way back to Brooklyn, though he stayed on in Manhattan!" A recent congregant commented, "I don't understand Aaron and his group who endorse Orthodoxy which denies gays and holds them in contempt."

But on another occasion Simon expressed his astonishment with Aaron's decision to carry on the Talmud class at CBST. He assumed that Aaron could hold meetings at his apartment and avoid the trouble of travel with no loss of attendants. Simon concluded: "This is Aaron's statement that he is still part of the synagogue." And when preparations were being made for CBST's eighteenth anniversary celebration, it was Simon who suggested that Aaron be invited to lead the commemorative Friday night service (an unusual gesture considering their latent competition, for when Aaron gave up his position at CBST Simon was among the first to take over his spiritual leadership.) On the same note of reconciliation, a member of the education committee suggested that Aaron be invited to deliver a series of lectures on Judaism on a level equal to that of his Talmud class. The surprised committee agreed but had difficulty finding an intermediary to make the offer. Finally, I, a quasi outsider, was enlisted for this mission.

If these attempts were sometimes awkward, three members of the Talmud class regularly crossed the bridge over the schismatic divide. Despite decreased participation of the Talmud circle in CBST services, Edward and Dov were still regularly attending and, often, giving sermons. Nathan was a frequent visitor and occasionally acted as service leader. These three were the most active "go–between" members and were respected at CBST where they had close friends. They regularly brought back information to the circle about developments in the synagogue. During the Rosh Hashanah party, for example, Dov described the "superfeminist" service he had unhappily attended, which led to a discussion of the plan to appoint a professional rabbi at CBST, a position the leader of that service might fill. This radical proposal, announced by the synagogue's board several months before, was no less hotly debated by the circle than by CBST itself. Though they had grown apart, Talmud class and synagogue were not indifferent to one another. Despite its apparent alienation, as expressed by both sides, the Talmud class was still woven into the fabric of CBST.

The Talmud Class as a Social Text

On rereading Heilman's (1983) description of Talmud classes he observed in Orthodox and Modern Orthodox synagogues in Israel and the United States, I was struck by how closely the gay Talmud class I observed conformed to the general phenomenon of Talmud study (*lernen*) in traditional Judaism. It conformed in the structure of the social relationships, the content of the activity, and its impact in terms of "cultural performance." Aaron is not unique in his position as an admired teacher and moral guide. In all Talmud circles Heilman observed, the rabbi was a central figure, at once warm and authoritative. The notion of fellowship among the *lerners*, their deep attachment and commitment to one another, was another shared characteristic. Applying an idea Clifford Geertz developed elsewhere,[3] Heilman interpreted the Talmud circle activity in the following—a description equally valid for the CBST group:

> Attending a *shiur* in the intimate atmosphere of the study circle may be understood as "a kind of sentimental education," during which what one "learns is what his culture's ethos and his private sensibility look like when spelled out externally in a collective text." (61)

Or,

> Both the process and product of such lernen provide "the structure of meaning through which men give shape to their experiences." . . . The result of all this may be not so much a scholarly education as a sentimental one, an infusion of cultural ethos and worldview. In the cultural performance of lernen, men . . . express and act out Jewish beliefs and ideas . . . while exploring the contemporary in light of the tradition. (109)

If not for its location in a gay synagogue, the uninitiated might not be aware of the unconventional identities of the members of the Talmud circle at CBST. The visitor might notice that during class the lerners wandered into subjects unrelated to the text, a process that enabled all to take part and made the Talmud study more relevant to contemporary life. But the difference between the CBST and other Talmud groups was more evident when the group met together outside the context of lernen. For other groups these social occasions were often dictated externally by events such as birth or death and involved family members not otherwise engaged with the group's activities. In contrast, the CBST circle's seasonal parties were opportu-

nities for forceful expression of the members' unique identity and existential circumstance. The additional participants involved were not outsiders but a wider constituency supporting the core from which these activities grew.

Heilman was inclined to see Talmud shiur interaction in terms of Victor Turner's "social drama."[4] In the CBST circle I found less social drama during the analysis of the Gemara. The close relationships between the participants going back to their own past at CBST and the intimate knowledge they shared about members, old and new, muted any competition between actors as well as confrontations at difficult textual points. The bonds engaging the circle carried an emotional and moral commitment far stronger than that described by Heilman. The social drama I witnessed played to a wider audience and followed a different script.

The dramatic tension of the Talmud class was in its challenge to several worlds. As actors, the members forced their presence and particular configuration of religious and sexual identity on both their Orthodox and gay Jewish audiences. They were active in Orthodox synagogues but at the same time preserved their stronghold at CBST. True, they kept their sexual orientation secret in their newly adopted "Brooklyns," but it was a secret known to many nongay fellow congregants. They were not revealed, nor were they denied the right to full participation in ritual and communal affairs. This unwritten compact was based on their acceptance of the basic tenets and ideals of traditional Judaism, including those most relevant to their existential situation.

Aaron told me he never gave up the hope of raising children. He had a dream of one day finding a woman who would cherish his promise of an affectionate relationship and devoted parenthood, but without sexual passion in their marital life. Aaron and his lover agreed that neither would stand in the other's way if this opportunity arose. I assume Aaron knew it was an impractical idea, even though he could relate a few instances where it had occurred, one involving a former member of the Talmud circle. Aaron admitted he was conservative in his view of Jewish life, and assumed that the continuity of Judaism required that of its people. He regarded his hope of fathering children—a belief that might materialize—as he did his strong conviction of the coming of the Messiah.

Aaron's vision was not shared by most of the other Talmud class members, who wished to adhere to Orthodox Jewish life without conforming to its norms of sexuality and reproduction. That approach was clearly expressed by Nahman: "Yes, there are problems, but a life of Torah and *mitzvos* is worth maintaining, even if one is negligent in one area of observance. Aren't there countless fine people in all committed Jewish circles who neglect one major mitzvah or another?" In another conversation Nahman differentiated between desire and action: "*Taieva* [lust] is not an *aveira* [sin]," only acting on it is. This distinction may be drawn from traditional assumptions that distinguish between transgressions forced on the individual by drives beyond his control and those deliberately undertaken with a free will. Rather than a clear-cut distinction between observance and sin, Nahman suggested an incremental scale in the failure to observe the halakhic prohibition against homosexuality. Though he himself didn't long for offspring, Nahman, no less than Aaron, accepted the normative expectations of a full Jewish life. Both endorsed the historical power of religious law, Halakhah, to preserve the Jewish people and culture precisely because it did not submit to frequent changes.

This doctrinal position was contested by several others in the Talmud circle, including Ralph and Dov. Ralph argued, "I refuse to believe that my loving a man is sinful. I think that the Halakhah is wrong in this area. Unfortunately, Halakhah changes very slowly." But only the strictly observant Gary refused to accommodate on any terms. He demanded that his Modern Orthodox congregation accept him as an openly gay Orthodox man. His claim was denied, and he was not supported in it by his gay friends in the same synagogue. But, at the same time, the straight congregants, who must have suspected the bonds between Gary and other unannounced gays, have not denied the others the honors and privileges of congregational life that Gary lost because of his conspicuous behavior.

The majority of CBST members did not differentiate between the delicate shades that colored the Talmud circle's theological position. Their synagogue was a haven (a "safe space") where they could express their Judaism as determined gay Jews. The concealment of sexual identity in the house of prayer, where one comes for comfort, assurance, and spiritual fulfillment, was considered a complete surrender to oppression. In this context the continuing presence of the Talmud members in the middle of CBST appeared like a scene from the theater of the absurd. "The Jews," as Leon derisively nicknamed them, appeared as "Orthodox impersonators"—gay men masquerading in the role of their major adversaries in Jewish society. Were they giving in to Orthodoxy? Or co–opting it, forcing it into the society and house of sinners?

Esther Newton (1972), who observed female impersonators, analyzed their impact on gay audiences and emphasized the duality they represent. They are evaluated positively "to the extent that they have perfected a sub–cultural skill and to the extent that gay people are willing to oppose the heterosexual culture directly. On the other hand, they are despised because they symbolize and embody the stigma" (104). Above all, the drag queen expresses the incongruity that is basic to the homosexual experience. The Talmud class was not performing in a rehearsed gay play but nevertheless contained elements of Esther Newton's portrayal. In the context of CBST this company of men seriously engaged in Talmud study, many in Orthodox garb, presented a social incongruity. But as skilled students of the Talmud they were also an implicit challenge to the tradition and institutions of Orthodox Judaism, which explicitly deny gays the status of moral personae. The return to Talmud study, which represents the highest intellectual achievement and purest scholastic occupation in Orthodox Jewish society, was a triumph gained after many years. From the vantage of the general CBST membership, however—much as they might applaud the Talmud circle's skill—the scene that it presented was taken from the most oppressive element of Jewish society. And as such it was a reminder of the stigma imposed by its people and theology. These mixed feelings of fascination and resentment, anger and affection that were often manifested by CBST observers poignantly communicated the duality embodied by the Talmud class.

My sociological imagination leads me to interpret the intricate relationships I observed at CBST's "Tuesday Play" in a Geertzian tradition—that of the images and cultural strategies employed to symbolize and give meaning to the individual's existential position and social identity. Resented or beloved by their spectators, Aaron and his circle embodied Orthodox authenticity at CBST. How else are we to understand the invitation to lead the commemorative service or to deliver a lecture series on Judaism? No doubt nostalgia for the synagogue's

early days played a role here. But if the Talmud shiur was a permanent reminder of CBST's institutional past, it was no less a reflection of
the spiritual and social alternatives available to all Jews, gay included.
For both audiences the Tuesday Talmud activity made possible a regular observation of their gradual development since their first reconciliation with, and open expression of, their yearning for Jewish life.
That juxtaposition, irrespective of the growing difference and
self–assertion on both sides, has offered a continuing link with the
historicity of Jewish culture and Jewish identity on the part of CBST's
congregants. And on the part of the Talmud class, their use of the
premises of the expanding and prosperous gay synagogue has offered
the vicarious experience of observing the unrestricted display and
expression of homosexual identity in a Jewish milieu. Here they could
witness the harvest of Jewish gay liberation, which they abandoned in
their search for Jewish authenticity.

▼

CHAPTER EIGHT

The Politics of a Lay-led Synagogue

During my first meeting with Simon he expressed his delight and astonishment at CBST's longevity, especially in view of the short life span typical of many gay institutions. The "miracle" of the synagogue's inception, survival, and growth, beyond its founder's dreams, was reenacted yearly at the synagogue's anniversary celebration, but nowhere was that self-congratulatory mood more in evidence than at the Rosh Hashanah party Morris hosted for fifty of CBST's "elite" at his impressive Greenwich Village apartment in September of 1990. As his well turned-out guests gathered round, Morris toasted the synagogue with pride and a feeling of accomplishment on its eighteenth year—a year auspiciously linked to the Jewish symbol for life (through the numerical value—eighteen—of the letters in the Hebrew word *chai*, "life"). And he singled out other past and current board chairs—Leon, Larry, Ruth, Norman, Saul, and Martin—whose presence symbolized the continuity of their institution.

I am unable to assess the role of the synagogue's leaders in the longevity of that voluntary organization, unaided by institutional Jewish support, but considering the many stories I was told of conflict that had erupted—some of which I witnessed—the mere fact of its survival, let alone its continuing growth, does seem remarkable. I can only attempt to portray some of its inner workings and sketch a few of its major actors.

Board Chairs: Styles and Strategies

My first months at CBST were marked by ongoing arguments and unveiled animosity—barely checked by the norms of public discourse—between what were called the two "factions." One faction was headed by Norman, a former board chair. Herbert, his lover, and two of his close friends, David and Lee, were on the synagogue's board, and Norman continued to attend its meetings and to take part in discussions. Once the board's members expressed their opinions, Norman usually had the last word from his rear seat. The other faction was a more diffuse group opposed to Norman's initiatives, and ultimately coalescing around Martin, a board member.

Saul, the board chair, tried to remain neutral and friendly toward all participants, but conflict often erupted when Martin forcefully voiced a different position from that suggested by Norman and his supporters. The tension underlying board meetings was also evident in other committees I attended, the Religious and Education Committees in particular. Norman's friends David, who was treasurer, and Lee, the board's liaison to the Religious Committee, often attended meetings of various CBST committees where they expressed criticism of the committees' fiscal laxity and deficiency in budgetary planning. They were also both adamant in demanding that decisions be brought to the board for confirmation, although the decisions often appeared to be part of the committees' routine work.

Norman and his colleagues were considered newcomers to Jewish tradition by their opponents—"They learned their Judaism at CBST," I was told—but had become the self-appointed custodians of that tradition. They were seen as opponents of any change that might affect their acquired familiarity and comfort with the ritual and religious style they first encountered at CBST. At the same time they were accused of viewing the synagogue's operations in purely business terms.

During the first board meeting I attended in February 1989, the vice chair presented a $1,300 budget for the Purim party, based on a forecast of 130 participants paying $10 each. David disputed the figures, predicting a lower attendance that would not cover expenses. He was answered that the Purim party was a religious activity and as such any loss would be covered by the synagogue. Saul called for a vote on the issue, and David remained in the minority.

▼

A more volatile discussion took place later when Martin delivered a report on attendance at courses and films sponsored by the Education Committee to which he was liaison. Norman, exercising the right of any CBST member to attend board meetings and speak to an issue once it had been discussed by the board, questioned the wisdom of spending money on programs so poorly attended. Martin, who was furious, reminded his colleagues of their obligation to promote Jewish education, and angrily concluded: "We are not running a business here." David, consistent with his prior argument concerning the Purim party, supported Norman's call for the cancellation of courses that attracted only a few congregants and again found himself in the minority.

The same debate was resumed at the next board meeting a month later. When Norman suggested the poor attendance at courses run by the Education Committee implied that they didn't fulfill the congregants' needs, Martin retorted that attendance was also poor at elections for the board. He continued: "I don't want to quarrel with you. We are a synagogue and we must care for education. We are therefore obliged to support also those activities which are not paying off. It is not in our interest to support popular activities only because they attract more people."

Later the same evening I attended a synagogue discussion group on being gay, which Martin conducted, called "Gay Sensitivity." Martin was still wrought up from his earlier encounter, and much of the session was an opportunity for him to vent his frustration. He thought the synagogue was too much like a business, involved with organizational issues rather than spiritual matters, and angrily declared: "The board is concerned with the quality of the toilet paper." Maybe it was time to start a new synagogue to serve those who were looking for something "more serious and more spiritual." Moreover, Martin continued, although the synagogue has a "million-dollar" building fund for the future acquisition of a permanent location, in the meantime there was no money for urgent present needs. Since CBST had recently signed a seven-year lease on its present space, Martin thought this was a good time to refurbish it: "The synagogue, as it is now, is dirty and shabby; it reflects on our self-image." As evidence of the general frustration felt with the present affairs at CBST, he mentioned his own membership in another mainstream synagogue and added that he wanted to see a rabbi appointed at CBST: "We have the money, but nobody would even give a thought to that option, because with a rabbi there would be somebody to tell them [the board members] what to do." With an eye to the elections two weeks hence Martin concluded that it was difficult to make changes at CBST because the majority of the one thousand congregants didn't really care, and a small organized group could implement its own interests. And he thought the proxy voting system that allowed those attending the election to cast five ballots on behalf of absent members enabled that group to preserve its control on the synagogue's board.

159

A similar atmosphere prevailed at the Religious Committee meeting I attended in March 1989. Although both Lee, the board's liaison, and Jack, chair of the committee, were usually relaxed and amicable, the long meeting was often interrupted by disagreements between them. The tension started almost immediately when Jack asked Lee to keep the minutes of the meeting, making him a party, albeit nonvoting, to the actions that he would have to communicate and defend before the board. Jack also argued, sarcastically, that since the liaison was apparently a full committee member—which was not the case, but expressed Jack's annoyance with Lee's interference—he should share all the tasks performed by the committee members. The issue was raised again later when Lee introduced the board's specific instructions and reminded the committee of its position with respect to the board. Jack then repeated his demand that the liaison should share the committee's administrative burden. Simon supported Jack in suggesting that they appoint the liaison secretary of the committee. Jack enthusiastically greeted this idea, which was obviously intended to annoy Lee, and called for a vote. In spite of Lee's objection Jack went ahead, but only three of the seven members ultimately voted in favor of Simon's proposal, with most of the rest abstaining. The vote was no doubt an act of protest on the part of the committee members, who saw Lee as a watchdog ready to report any change that departed from the synagogue's "tradition" to those on the board who objected to the growing independence of the Religious Committee.

The evening of March 30, 1989, I attended the election, which, despite Martin's pessimism, many hoped would result in a leadership change at CBST. As soon as I arrived I was immediately told that the proxy system had been grossly worked by the two factions. Norman in particular was accused of abusing that privilege by soliciting votes by telephone. The meeting was called to order, and the candidates to replace the five board members whose two-year terms were expiring

▼

were invited to introduce themselves and answer questions. Two of the eight candidates had been CBST members for less than one year. Saul defended their ambition: "If there is a young man who believes he can contribute to the synagogue, we have to encourage him." Beaming with satisfaction, he asked rhetorically, "Do you need an example? Four years ago there was a young man who wanted to be a candidate although he joined the synagogue only eleven months earlier." It was now evident he himself was that young man.

The vote was then taken by paper ballot and the election results announced later to those who remained in attendance. Despite the forecasts Norman did not in fact consolidate his influence. Most of his friends on the board were among the half whose terms were expiring, and of the eight candidates the only one who was clearly associated with him was rejected. But Joel, for one, greeted the changes with amused cynicism: "Look who is on the board. Five years ago who knew anything about Martin. On the eve of the elections, people search for new faces in order to avoid the monsters. But eventually the new ones are not much better than the old monsters."

At the first meeting of the new board meeting in April, Norman attended as usual, accompanied by his lover. During the meeting the head of the Election Committee, Leon, whose reputation for sagacity and diplomacy was often put in the service of the board, reported on the recent balloting. He summarized a document distributed to the board that analyzed the results of proxy voting, a relatively new innovation. The written report was very critical of the practice and called for major changes in the bylaws. It found that 70 percent of the ballots had been by proxy and continued: "Validation of proxies against membership lists took close to two hours. Several proxies were invalidated because the names of the members were ineligible and the proxy holders did not know who they held proxies for." The report reiterated the conclusions made by last year's Election Committee chair, "The system encourages proxy soliciting, and the consolidation of voting power behind those who collect the greatest number of proxy ballots," and called on the Board of Trustees "to repeal the ill–advised multiple proxy clause, and replace it with any system that returns CBST to a true one person–one vote system . . . and thereby return sanity to CBST's electoral process."

In a later conversation Leon expounded on the recent election, disclosing information that was not included in his report. Despite the common belief, Saul, the incumbent board chair, as well as Norman, secretary of the Election Committee, had been active in proxy solicitation, but Saul had been more successful.

Norman asked for a short break in the meeting and brought out a bottle of champagne to toast the new board. In his short speech Norman made two points: board members should realize that they are no longer regular synagogue members. From now on they would be looked up to and must prove themselves a model of proper behavior. If, for example, they see some litter in the synagogue and don't bother to pick it up, others watching them will do the same. Second, as new board members they are naturally anxious to implement change. But since they are not familiar with the reasons for earlier decisions, they may ignore or underrate them. They would do well to consult members who were on the board when these decisions were made, and he himself was always at their disposal, happy to offer his advice and help. He wished the board good luck and left the meeting. Norman, himself, had become increasingly engaged in his new career in local politics, and, too busy with his new tasks, he was satisfied enough and only rarely attended CBST board meetings.

Saul was reelected to a second one-year term as board chair, a term notable for several tentative initiatives: appointment of committees to explore the possible renovation of the synagogue and the hiring of a professional staff. Neither initiative, however, reached a firm conclusion.

A year later the new board elected Martin as its chair. That development would have been deemed improbable just over a year earlier when he seemed so weakly positioned versus Norman and his faction. But Martin was now the most impressive figure among the veterans left on the board and, having retired from a top administrative post in health care when he discovered he was HIV positive, the only one who could spare the time for the job. (I was often told that the position of board chair was so demanding that only those having independent means or freedom at work could undertake it successfully.) Now that at forty he had been so unexpectedly given the power to do something about the shortcomings he had complained of to the Gay Sensitivity group, Martin was no less adamant about running the synagogue his own way than had earlier chairs reputed for their strong will and benevolent authoritarianism.

▼

As chair Martin immediately sought to realize the two goals he had earlier articulated: renovating the synagogue and appointing a rabbi. Both projects had already been tentatively explored under Saul's leadership. But Saul was always looking for compromise: "He tried to connect the extremes," Jack observed, "but then nobody was really satisfied." Speaking from his position as chair of the Religious Committee, Jack went on, "It's better to have a clear-cut decision even if you are not comfortable with it. Then, you can decide if you go along or not." And it was Martin who would not rest until his aims were implemented.

The renovation of the synagogue was almost complete in time for the High Holidays of 1990. A new dropped ceiling housed the improved lighting and air conditioning. Now painted throughout in grey tones, several elements were in faux marble, while the eastern wall of the sanctuary containing the holy ark abstractly suggested the stones of the Wailing Wall. But not all were pleased with the colors and style; Norman, for instance, commented that he wished the eastern wall had been more representational.

The appointment of rabbi was a more difficult project, and many thought unattainable. But in May, only a few weeks after his election as chair, Martin received the board's unanimous endorsement for his plan to appoint a rabbi pending congregational approval. At the Friday night service, June 29, 1990, Paul, the board's secretary, announced the first public meeting, scheduled for the next week, to discuss the board's decision. That it was Paul who made the announcement, and not Martin who had just addressed the congregation minutes before, suggested Martin's desire to have the project be seen as one of the full board and not just its chair.

But it was Martin who explained the decision in the July–August *Synagogue News*. He detailed the urgent need for a rabbi, pointing to the AIDS crisis, the growth of the synagogue, and the need to improve the quality of its services and educational activities. At the same time he announced the board's decision not to affiliate with any of the major Jewish movements. The first decision, it would appear, marked a step toward the Jewish mainstream and a break with the synagogue's "tradition," while the latter decision suggested a reaffirmation of CBST's unique position. Presented together, it seemed that these somewhat contradictory decisions could appeal to a congregation often conflicted between change and continuity.

I have already presented much of the debate that followed the board's decision to appoint a rabbi. Suffice it to say here that at the first public meeting held to discuss the decision, Martin expressed his wish to have a rabbi installed in time for the High Holidays of 1991 a   163 year hence. He succeeded in his essential aim, but one year late—the candidate search and screening process having taken much longer than anticipated. Rabbi Sharon Kleinbaum was formally installed before eight hundred members and guests by Rabbi Alexander Schindler, president of the Union of Hebrew (Reform) Congregations of America, on Friday, September 1992, in time for the High Holidays. Martin, however, succumbed to AIDS ten days before the ceremony that represented his legacy to CBST.

The history of CBST has included powerful board chairs who left a clear mark on the synagogue and others whose terms were less memorable. Contrasting two types of leaders, an administrative leader and one of change, Morris observed: "Martin is a leader of change." It would be wrong, however, to suggest that Martin alone had manipulated the congregation and its most influential members to realize his personal ambition for the synagogue. Those congregants appointed to the committees responsible for eventually hiring a rabbi were among the most impressive members of CBST in terms of their education, personal integrity, and reputation beyond the synagogue's realm. At least three had at the start publicly expressed their serious reservations about the hiring of a rabbi, though once involved in the process they gradually came to support it, lending it added credibility. By the final stages of the over-two-year process, the hiring of a rabbi had gained the legitimacy of the synagogue's formal and informal leadership. One might see Martin's enlistment of respected members of the congregation, despite their reservations, as a clever maneuver to achieve his ends. I believe, however, it was the dynamics of committee work and the discourse between those veteran leaders rather than one man's smart strategy that carried them along the path of consensus.

Morris himself was another member well known for his effective leadership and admired by most members for his continuing contribution to CBST. But I was often told about his authoritarian style, and how he would short-circuit the decision-making process: instead of waiting for a committee to complete its laborious deliberations about some expenditure or other, he would go out and buy the item in question with his own money or that donated by people he had solicited.

▼

Such had been the case with the silver Torah ornaments. Many years before, when he thought the sanctuary could be expanded to comfortably seat more people, he hadn't waited for a committee to consider the proposal but brought his own workers in, pulled down the wall separating the sanctuary from the community hall, and installed folding doors. For most, Morris was evidently well-off and obviously generous, and it seemed futile to argue with him over democratic procedures when he took upon himself both the work and expense.

If Morris sometimes ran roughshod over its protocols, his long-term personal devotion to CBST seemed clear. Morris saw the synagogue as home in a very intimate way. It was he who had instituted the congregational dinners and would come in early to drag the heavy tables out of storage and set them up. One evening, having responded to a call for help preparing the synagogue for the High Holidays, Morris was working along with present board members and a few other volunteers rearranging the chairs, the tables, and the heavy bookcases. When the group was asked to use some sheets to cover the boxes containing prayer books and handouts stacked in a corner of the sanctuary, Morris reminisced that ten years before he had lugged big potted plants to the synagogue for a decorative screen, "but then I was fifteen years younger," he wryly noted.

Morris's leadership was assessed in the context of other recent board chairs by a longtime CBST observer:

Saul tried to stay friendly with everybody and didn't leave his imprint beyond expanding the bathrooms. . . . Norman didn't decide all alone, he had his group of supporters to consult with. . . . Martin was different: he carried out the goals he believed were absolutely important. . . . Morris is the model for leadership in the synagogue. He projects confidence, but is not ashamed to acknowledge his weaknesses. He used to say, "I am ignorant in Judaism."

If the history of CBST's board chairs includes those of different character and style, it frequently demonstrates a pattern of a strong leader followed by a more amiable one. Those who served less than the usual two consecutive one-year terms permitted were usually forced out by more ambitious and strong-willed individuals. This was true of Ruth, whose selection apparently resulted from the competition between two equally forceful male candidates, one of whom, Norman, succeeded her, the other being the easygoing Larry. In that leadership pendulum, which seemed to accommodate the pace of change the congregants were able to absorb, Martin replaced the conciliatory Saul, and in turn was expected to be followed by Paul, who was far less authoritarian and endeared to the congregation. But Paul resigned from the board because of deteriorating health, and the remaining members seemed to lack the stature of chair. Assuming the synagogue had reached a dangerous leadership void, Morris decided to return to the board. Winning election, he was then selected by his colleagues to be their chair. I was not in New York to observe him in that position, but I was told he led the synagogue with few constraints from its governing bodies. AIDS, it seems, interrupted the "natural" cycle of leadership at CBST.

165

Board Members and Committees

In addition to the chair, responsibility for governing CBST was vested in the other nine members of the Board of Trustees. Along with their collective duties, each was granted a specific role in the synagogue management. These included the positions of vice chair, secretary, treasurer, and either liaison or chair to one of the six major permanent committees: communications, events and activities, membership, education, house, and ritual affairs (the Religious Committee, as it was generally known). In addition to the these, there were ad hoc committees and subcommittees as well. The High Holidays Committee, for instance, discussed in chapter 5, was a permanent committee from which a subcommittee was appointed to allocate honors. Every year the board appointed Election and Fund-Raising Committees. (The latter was particularly sensitive, dealing with annual pledges, and apart from its three members only the board chair had access to its confidential information.) The network of committees was large, but its membership often overlapped, being drawn from a limited pool of volunteers.

The committees did the work of the synagogue, and board members and committee chairs devoted a great deal of time to the daily running of CBST. On any given week night one or more could be found in the synagogue attending meetings, reading mail, decorating the sanctuary, mailing out the newsletter, etc. Rarely was there any activity without a board member present. Some jobs were particularly demanding, and members were reluctant to take them on: chairing the House Committee was one. Late one night I happened upon

▼

Shelly, the board member responsible for that committee, cleaning out the kitchen's storeroom. Responding to my surprise at finding her still at work, she explained: "I'm dating now; but if I had a relationship, I wouldn't have all that time."

Board members were not alone in carrying a heavy burden at CBST. The chair of the Religious Committee was responsible for supervising all regular services. Jack told me he was tired after three years but that there was no one immediately available to replace him who had sufficient knowledge and was able to take the time from work. Jack himself had a full-time job, and had to juggle its demands with the need to make numerous calls each day attending to the religious affairs of the synagogue. Though few at CBST were aware of the immense time and effort Jack invested in his position, he at least was fortunate in having an understanding lover equally interested in the smooth operation of the synagogue.

Joseph, who had twice served on the board and been active in various committees during his first years at CBST, felt the volunteer structure was overwhelmed and had himself retired from it: "In 1978, we had 120 members, and 50 of them were active in committees. With this number you could do a lot for the congregation. But now, there are still 50 active members, but the synagogue has 1,000 members." If CBST continued expanding, Joseph believed there was no alternative to hiring professional staff. Personally, he thought it might be better to have new gay congregations that could serve the needs of various groups: "We can't be everything to everybody; I resent the idea that bigger is better." But barring that, he felt the volunteers' growing exhaustion, and the board's inevitable engagement with trivial issues, required the hiring of an executive to handle administration, freeing the board to deal with "serious issues." Perhaps paradoxically, however, Joseph opposed the synagogue's first concrete step toward professionalism, the hiring of a rabbi, believing that no candidate could satisfy their congregation's diverse tastes and needs.

Joseph was not alone in complaining about the workload borne by a small group of volunteers. Some pointed to Morris and Norman, whose willingness to roll up their sleeves and undertake the most menial tasks, admirable as that was, set an unrealistic standard, they felt, for the operation of so large an institution. Both Morris and Norman were reluctant to authorize expenditures that could be avoided using volunteer labor. "They think it's a Cousins' Club," Joel complained.

The overworked leadership was not without public recognition, however. During the High Holidays they were given ritual honors. At Kol Nidre, all past chairs and present board members were invited to the bimah to attend the opening of the ark, and again called up for the same honor during the Ne'ilah service the next afternoon. Morris was granted the honor of leading the Torah procession around the fully packed sanctuary, and regally accepted the affectionate greetings of the congregants who pressed forward to kiss the sacred scrolls. 167

There were other dedicated volunteers who did not aspire to positions of influence and whose efforts were less publicly recognized but no less indispensable. These were the members Martin once cautioned his board colleagues they should be careful not to offend. Among them was Lenny, who took charge of the kitchen and prepared the food for the kiddush, the congregational dinners, and other special events. He held complete monopoly over the kitchen, and the results of his efforts were not without complaint, but his sudden death shocked the congregation. Several hundred congregants attended his funeral where his dedication to the synagogue was eulogized by the CBST leadership and his friends. At the following Friday night service Saul again mourned his loss, concluding: "Ten members could not replace Lenny's work here." Martin, the current chair, announced the appointment of a kitchen committee to take over Lenny's job and called for volunteers.

Lenny's death dramatically highlighted the love individuals had for CBST and reminded many congregants of those other members who freely contributed their time, energy, and money to the synagogue. No doubt had CBST employed professionals to perform these roles it would have been a different institution. When Larry volunteered to rejoin the Religious Committee sometime after concluding his term on the board, with one year as its chair, he was asked about his motives. He explained that rather than just be "on call," he felt he needed to be part of some ongoing synagogue activity. Otherwise, "I feel I am floating."

The Case of the Religious Committee

Within the organizational structure of CBST, the Religious Committee was uniquely constituted. Its members were neither elected by

▼

the congregation nor appointed by the body to whom the congregants had delegated their authority: the Board of Trustees. Rather, it was, as Joel, its former chair, described it: "A self-selected committee."

Any congregant who attended its meeting for six months could ask to be voted onto the committee if there was a vacancy among its seven members. One member was selected as chair. Its unique autonomy in a democratic organization, however, was checked by its lack of institutional authority. For it remained clearly subordinated to the board. All actions taken by the committee required board approval before going into effect. In addition, the committee chair did not sit on the board or even report to it. Rather, a board member was selected to act as its liaison, though not always one with an extensive Jewish education. As we have seen above, conflicts frequently existed between the committee and its liaison as surrogate for the board.

The weakness of the Religious Committee vis-à-vis the board was demonstrated in a discussion I attended in early 1990. The board had decided to celebrate the synagogue's anniversary with an oneg[1] program following the Friday night service and had selected the Charlotte Russe band. The group had performed its classic Jewish and contemporary repertoire at Martin's commitment party as well as at a prior CBST anniversary dinner held outside the synagogue. But the committee deemed them less appropriate for a function held in conjunction with a religious service than another group of klezmer musicians who had performed at CBST on Chanukah. After Jack's introduction, Simon opened the discussion: "We are the seven rabbis of the synagogue and we have a responsibility. We want a Jewish place. . . . We want a Jewish feel. We have to advise the board about our feelings in a way they will listen to us."

Others felt that the committee wouldn't be listened to, and that Martin, the board chair, wouldn't accept a change because Charlotte Russe was a bigger draw. One member unhappily reminded the group that the Chanukah Dance had been postponed to a Friday evening because it was a more popular night. Ze'ev responded: "If Friday night is our island in time, we have to do everything in our power to make it more Jewish in kind." It was finally decided not to demand a change in the board's decision but instead to request that Charlotte Russe perform mainly from its Jewish repertoire. Henry, the liaison, taking the committee's side, added: "We have to consider how to sell our advice to several people [on the board]."

The Religious Committee's weakness was a continuing source of frustration to its members. Naomi, among its most knowledgeable in Judaism and one of its few women, resigned from the committee because, as she told me, all important decisions in religious matters were made elsewhere. She cited the board's exploration of the idea of hiring a rabbi and joining a mainstream movement, which was done without consulting the committee, and neither was the board's task force drawn from the committee membership.

The Board at Work

Although the board—apart from reviewing actions of the Religious Committee—was not often directly involved in religious matters, its decisions frequently did have religious implications. At one board meeting I attended the discussion turned to CBST's upcoming Eighteenth Anniversary Party being held at a restaurant in Queens. Sheila asked, "Would it be a kosher meal?" In reply, David, the vice chair, told her: "It's going to be kosher-style, but not strictly kosher." The food would be kosher, but the kitchen, the dishes, and the cutlery would not. Had they required a strictly kosher meal, the ticket price would have to be $100 per member instead of $72. But Sheila, who had recently joined the Religious Committee as well, was not satisfied, commenting: "If we are the shul that we are, we have to address the issue of kashrut." She went on to argue that CBST events should conform to the same rules whether they are held inside or outside the synagogue. Henry commented that last year he had noticed a few congregants who wouldn't touch the food when they learned it wasn't kosher and who might be offended by a repetition. A congregant, a lawyer, attending the meeting summarized the dilemma: "There are two issues we have to address: inclusion versus exclusion. True, there are those who would be offended by that caterer whose food is really *treif* [ritually impure]. But there are more people who would be hurt by the price of tickets." He said he himself would consider a $200 per couple expense differently from a $150, and felt many people would be offended by the increase if it went to satisfy the "people of kashrut." Sheila was not convinced, reiterating: "We must be aware of who we are and who we represent." The lawyer replied: "If this is the case, we have to accommodate our events to our rules [consistently and] well in advance, rather than accommodate, ad hoc, the rules to the events."

▼

Jack, the chair of the Religious Committee, who happened to be at the meeting, suggested that the issue wasn't so clear-cut. The synagogue hadn't completely solved the problems of kashrut in its own kitchen, and for practical reasons was not a model of observance itself. Following Jack's comments, a vote was called. The board accepted the restaurant proposed by the Events and Activities Committee, with only Sheila and Henry, the Religious Committee's liaison, abstaining.

Later in the evening Jack raised the issue that had impelled him to attend the meeting, one that related as well to the question of how far the majority should go to accommodate the strongly felt needs of the minority in a "diverse" congregation. Visibly upset, and speaking only for himself, he urged the board to reconsider its recently adopted policy on the use of congregants' names. The policy declared that a member's name was not to be printed in any CBST publication or announced from the bimah without the member's prior approval. This decision followed a member's complaint that an article she had submitted to the newsletter had been published under her name, an "outing" that potentially compromised her position at work.

Jack began by reading a letter recently published in the Reconstructionist movement's journal, a letter that declared homosexuality an obscenity. He exclaimed passionately: "We are oppressed in our daily life, and the board's decision means that we must think all the time that something is wrong with us!" Jack argued that the policy was completely unacceptable; that it was not CBST's business to accommodate those members who hadn't solved their own problems: "Our synagogue is a strong statement on being gay and proud. . . . It doesn't make sense with this being a safe space and not part of the oppression surrounding us." He asked the board to rewrite the policy, particularly as it applied to announcing names from the bimah, insisting that it was the responsibility of those members who feared exposure to make their reservations known.

The board heard Jack out but took no action at that meeting. Ultimately, however, the policy was modified to balance the responsibility. As a result, the Religious Committee, for example, sent a letter to the one hundred members on its list of qualified cantors, service leaders, and drashah speakers declaring its intention to include the names of the cantor, leader, and speaker in the announcement of upcoming services. Those having a problem with this were asked to make that known and in the absence of a reply would be assumed to have none. Only one replied that he did.

The responsibility to accommodate diverse needs in its embrace of the wider gay Jewish community also arose with the issue of the syn- agogue's membership fee. The annual membership of $72 (in 1990) was nominal compared to other gay—and especially other nongay synagogues—and was frequently cited as an example of CBST's "open door" policy, its ethos of an institution unbounded by background or class. When Martin introduced the board's plans for hiring a rabbi, he emphasized that it would only require a membership to go up to $125, compared to $200 at the gay synagogue in Philadelphia and $400 in Los Angeles. Similarly, except for the elaborate anniversary party mentioned above, ticket prices for dinners and parties were also modest, $10–$15, barely enough to cover expenses.

With its membership fee intentionally kept low, the financial operation of CBST was largely dependent on the congregants' donations, the overwhelming majority pledged during the High Holidays. Martin, the board chair, claimed that 70 percent of CBST's budget came from contributions and the rest from memberships, the reverse of most synagogues. In 1990 High Holiday pledges totaled $104,187, of which $65,000 was paid in the first two months, out of an annual budget of about $250,000.

As mentioned earlier, individual pledges were kept confidential, but rumors about the more generous donors and their largesse endowed them with some special standing in the congregation. When I expressed my surprise at the board members' indulgent attitude toward David's many time-consuming comments, it was remarked that not only was he ready to take on jobs refused by others but he was also a generous contributor to the synagogue. It was clear, however, that monetary contributions were not enough to endow a congregant with a leading position at CBST. I was told the story of a congregant who was disappointed to learn that his wealth did not confer on him the honors his father and grandfather had effortlessly enjoyed in their own synagogues. He finally reached a position of respect and influence, but only after he accommodated CBST's expectation of active service. "Money doesn't talk here," Joel declared, "here you must work."

The confidentiality of pledges was a long-standing policy at CBST, dating back to a generous supporter's wish for anonymity, but it was

▼

criticized by some. Saul, who as chair had been privy to individual pledges, discovered that some members were contributing far less than their means would allow, while others reneged on their pledges.

Of the one thousand members, four hundred contributed nothing beyond the membership fee. Lee agreed with Saul that fairness required that contributions be made public: "Those for whom the synagogue is important as a means of identity have to prove it." But though confidentiality may have allowed some to avoid giving their "fair share," it served the synagogue's egalitarian ethos by damping the status of wealth. If one had the time and energy, the avenue to leadership in the synagogue was open to all regardless of net worth, age, occupation, or length of membership.

The trustees were careful not to alienate important audiences while preserving the synagogue's authority. That strategy displayed the leadership's policy aimed at preserving the position of CBST as the only dominant gay and lesbian synagogue in New York. Martin, who professed the need for various gay congregations, once he became board chair made all efforts to ensure the synagogue was the "right" place for everybody. On one occasion he suggested introducing movable walls in the community hall to allow for two services to congregate at the same time. The Religious Committee, for example, had practically no authority over the practices, the texts, and the rituals conducted in the new services. Similarly, the synagogue had never endowed its rabbi members (among whom a few have officiated as rabbis of Conservative or Reform congregations) with any special leading status. They were not called to serve on advising committees or decide on religious matters. They were treated as most other members to the extent that they wished to take an active role. "That would have raised strong opposition, we are a lay–led congregation!" I was told when I inquired why the group of rabbis, members at CBST, were not approached (except for one) by the board to consult with on the merit of the new siddur declined by the Religious Committee.

The appointment of Rabbi Kleinbaum indicated a major change in a tradition of twenty years. It is beyond the context of my observations to conclude about the impact of that change on future congregational life at CBST. Nevertheless, one could suggest that the style of a lay-led congregation had been institutionalized at CBST to an extent that guaranteed a continuity of its unique style of congregants' participation and deep involvement in religious and organizational affairs.

That lay participation was one of the components that must have contributed to the "miracle" of CBST's survival and continuing growth despite the centrifugal forces that fostered serious divisions, the potential for the emergence of separatist lesbian and gay congrega- 173 tions in New York. Other elements and mechanisms supporting CBST's institutional durability included an open avenue of leadership for newcomers regardless of age, occupation, and wealth, together with the continuing participation and gratification of veteran activists, the lengthy processes of decision making, and, particularly, the reluctance to impose one dominant theological commitment. For a long time, however, the open avenue mentioned above most probably was not equally applicable to women's opportunities for mobility into positions of leadership, among the issues to be discussed in the following chapter.

▼

CHAPTER NINE

Getting Around the Gender Issue

When I first began observing CBST in January 1989, women accounted for a third of the synagogue membership. At regular Friday night services, however, most sat clustered together in a few rows in the center of the sanctuary, a disproportionately small presence. That underrepresentation of women characterized most CBST activities, committees, and leadership positions. Few women were service leaders, cantors, or drashah speakers; the Talmud class contained no female members; of the seven members of the Religious Committee, there was only one woman; none was currently sitting on the ten-person Board of Trustees; only one, Ruth, had ever been elected its chair—a choice resulting from a stand-off between two men, and then for only a one-year term. During my stay women seemed to leave CBST's premises earlier after spending some time at the kiddush and the social hour following the Friday night service. That, however, could be my impression because of their smaller number. As indicated in earlier chapters, only at High Holiday services and congregational dinners was the percentage of women in CBST's membership fully revealed—when, in fact, it was overrepresented.

During the first election I observed in March 1989, Sarah, a writer for the *Synagogue News*, asked several of the candidates, all of whom were male, why there were so few women at the meeting and none running for the board. One candidate told her to ask the missing women. Another, Paul, expressed his disappointment with the absence of women but pointed to the great change in their position at CBST: women could be found leading services on several consecutive Friday nights, something he declared was unimaginable a few years before. "Who would have thought a woman could lead a service!" 175 And he concluded that there were no conflicts today between men and women.

During a memorial service for Penny, a legendary congregant who passed away in 1990, a CBST veteran, Sam, commented on her loss, telling me about the changes he had witnessed in recent years in the relations between men and women at the synagogue: "Except for Penny, you couldn't talk to them. They were so resentful toward men, they didn't see you, they looked through you. They showed up like dykes."

In spite of Penny's close relationships with many leading congregants, she was never elected to the board. "She was too opinionated for the congregation," Jack explained to me. Her relationships had been forged as the only woman involved in the Community Development Committee, where she had shared with the synagogue's male leadership the intimacy of revealing their inner feelings and hopes for the synagogue. During the memorial service Leon described one of these sessions, when she had burst out in anger at her colleagues, telling them that they treated her as a nonperson. Leon quoted her complaint: "You don't care about me. When we finish our meetings . . . you guys, three go out for dinner, two go on to a bar, two go out cruising, two go home together to bed, and I go home alone. Am I not a human being? Can't you invite me to join you for dessert?"

Relationships between men and women were developing toward greater joint participation, and one could often observe expressions of affection—hugging, kissing, and other signs of close friendships—between some men and women. But that growing participation and partnership was not devoid of mutual suspicions and occasional outbursts of bitterness (as demonstrated in chapter 5 in the case of dukhanin). Dov, considered traditional, claimed that had Aaron stayed at CBST he wouldn't have encouraged great changes in the position of women (against the belief of his female admirers). But a few of the men as well—strong supporters of feminist goals—expressed some doubts about the true feelings of other male congregants with regard to full equality between men and women. "They *do* follow the degenderized texts, but they don't really comprehend the essence of

▼

feminism," exclaimed a leading male congregant who witnessed an expression of resentment toward women he didn't expect from another influential male congregant.

What was the experience of women at CBST and how had it differed from that of men? Was it as bleak as Penny's poignant assessment made in the late 1970s? A group of eight women were invited to brunch during a visit I made to New York in January 1993 to share their feelings and experiences as members of CBST. A number of them were veteran members—one going back to the early years of the synagogue—others were newer to CBST. Most of them were engaged in stable partnerships though not all attended the meeting with their lovers. The majority were professionals occupied in (or recently retired from) comfortable positions.

After a short period of socializing Annette suggested we get down to business. The group seemed willing, even eager, to express their views and had no hesitation being recorded. Naomi began by describing her Jewish background and the alienation from it that resulted from her sexual orientation. The personal history she recounted was very similar to that of other (i.e., male) CBST members, as were her initial feelings on arriving at the synagogue, but her account soon diverged:

> I think, at least my perspective was, when I came into the synagogue, that I was comfortable with the service, part of it. It felt like home. It felt good. I had been away from it for a long time. But that grew old very quickly for me because I found that although it was degenderized there was no place for me . . . it was uncomfortable. This was in '83 or so."

Other opinions were offered:

> "I've always felt at home."
> "That's not true."
> "In the beginning I was uncomfortable."

Annette commented: "I think some of it might have had to do with various Jewish backgrounds coming in. I mean if you felt comfortable in the synagogue, then it was easier to get around the gender issue." Naomi agreed: "I think it's an important point, because for a lot of women raised in the '50s and '60s . . . a lot more training occurred for the boys than for the girls." But as a member of CBST who had been trained.

there was such fear that we would get the men upset, that I was sitting there feeling that this was '63, not '83. Just as an example of that, when Esther and I conducted a service, you would have thought that the whole place was going to explode. There were guys who were sitting in the front row making comments through the whole thing—absolutely threatened. It was unbelievable. Every week two men got up there together, two men, or it could be a man and a woman, but two women?!!

Jill continued:

If you were leading services, you always had to be aware of who you were inviting for a reading. . . . From the male perspective it didn't matter if it wasn't only men called up, but it couldn't be all women that you called up. And if you called women up, you had to make sure there was "balance."

Annette offered a historical perspective. She argued that the atmosphere in the early years was not supportive of women, but she credited Aaron for having included women in CBST's ritual, despite his Orthodox background: "As I said, Aaron set it up so women would be called to the Torah. It was there, and yet the culture was different because there were very few women." Judy asked Annette: "Were you there for the First World Congress? I understand that the pivotal point that sent a lot of women out was a play." Annette answered:

Actually it was the Second World Congress, but it was the first big one that was held in our shul. Let me describe what happened. The incident that I'll relate had nothing to do with religious participation. It had to do with bad taste—antifeminist bad taste.

The conference was designed, overproduced, in typical CBST style, with activities every second of the day, and the Friday evening had a service, and an oneg, and a play. And the play was a production written by a burgeoning playwright member whose name I won't mention. We had seen the play before, and it was in exceedingly poor taste. And I got wind of the fact that it was going to be presented to the world congress, so I wrote a rather strident letter to the board, who ignored it. That's where numbers were so tough, you know. There were just a couple of people who were in a position to say they were going to put on

▼

the play. But, unusual for the shul, there were a lot of women there that Friday night. And we actually walked out on the play. . . . It was a story about a Jewish dentist and his mother. You know the negative stereotypes of the Jewish mother—real bad comedy.

It was the best thing that happened that weekend because all that very formal structure, that content which was overproduced, got put aside, and the whole next day was devoted to really looking at these issues. . . . It was a really superb discussion of these kinds of things—saying you can't roll over people's feelings. It was a change. It was very interesting. . . . And that was 1977, and people really learned from that.

Naomi asked, "Degenderization had to follow that?" Annette replied,: "Well, certainly . . . if you remember the copyright on the Siddur was '79. I remember sitting on that committee, and that was a long process."

Naomi continued,

By the time I got there in '82, there was no question women were a timid minority. They felt like the sisterhood. And the board was scared to do anything which was women-only in terms of having any events. That was against synagogue policy. Women felt it was not their organization.

Jill agreed.

There was not the consciousness that when you have a very small minority you have to have women-only activities. There was no understanding that to have a synagogue dance meant you had a men-only dance because there were too few women to make the women willing to come. Because a handful of women would feel lost among two to three hundred men. And that was not totally ill will: it was total lack of understanding.

In 1990–91 there were three women on the board. Only two remained in 1991–92, but a third woman joined them at midterm. Three women served again on the board in 1992–93. Jean, who was not elected to the board in 1992, assumed it was the superior number of men that made it difficult for women to run for the board. She thought they should have been entitled to 50 percent representation on the board. But when I asked at the 1993 brunch why it was that even now, when women are apparently entitled to full participation and could effect considerable changes in the synagogue, they are still poorly represented on the board, the responses didn't blame the men in a direct manner.

In the ensuing discussion Jill argued that women were less inclined to take part in politics and strive for positions of leadership. They reflect the value system and education in America that expects men to achieve goals and strive for authority while women are educated to be passive. Other women supported Jill's interpretation adding that women back off from the investment of time and the unpleasantness one must endure as board member. Women are reluctant to continue in leadership positions because they don't consider it an important outlet for self-expression and creativity. As evidence, they mentioned Naomi, who resigned from the Religious Committee, and Jill, who refused to run for the board. They indicated Sheila as the only woman on the present board (of 1992–93) who seemed to possess the ambition for power typical of men.

There were, however, a few other women who seemed inclined to run for office. Carol, in particular, wished to join the board. But as far as the men were concerned she was too "opinionated," as displayed in her uncompromising position during the deliberations on the hiring of a rabbi. She was not popular among the female congregants, either. Jean, a new member, was soon interested in joining the rank of leadership as well. With her professional background and eloquence she appeared to be ready to fulfill that ambition. But she failed on her first attempt in 1992. I think she antagonized men because of her combative style during arguments. Sheila, in contrast, combined her interest in politics with a more relaxed demeanor that appealed to many men. Nevertheless, she didn't escape some criticism in her drive for leadership, including the suggestion, made by women, that she was thriving on the tragedy of men inflicted with AIDS who were vacating the theater of power.

Although women have not been strongly pressing for a greater share in the running of CBST, it seemed inevitable that they would take a growing part in the organization, since the supply of active men was dwindling. When Paul's health rapidly declined, Sheila's candidacy for the presidency became a real possibility (Paul was considered by many men and women as Martin's successor). Rumors spread about the growing tension between Sheila and Lance, who also became very

▼

prominent on the board. They seemed equally skilled, but both were not yet considered by their colleagues to be ready for the job. Morris, who ran for the board and became its chair, actually postponed the competition between the two. They were both appointed co-vice chairs. That organizational innovation of two vice chairs signaled a new parity between men and women. The women on the board served in various positions as chairs or liaisons to the committees of education, membership, house, communication, and secretary of the board.

The superior power of men in the synagogue's organization was also related by a few women to their economic advantage. Men still earn more than women, and most among the generous contributors to CBST's annual appeals were affluent men. Ruth argued that the official ideology of maintaining a low membership fee was actually a strategy of control employed by the male leadership. Since the synagogue's budget was greatly dependent on the male benefactors, they naturally had a greater say in the synagogue's affairs. But women's weaker stand in the synagogue was more often related to the strong lobby of "Orthodox" men. Nevertheless, the latter's influence was discovered by the women themselves to be much exaggerated when a woman was elected as first rabbi at CBST. "It was a loud-mouthed minority that carried much influence for a long time" was Naomi's conclusion after the election of Rabbi Sharon Kleinbaum.

The growing visibility of the women's constituency and their demands was most dramatically displayed with the establishment of the feminist service. Actually, when the plan was first introduced to the board, in January 1991, it was not immediately called a "feminist service." Naomi, who had previously resigned from the Religious Committee, was most instrumental promoting the new project. At the start of her presentation she told the trustees the Religious Committee had already confirmed her request for an alternative monthly service (see chapter 5). She went on to explain that the new service would be more liberal in its orientation and introduce changes in the English as well as in the Hebrew texts.

The discussion started with the issue of space. The monthly Friday service was planned for a late afternoon, at 6.30 P.M., early enough before the regular evening service at 8.30 P.M. Naomi asked to use the back wing of the community hall. She promised it would not interfere with other activities that might take place in the synagogue and be open to everybody. "It is not going to be our space" she concluded, in a tone that satisfied the trustees. But the major problem during the ensuing discussion was focused on the name of the new service. Henry, the board's liaison to the Religious Committee, argued, with a strong notion of indignation, "I object to any name such as 'alternative,' 'innovative,' or 'creative,' which would indicate that other services are less innovative or creative. We must have a nonjudgmental name!"

Only at that stage did Naomi stress that the service would carry a distinct feminist orientation. It was decided to advertise an "additional service" and explain in the newsletter its special characteristics. The new service, which recruited many women and a few men, was later referred to and advertised as the "feminist service."

Another issue raised during the board's meeting concerned the liturgy to be used at the new service. Naomi explained that the organizers had not yet decided about the preparation of a specific prayer book. In the meantime they intended to use various texts assembled by the service leaders. Henry raised the issue of supervision, which he had already introduced during a meeting of the Religious Committee (December 1990). The trustees requested some sort of supervision by the Religious Committee, but not the control to impose its authority over the new service activities and choice of texts. It was finally agreed by all present that the new service would perform "under the auspices of the Religious Committee."

The intriguing observation at the meeting was why Naomi didn't introduce the new project as part of a feminist agenda in the first place. She was known for her candor and strong convictions as much as for her knowledge of Judaism. She could be as eloquent and forceful as any among the trustees and could also rely on the strong support of the female trustees. Similarly, why didn't the trustees suggest that title for a service obviously feminist in its orientation?

It seems that at the time both parties preferred to avoid a public indication of a split or of conflicting interests between clearly defined constituencies. It was only when another new monthly service catering to a well-defined audience was constituted, the early (or traditional) minyan (Orthodox in style and composed mainly of men) that the door was also opened for the feminist service to be publicly identified as such. Now the synagogue was conceived as being able to

▼

accommodate the special needs of its various constituencies without the danger of exposing separatist tendencies that threatened its integrity. Naomi's strategy in presenting the new service could suggest no less the basic weakness of the lesbian members of the congregation at CBST. Nevertheless, the de facto establishment of a viable feminist service indicated the gradual erosion of male hegemony in the synagogue.

Ruth, who served as board chair in the early 1980s, survived only one year in the role. When I first met her in 1990 she claimed that the women have usually been pushed aside by the men, who welcomed them only as a sort of ornament. True, she added, the women didn't know the rules of the game and they haven't always cooperated among themselves—"they stabbed each other in the back." But at the 1993 brunch Ruth considered the situation to have changed, with three women on the board (she was alone among the trustees).

My description of the lesbian constituency might leave the notion of little cooperation between women in spite of their apparent shared interests. But whatever the "true" picture of that social reality, which might have probably been differently constructed by a female observer, there is no doubt that the feminist service offered a new arena for women's mutual support. That new field of interaction and joint agenda was due to influence the growing visibility and participation of women at CBST far beyond the borders of time, space, and activity of the feminist service.

Observing the success of the feminist service, the appointment of Rabbi Sharon Kleinbaum, and the election of Sheila a few months later (April 1993) as board chair, I felt a new era had opened for women at CBST. The 1993–94 new board was composed of five men and five women. Moreover, on my last visits to CBST in July 1993 and February 1994, I observed a significant increase in the attendance of women. Compared with the observations on my first visits of five years earlier, the gender representation appeared extremely different.[1]

182

▼

CHAPTER TEN

The Social Component at CBST: Couples, Gentiles, Cruising, and Talking Sex

The mere term *gay synagogue* seems to raise a list of contradictions of which a most unsettling one might be: spirituality and cruising. How does a gay synagogue compare with other gay institutions that offer an opportunity for blatant or more latent cruising, such as the gay bar, the gay sauna, and other gay circles whose agenda is more or less conspicuously sexual? That contradiction was succinctly expressed by Mark—whom I first met in the company of mutual heterosexual friends in New York—who had eloquently written the following narrative. Mark was too perceptive about his life to let his story be told and framed by anyone else.

> I was twenty-six before I first touched anyone. And that was in the Park-Miller all-male porn theater. But I had a life of friends from high school, college, and the army. I began to "fool around" and meet other people, which was fun, but I wasn't motivated to form any lasting friendships. In part this was because I felt this new life was a threat to the one I already had. But I also had the feeling that the people I was meeting were not like those I had become friends with earlier on the strength of shared interests and background, irrespective of physical attraction. I don't know how I became aware of the gay synagogue, but I thought this might be a place to meet the kinds of people I wasn't seeing in my rounds in the Village.

I remember arriving alone—somewhat anxious as I would be in any new situation—and being instantly relieved. It seemed so familiar. There was an older man, looking very Jewish, at a table greeting people as they arrived. He reminded me, generically, of Hymie Goldstein, a kind of lay elder of the temple I grew up in, who would hand you a prayer book, find you a seat, and on week nights make sure there were enough for a minyan.

But if it was so reassuringly Jewish and familiar, that presented a problem for me. How could I approach this familiar place with my trashy intent? I associate going to temple with showering, putting on a suit and tie, and joining my parents and their friends in a place which if not quite holy—I wouldn't get carried away—has a purity about it and a sense of elevation.

After the service there was a kiddush, and I remember there was one very attractive fellow. But if he was attractive to me, I'm sure he was attractive to everyone. What was I going to do, go up to him and start a conversation because he was attractive? The whole thing seemed so sleazy, so obvious, and so inappropriate. Maybe I didn't know what the question was, but this wasn't the answer. I didn't go back.

Mark's scruples—or hang-ups, depending on one's point of view—were obviously not shared by everyone at CBST, nor was his separation of the religious from the social/sexual. He himself recently reported overhearing two men—at least one apparently a CBST member—dressed only in towels discuss the "Holocaust Torah" at the Wall Street Sauna, one of Manhattan's two remaining gay bathhouses. And in chapter 4 we have already seen a category of members whose attraction to CBST was essentially social.

But the field of sociosexual behavior at CBST was more complicated than a "cruising versus spirituality" contradiction might suggest. It was actually Mark's surprise at the synagogue's official policy concerning commitment ceremonies that made me start the following discussion with the position of couples at CBST.

Couples: an Invisible Majority

I did not conduct a survey of the congregation and cannot claim my data are "representative," however, during my observation of CBST I met at least seventy-five congregants at services and other synagogue activities about whom I have demographic data. Nearly 60 percent of them were engaged in committed relationships. Of those involved, nearly 40 percent met their mates in the synagogue. By way of comparison I attended a regular monthly meeting of the Gay Fathers Forum at the Lesbian and Gay Community Services Center. After dinner the attendees were arbitrarily split into two groups for a discussion about how to find Mr. Right. In my group of thirty there was only one couple who had met at these gatherings and had been together a while. The chairman of the organization, commenting on this dismal finding, argued that Hollywood movies had brainwashed people into looking for perfection.

Congregants were eager to tell their own stories of long-term relationships begun at CBST. So much so that in the short descriptions of themselves two candidates for the board gave during the 1989 election, they emphasized that they had met their lovers in the synagogue. Ron—among my first acquaintances at CBST—told me how he met Jack nine years before. He was visiting New York during the Jewish holiday of Shavuot and, as a member of the gay synagogue in Los Angeles, it was only natural for him to attend services at CBST. Ron was very impressed with the service leader who was highly skilled in Torah cantillation and who honored the guest with an aliyah during the Torah reading, the crowd being small as usual at the morning service. Afterward Ron thanked him and expressed admiration for his performance. Jack, the service leader, offered Ron a lift to the place he was staying in New York and phoned him the next day. They made a few short trips to visit each other, often talking on the phone. One year later Ron moved to New York, and since then they have lived together and have both been very active in CBST.

Many if not most of those who met their mates at the synagogue had done so early in their involvement with CBST: some, like Ron, on their first visit, others, a few weeks later. In chapter 4 I wrote about Harry who, having broken up with his Gentile lover, came to the synagogue in search of a Jewish mate. At his first Friday night service he met Edward, the man with whom he shared his life for fourteen years. In the same context I related the story of Joseph who, until he joined the synagogue at twenty-nine, had experienced only a few brief, unsatisfactory sexual encounters. Shortly after joining one of CBST's committees he met a synagogue member and embarked on his first serious affair, which lasted for three months. Soon after he met another member with whom he lived for nearly ten years.

▼

Couples sat together in the synagogue, female couples more noticeably expressing their affection in gentle body gestures. CBST provided a safe social environment for couples. When I first met Jeff at a Rosh Hashanah party, he immediately introduced me to his lover, whom he had met in the synagogue two years earlier but who was less involved in synagogue affairs. Later that same evening Jeff described his first meeting with one of our hosts. He had come to the synagogue three years before and was sitting alone in the back row with our host seated in front of him. When the service leader announced the concluding Shalom Aleichem, they stood, turned to each other, and joined hands for the communal singing. Later, during the social hour, they carried on a lively conversation. Jeff was pleased to have met such an educated, good-looking, friendly man—one who seemed the perfect mate. His excitement was short-lived, however, when his new friend introduced him to his lover. "I felt as if somebody had pulled the carpet out from under my feet." But in spite of his evident infatuation with his new friend, Jeff retreated once he discovered he had a mate. They were able to remain friends, and Jeff was often invited to the couple's home. I do not think that was atypical, for despite the closeness with which couples were watched, I heard almost no stories of infidelity or abuse of trust occurring within the synagogue society.

The most famous story of "mate swapping" at CBST was as much an indication of the ethos of stability. Jill and Susan, who had been together eighteen years, suddenly separated, and the two women were soon involved with new partners they each had met in the synagogue. None of the gossip about their split and new unions implied any infidelity preceding their separation. The four women all remained active congregants, and each of the new couples—Jill and Alice, Susan and Naomi—has subsequently celebrated its union.

The deep affection I witnessed between couples, both male and female, who had been together for many years often impressed me, as did the protective attitude they took toward their mates. In chapter 5 I recounted Jack's angry defense of his lover Ron when Dov publicly stopped the latter's Torah chanting to correct a mistake in pronunciation. Never had I seen Jack, who was usually restrained and civil, even under the heavy pressure as chair of the Religious Committee, so angry. He screamed at Dov, who he thought abused his role as gabbai, as he comforted Ron, whose chanting had been thrown off by the interruption. I knew Dov, Jack, and Ron very well. They were all gentle and caring people. But Dov was a purist in ritual matters—as much as Jack was a master of Jewish liturgy and ritual—and reacted in this case exactly as he would have done with anyone else. I doubt that Jack would have lost his temper had another congregant been involved. But he reacted spontaneously in defense of Ron, his lover, who had gone through an intensive process of Jewish training and whose proud moment before the congregation this reading represented.

On a later occasion when I spoke to Dov of my admiration for the devotion I witnessed between couples at CBST he explained: "Heterosexuals take their relationships for granted; they enjoy the support of society. Homosexuals have no source of external support and they rely completely on each other." Dov went on to observe that not only did gay couples lack the support of straight society, they often found themselves undermined within their own. He recalled that when he and Jack had cooled off after the unfortunate incident of his criticism of Ron's Torah reading, Jack told him of the interest the incident had generated and the great number of phone calls he received. Dov interpreted this as "unhealthy gossip," complaining, "You wouldn't believe it, but there was a tendency in the synagogue to exacerbate conflicts among couples. Gossiping contributes much to the escalation of a rift between lovers and friends. Therefore, gay couples must continuously cultivate their relationship."

Whether Dov's interpretation of this "interest" was accurate or not, the relationship between partners was frequently a subject of conversation, either in admiring or doubtful tones. The same couple would sometimes be introduced as a model relationship, while other observers would raise serious doubts about their viability as partners. Someone might insinuate that he saw one partner engaged in anonymous sex. When Ron was unemployed and showing signs of stress, a few congregants commented on the difficulties he and Jack must be having. But when Jack and Ron celebrated their tenth anniversary, Isaac, who attended their party, told me: "They have problems, but they are a couple for life." Isaac thought of himself as a victim of a homophobia that had made him marry against his strong sexual preference and now left him, in his late forties, in the process of divorce after twenty years of a sad marriage. He looked at Jack and Ron in admiration. They were the first gay couple he had met and were supportive of his late "coming out." They were also a source of hope that

▼

gay life might still offer happy companionship instead of the loneliness and stigma he so feared in his youth.

Despite gossip and perhaps occasional cattiness, CBST's couples were spoken of with pride. They reflected on CBST as a society where one can come and find fulfillment. But in other respects, particularly in a strictly institutional sense, both the presence and the role of couples at CBST was more ambiguous, if not ambivalently viewed. I have already pinpointed the central role of the family in American synagogues. At CBST, however, couples did not occupy an analogous position. Though it contained them, in its daily life CBST was not an institution of couples. Except for the occasional invitation of couples to the bimah for a joint aliyah or to make the blessing over the Sabbath candles, members performed—and often presented themselves—as individuals, not social units. So much so, that in several instances I witnessed congregants were surprised to discover that an old acquaintance had a long-standing partner they had not known about—typically one who didn't attend services. In addition, a common view ascribed what was seen as the increased number of couples to the fear of AIDS, though many partnerships dated back before its advent. More trivially perhaps, considering the sums involved, a call to the CBST office inquiring about membership fees elicited the response: "An individual membership is $125, a couple is $250."

When I first told Simon of the number of couples I noticed in the synagogue, he insisted there were not that many and argued that only among the leading members was it typical to be "married"—a term he used but warned me about using. He was not alone in ignoring the strong presence of couples at CBST. We immediately checked the conjugal situation of the ten members of the board and discovered that five were in long-term relationships—many over five years—and one had recently lost his mate. A few months later Simon discovered that another was, in fact, in a relationship of many years. The percentage of "married" board members mirrored my wider sample. A few other leading congregants were also engaged in long-term relationships: Jack, chair of the Religious Committee, had been together with Ron for ten years, Guy, chair of the Education Committee, with Sean for nearly eighteen years. But not all CBST leaders were. Leon and Larry, both former board chairs, Joel, former chair of the Religious Committee, and Simon himself were not in long-term relationships.

Assuming that my data reflect the broader membership of CBST, an intriguing question arises: why was the frequency of couples less evident in the public consciousness than it was in fact? Is there some incongruity between individuals' desires, the folk model, and the normative ideology prevalent at CBST? The area of mate selection, bonding, and sexuality have long been codified and ritualized in heterosexual contexts—whether it is the "church social" or the "singles club"—with the behavioral norms and expectations clearly charted. The social-sexual territory in a gay synagogue is a less well mapped— perhaps the least well mapped—terra incognita, both in terms of specific ritual and the attitude toward it. Several models exist for defining its contours, but none seemed immediately applicable.

Ceremonies of Commitment: "It's a Problematic Issue"

The paradox surrounding the visibility and public confirmation of gay and lesbian couples was most evident in the continuing discourse on the status of their most symbolic expression: the commitment ceremony.

In 1988, when Naomi and Susan wished to have a commitment ceremony at CBST, they were surprised by the reaction. They were told the synagogue did not have a tradition of celebrating such unions and, on the technical side, wasn't insured for events sponsored by individuals. It was suggested they hold it in the synagogue of the rabbi who agreed to perform the ceremony. Two years later Naomi, in recounting the story, had still not forgiven the synagogue for the lack of support she and her lover encountered: "We wanted to have it at CBST because this is our synagogue!" she exclaimed. Faced with Naomi and Susan's persistence, the leadership eventually agreed, and the ceremony was performed at CBST with a ritual the couple and their rabbi devised.

As Naomi and Susan discovered, rather than fully embrace a visible and symbolic confirmation of gay and lesbian couples, the synagogue had not adopted an official policy on the issue, a position that was tantamount to a refusal to condone the ceremony. A review of its history at CBST reflects the synagogue's ambivalence toward it.

Aaron held a commitment ceremony for himself and his lover in CBST's founding year of 1973, which was the synagogue's first. In the program for the ceremony prepared by Aaron and his close friends, they acknowledged an awareness of the delicate ground they were treading. Its introduction declares:

189

▼

In performing this "ceremony of loving dedication" we *do not* seek to duplicate, approximate, or imitate the marriage ceremony as performed at the wedding of a man and a woman. The traditional Jewish understanding of marriage as a social and legal institution is based on considerations quite different from what applies to the needs and wishes of Gay people. . . . It is as a joyous recognition of what already exists between two individuals, as an established fact, not as a ceremony intended to create or legitimize it. Precisely because we do cherish our [Jewish] tradition, and see ourselves part of it, the celebration draws freely upon the traditional formulations, but does so with appropriate innovation and change. . . . What has been selected are those blessings which praise God for the creation of humanity and offer thanks for the joyous love we have been enabled to share with one another. We speak not of "bride" and "groom" who "take" each other in marriage, but of loving individuals who have been moved to express their mutual commitment.

The text of the ceremony itself, in Hebrew and English, bore little resemblance to the traditional wedding liturgy. A large section included excerpts from the biblical stories of David and Jonathan and Ruth and Naomi, each referred to as "a model love after which we might pattern our love." The traditional Sheva Brakhot, marriage benedictions, were adapted to gay and lesbian couples called *benei ahavah* (sons of love) and *benot ahavah* (daughters of love). The ceremony included the traditional kiddush over wine and the breaking of a glass, but there was no mention of exchanging rings or a ketubah (marriage contract) between the lovers. In keeping with its introductory remarks the ceremony Aaron celebrated with his Gentile lover was not simply a transposition of the traditional marriage ritual but a creative invention characteristic of his style as "rabbi." It manifested an almost Hasidic enthusiasm, involving the congregation in a display of joy and sentiment that might be described in terms of Turner's communitas.

Despite Aaron's example there was never any official encouragement for further commitment ceremonies. It was not presented as a model in CBST's drashot, speeches, or newsletters, and, with the exception of one other early ceremony between male Jewish and Gentile lovers, not repeated until Naomi and Susan's request. Aaron himself separated from his lover about the time he left CBST, and more.

than once I heard it said that a commitment ceremony was no insurance against the breakup of a relationship. On the contrary, it was claimed that the few couples known to have celebrated such a ceremony hadn't lasted together long after. CBST couples did, however, often celebrate the anniversaries of their life together and invite the congregation to join them in a kiddush after the Friday night service.

When I arrived at CBST early in 1989 the issue was far from resolved. Naomi and Susan had celebrated their commitment ceremony at the synagogue the prior March, a privilege begrudgingly granted fifteen years after that of Aaron and his lover. According to witnesses as well as published reports,[1] their *brit ahavah* (covenant of love), which was conducted by the associate rabbi of the Stephen Wise Free Synagogue (Reform), was far more formalized than Aaron's. The lovers stood elegantly dressed under a chuppah (wedding canopy) they had made themselves from pieces of cloth and embroidery contributed by their relatives and close friends. The ceremony included most of the traditional wedding ritual adapted to their shared gender: the kiddush over wine, an exchange of rings, a reading of the ketubah, and the breaking of a glass. Joel viewed the elaborate ceremony, which was open to the entire congregation, with a jaundiced eye: "The synagogue was flooded with trees and flowers. What a sight. Who could compete with that?"

Just after my arrival Nora and Liz, a member of the Religious Committee, celebrated their union outside the synagogue. The ritual, which they described as a *brit neshama* (soul covenant), was conducted at home on a Sunday morning in the company of a select group of family and close friends, an arrangement some congregants criticized for its "secrecy." But a group of 120 guests were invited to a festive dinner the same evening, where the wedding blessings, the Sheva Brakhot, adapted to their gender, were repeated and the guests offered the couple gifts of bread and salt, water and oil, rocks and minerals, each symbolizing various aspects of happiness and prosperity. Nora and Liz had actually moved into a new apartment together two years before and had given a party on that occasion.

Shortly after Nora and Liz's commitment, which followed that of Naomi and Susan, I asked two CBST members why it was that only women were celebrating their unions. Sarah answered that women have been educated to expect marriage and they wanted to be brides. Not so men. Simon rejected this interpretation, pointing to the earli-

191

▼

est CBST commitment ceremonies, both of which involved male couples, and concluded that it was the personal attraction to ritual that
made people fond of these celebrations. In this context he mentioned
Naomi and Susan's elaborate ceremony. Sarah responded that Jack
and his lover Ron were deeply involved in ritual and liturgy, but had-
n't contemplated a ceremony to mark their ten years of shared life.
The issue remained unresolved at that point.

An old-time member of CBST commented when the subject of Liz
and Nora's commitment came up: "These are silly ceremonies. Why
should we imitate the habits of a society when we don't live according to its rules?" He said he hadn't attended Aaron's ceremony because
he couldn't stand the extravagance but had attended the second one
out of curiosity. And added, in a note of triumph, that both couples
had separated a few years later. In contrast, he pointed to the first editor of the *Synagogue News* and his lover, who have maintained a "wonderful Jewish home" together since the early days of CBST but never
entertained a desire to perform a commitment ceremony.

Morris and Leon expressed a similar attitude a week later. Both
confessed they couldn't understand the merit of the ceremony, and
claimed that those who went through it ultimately separated. They
argued that a good voluntary relationship is often doomed when it is
transformed by the exchange of vows into a compulsory one. Morris
and his lover had been together for many years and never desired a
public ceremony. When Martin mentioned that his lover Job wanted
one, his colleagues responded unenthusiastically. About a year later I
heard Norman, past board chair and himself in a ten-year relationship, explain CBST's traditional resistance to commitment ceremonies
from an institutional standpoint. How could you decide when a couple was eligible for a ceremony that implied the synagogue's endorsement? How could you avoid sanctioning relationships that turned out
to be short-term, especially in the pre-AIDS era "when guys went to
bed first and then examined the prospects for seeing each other
again?" How long should the couple have been together? Would they
have to prove their partnership by means such as a joint bank
account? Would they be expected to follow the rules of "a Jewish
home?"[2] How long should they have been members of CBST? What
were the terms for "divorce?" Until the synagogue could resolve these
issues he didn't see how they could sanction commitment ceremonies. Finally, he claimed that there really hadn't been any demand

for the ceremony among CBST's many couples, and pointed to his lover and himself who had been together for ten years without contemplating one.

Mark, whose nominal membership at CBST didn't reflect an enthu- siasm with its style, perceived Norman's explanation as projecting an acceptance on part of the synagogue's leadership of the stigma of gay society. They themselves, he concluded, have apparently considered the relationships between gays as "frivolous," which is a cornerstone in the low evaluation of gays in mainstream society. A similar conclusion was expressed by Naomi, who defined the synagogue's reluctance to endorse the ceremony as a sign of "internalized homophobia." She thought it reflected the feelings of discomfort with habits and beliefs implanted by society. That is, ceremonies of commitment are associated among gay congregants with weddings appropriate only for heterosexuals.

The pragmatic difficulties that Norman characteristically pointed out presented themselves in a Religious Committee meeting I attended at about this time. Jack introduced the request of a male couple, new to CBST, to have a commitment ceremony at CBST. He reminded his colleagues that they had discussed the need to establish a policy governing these events but had only come up with a "vanilla decision" stating that the synagogue would have the authority to supervise these ceremonies. Specifically, they hadn't decided what to do if one partner were not Jewish, which was the case in hand. Complicating the matter, the couple had asked that both a rabbi and priest be permitted to officiate, and that the ceremony be held on a Sabbath afternoon.

Larry responded that he didn't mind the priest, but he objected to the ceremony on the Sabbath (which contravenes Jewish custom). Jack warned that if they didn't come up with a clear policy soon, they would cede their authority to the future rabbi; in which case, Sheila observed, the committee would be nothing but a "laughingstock." No one responded when a CBST old-timer attending the meeting brought up the precedent of "the wedding ceremony our rabbi [Aaron] had with his non-Jewish lover." Finally it was decided to appoint a subcommittee to prepare "an informal policy manual." (No policy, however, was implemented before the new rabbi's installation, and the couple making the request did not press the matter.)

About this time Martin, who was now in his term as board chair and involved in hiring a rabbi, was interviewed on the issue of commit-

▼

ment ceremonies for two articles in the December 21, 1990, issue of the *Jewish Week*. He told one reporter that the synagogue did not have a clear policy regarding these ceremonies: "At the moment, if people come to us and want to use our sanctuary for a commitment ceremony, we let them. We will not sanction it, endorse it or condemn it" (28). In another article Martin went on to explain his personal view:

> It has to do with people becoming people and legitimizing their relationship to the outside and themselves. It's not a "wedding." That is a word reserved for a man and a woman. But people who have had a commitment ceremony do consider themselves married. (37)

Even milder was the statement made by Simon, who also supported these ceremonies. He claimed it was intended to allow a public expression of feelings and the notion of "here I am—here we are." He compared the raison d'être of that event with the ceremony that celebrates one's moving into a new apartment. The occasion of celebrating a union of lovers, he argued, is a sort of an inauguration ceremony of a new connection. The vocabulary he used was thus far less associated with heterosexual family terminology.

One year later the issue of commitment ceremonies, which had periodically arisen, ebbed, and flowed throughout the life of the synagogue, was given an effective resolution—albeit a de facto one; two highly visible commitment ceremonies involving leading members of CBST were celebrated one week apart: the first, between Martin, still board chair, and his lover, Job, a rabbi; the second, between Alice, also a rabbi, and Jill—both prominent in religious affairs at CBST.

I attended the Sabbath morning service honoring Alice and Jill's impending commitment ceremony. In sharp contrast to the regular Sabbath services, a much larger crowd was present, prompting Martin to comment loudly that it would be worthwhile having many commitment ceremonies if only for the sake of better attendance at services. Jill herself led the service along with Gershon, a popular cantor. In a moving ritual moment both Alice and Jill opened the ark and removed the Torah scroll together. At the conclusion of the Torah reading the congregants joyously danced around the couple and showered them with sweets.

During the kiddush reception that followed I spoke to a number of congregants about the impact of the two commitment celebrations.

Many were still deeply moved by the events attending Martin and Job's ceremony the week before, which I was not in New York in time to witness. They pointed, in particular, to the drashah Job delivered during the Sabbath morning service that he led. In the presence of 195 both sets of parents and other relatives, Job expressed his gratitude to CBST and to Martin who had enabled him to retrieve his self-esteem and discover he could be loved. Both Job and his listeners were brought to tears, both by the sentiment and the knowledge that Martin was terminally ill with AIDS. The commitment ceremony itself, which was celebrated by six ordained rabbis, was seen as an emphatic declaration of the bond between Job and Martin against all odds.

Joel, who called the events "weddings," felt that the usually "closeted" Alice, in particular, had been liberated by the celebration in discovering that she could publicly express her right to love whomever she chose. Others saw the same lesson for their own lives. A congregant with a ten-year involvement told me, "It's a problematic issue": many would have wished to have a commitment ceremony because of its personal meaning for their joint relationship, but refrained because they perceived it as a surrender to the tradition of the heterosexual majority. No doubt, he commented, recent events have stimulated many discussions of the issue, although he was skeptical about the outcome. Gershon, however, declared that he planned to have a ceremony next year to celebrate his own ten-year partnership.

The history of commitment ceremonies at CBST presented above suggests several explanations for the synagogue's reluctance to endorse the union of couples. "Why should we imitate the habits of [straight] society?" was a frequent theme, one drawn from the rhetoric of gay politics.[3] But the relationship of the "copy" to the "original" was not a simple one, and often included a good deal of self-conscious irony. Long before their commitment ceremony, Martin and Job frequently defined their relationship in the language of heterosexual conjugality. Martin recalled a trip he and Job had taken together with straight couples. When Job was asked about his matrimonial situation he replied, "I am married to a husband." On another occasion, a public meeting at CBST, Martin buttressed his argument about the heavy load awaiting the new rabbi with the observation: "As the wife of a rabbi, I can testify it's a twenty-four hour job." With a wide smile, he pointed to his lover, who was in fact an ordained rabbi, and exclaimed: "My husband is sitting here!" Since Martin was a tall, pow-

▼

erfully built man, the metaphor of his role as "wife" bore a certain
intentional humor.

Gershon and his lover, Max, similarly used the language of heterosexual marriage. Max referred to Gershon's parents as "my parents-
in–law" and called Gershon's mother, with whom he was extremely
friendly, "Mom." His straight brother introduced himself to a lesbian
congregant as "Gershon's brother–in–law." One evening, as a group of
volunteers was sitting around a table at CBST mailing out the newsletter, Max asked another member how his "father-in-law" was.[4] He later
spoke of having threatened Gershon with "divorce" if he went ahead
with his plan to run for the board. Max described his wish to have a
commitment ceremony on their tenth anniversary: "I've always
wanted a grand wedding, but we'll do it with a small crowd." When
an older couple seated nearby learned that he and Gershon had only
been together eight years, they described them as "newlyweds."

The transposition of heterosexual terminology, which no doubt
underlaid sincere feeling, contained an element of camp humor, and
its use was situationally determined. When I introduced Job to a
friend of mine, he referred to his lover Martin as "my life companion"
rather than "my husband" as he would typically in a more intimate
circle. But not only was there sensitivity to its provocation to outsiders, there was concern that an outsider's misuse of it might offend
members of the in-group. I mentioned earlier Simon's warning me not
to use the term "married." I assume he thought I was insufficiently
attuned to the appropriate use of this argot, its nuance, its relevant
contexts, and its tone. In addition, as an "outsider" I had not yet
gained the privilege of a joking relationship between close friends.

An awareness of the potential confrontation of homosexual partnership went beyond its linguistic representation. In an informal
conversation Martin commented on the unrestrained way in which
Job publicly displayed his affection for him and, in that same context, referred to Paul as someone who made a point of dancing with
his lover at office parties. Paul agreed, observing that change would
only come if gays were willing to do "the uncomfortable." He recalled
the reaction that twenty years ago would have greeted the sight of a
black man dancing with a white woman and declared: "If we start
doing it now, people won't notice it at all twenty years from now"—
a projection he amended to fifty years in response to Martin's look of
skepticism.

In the introduction to Aaron's commitment ceremony quoted above, an acute awareness of the potential confrontation is evidenced and great pains are taken to distinguish it from the heterosexual marriage model. Aaron's ceremony was intimate, inventive, and Jewish in its world of images. It was a social claim expressed and witnessed by an audience of gay and lesbian friends. It was a ritual for the congregation, fully created and performed by its membership. Aaron's family, for example, was completely unaware of that development. If, despite the disclaimer, it was inevitably viewed in the context of a "straight" marriage ritual—"the wedding of our rabbi"—then it suggested a camp presentation in closeted gay society.

The commitment rituals beginning with those of Naomi and Susan, fifteen years later, were no less creative but far more patterned on Jewish customs and tradition. More important, these events were publicly staged and witnessed by a large mixed audience of homosexuals and heterosexuals, with close family members attending as guests of honor. But imitating the major patterns of traditional weddings did not detract from the provocation and challenge to mainstream social norms and images. One could argue these too, however refined, were expressions of camp and kitsch (Travers 1993). The major participants created an aura of sincerity that might be described in Travers's words (129) as "beyond the possibility of criticism by tightening the screw of 'here and now' to such a pitch that there can be no current self other than the self locked into its mockery." But this was camp that prompted tears and wonder rather than Travers's laughter. These grand ceremonies, in adhering more closely to traditional ritual, replayed the dominant culture's major drama of gender, social bond, and reproduction, with each element significantly altered, if not overturned, and included a new audience whose major symbols were affronted.

Given how complexly freighted "marriage" is in gay society, with multiple readings running from acquiescence to the dominant culture, to parody, and ultimately to confrontation, it is perhaps not surprising that CBST, an institution impelled to confine the scope of confrontation with mainstream society, should have responded ambivalently to the celebration of commitment ceremonies on its premises.

Gentiles: Lovers and Congregants

The synagogue society contained a small but noticeable component of Gentile members. To the surprise of some observers, these

▼

were mostly lovers of active members, including a few who have gradually inclined toward greater traditionalism. I identified ten male Jewish–Gentile couples who have been engaged in a long partnership of more than five years. I met five men who had separated from their Gentile lovers, mostly after a long partnership, and two who were still mourning their deceased Gentile lovers. I identified two female couples and one woman who had separated from her Gentile lover of many years.

One congregant of four years membership finalized conversion during my stay. His conversion was not initiated by an intimate relationship with a Jewish partner; on the contrary, his lover was a Gentile. Three women also converted, but only two had Jewish lovers. In fact, most Gentile lovers, including those who attended services frequently, had not considered conversion.

The synagogue's association with non–Jews already started with Aaron and his Gentile lover. Aaron admitted his return to Judaism and his efforts to found a gay Jewish community were encouraged by his lover, whom he met in a gay church. As I learned sometime later, the first couple I met on my arrival at CBST, Guy and Sean, represented a Jewish–Gentile partnership. As Guy told me at our first meeting, he never thought religion would be part of their shared life. He was always attracted to Jewishness, but they were too busy pursuing their careers and building their home. They had been together for more than fifteen years when on a Purim evening he suddenly felt an urge to get closer to Jewish life. CBST was the best solution. Sean, of Irish Catholic extraction, supported Guy's desire, and the two always attended services together. Guy was soon actively involved in committees and Sean was a great help. Sean attended a basic course in Hebrew, which enabled him to feel somewhat more comfortable during services. He was humorous about his dedication to services at CBST. He often repeated his decision to make a lent in the Catholic tradition: to give up church . . .

On Yom Kippur I was sitting near Guy and Sean and another Jewish–Gentile couple, Ted and Roy. Both Sean and Roy arrived for the Ne'ilah afternoon prayers and joined their lovers who had attended the service since morning. Roy, however, who also made efforts to learn Hebrew, told me he enjoyed spiritual activities and also regularly attended an Episcopalian congregation. The Gentiles who attended services seemed to follow the prayers, which were partly in

English; most other texts in Hebrew were also introduced in the siddur by transliteration (not a few Jewish congregants were unable to read Hebrew).

A few members in the Talmud class had Gentile lovers. Ralph, for example, couldn't attend synagogue on Fridays and Saturdays because his lover, who otherwise was very tolerant of Ralph's return to Judaism, preferred to spend the weekends in their country home. Ralph couldn't keep kosher either because his lover had special culinary skills. Ralph told me he had never had a relationship with a Jew. In his own words, he shared a cultural background with his lover as "children of the suburbs." They grew up in a mixed Jewish–Italian neighborhood. He described his lover as "the boy from the next-door neighbor's home."

Edward recruited his lover Matthew to attend the Talmud meetings. Matthew was actually able to follow the Hebrew text. Another dedicated Talmud class member had been together for many years with a Gentile. His growing commitment to Judaism didn't seem to disturb his situation at home. But Aaron, whose own growing traditionalism had resulted in separation from his Gentile lover, had some doubts about the future of these couples. He told me the story of another close friend who was together with a Gentile lover for ten years and who also performed a commitment ceremony; they separated when they couldn't accommodate the Jewish partner's growing religiosity. The latter also found a Jewish mate who suited his new spiritual needs.

Aaron explained the attraction of religious Jews to Gentiles as an example of that between opposites. The attraction of opposites was a common explanation for the frequent choice of Gentiles as partners of active participants. Another explanation related to the difficult character of Jews. Gilbert, a popular cantor who had much influence on the synagogue's liturgy and who for fifteen years had an Italian lover, claimed he was never attracted to Jews. To make his point, after being provoked by Simon who expressed his amazement at the attraction of leaders and traditionalists to Gentile lovers, he responded jokingly: "I love Simon's *neshoma* (soul), but his *shtikle* (piece–penis)—brrrr!!! (with an amused expression of disgust on his face)." However, Gilbert also made a more serious comment suggesting that the love of Gentiles balanced the strong dedication to another attraction, that of Judaism. He thus implied an ambivalence that educated congregants might feel toward their own growing traditionalism.

But having a Gentile lover was not necessarily an obstacle for the Orthodox. Sasha, a successful professional who enjoyed the respect and affection of many congregants, affiliated with CBST only after he met his Gentile lover, Robin. He couldn't attend services before he met his Gentile companion because he didn't drive on the Sabbath. It was only now that Robin did the driving that he could attend services. I was told that the loving partner also used to open the car door for Sasha and save him from the slightest infringement of Sabbath rules. Robin (himself a professional) attended services with him for four years, until they moved away and visited the synagogue only on holidays. He also became an expert in kashrut. Sasha claimed that Robin was more knowledgeable about kashrut than many other congregants. He was so careful to accommodate Sasha's religion that his own relatives had learned not to use their kitchen before asking him for specific directions. Their story was part of the synagogue's folklore. When I was invited to share a meal with them at the end of the Yom Kippur fast, it was Robin who prepared the meal for the hungry Jewish crowd.

Although Gentiles were not called to bless the Torah, they were invited to perform in other prayers and rituals. For example, Guy and Sean were together invited to bless the Sabbath candles and read a prayer from the bimah.

Once during a Sabbath morning service just before the opening of the ark, Ron stopped the service as his eyes searched through the small congregation. A man seated next to me commented smilingly that Ron just discovered that he had lost the kosher minyan since a man and a woman had left and the remaining ten attendees included Ned, who has not yet completed the process of conversion. He added derisively: "Women are not a problem, but this bothers some people. For me Ned is kosher enough, I don't need a Voodoo ceremony!" Ron later told me during the lunch following the service that he and Jack were involved in Ned's conversion. Ned had actually completed most of the requirements, but the last problem was scheduling a date convenient to all concerned for his visit to the ritual bath, the final act of his conversion. During the same meal Jack suggested that the group of Sabbath morning service regulars would contribute for a Friday kiddush to honor and celebrate Ned's forthcoming conversion.

Ned told me he was always eager to convert. He was convinced he had Jewish ancestors although he was born in a very small town in

California. He joined the synagogue four years earlier, soon after his arrival in New York. A rabbi congregant affiliated with the Conservative movement supervised his conversion. Sometime later Ned also went through a late bar mitzvah ceremony. He was extremely happy with his change of status and flattered to be told he looked Jewish. His Gentile lover supported Ned's desire to convert and joined him sometimes for services. He was also tolerant of Ned's insistence that they maintain a kosher kitchen.

The synagogue's bylaws entitled anyone over eighteen to join the congregation. Non-Jews, mostly lovers and a few converts, were usually perceived in affectionate terms. I never encountered an unpleasant description of a Gentile congregant. On the contrary, they sometimes enjoyed a more flattering reputation than their Jewish lovers. They never aspired for a formal position and their contribution to the running of the synagogue was purely voluntary. Although a small constituency, I believe their presence carried a significant role. They formed a link with New York's wider gay scene. Without them CBST might have carried the image of an isolated ethnic enclave. Their association with leading members added weight to their presence. Moreover, their presence had a latent influence on the theological-ethnic discourse at CBST. It encouraged the promotion of universalistic and humanistic elements of Judaism in contrast to the ethnocentric bias displayed in particular in Orthodox synagogues.[5] Their presence was also sometimes mentioned as another reason against CBST's joining a mainstream Jewish denomination that might have affected the status of Gentile congregants.

The role of the Gentile lover had an ideological–liturgical support in the story of Ruth and Naomi. The teacher in a course on Jewish sources offered by the Education Committee reviewed the cases of homosexuality in the Bible and in later Jewish texts of scholarship and poetry. Himself a rabbi congregant, he suggested the love between Ruth and her mother-in-law Naomi was a clear case of lesbian love. Ruth was an ancestor of King David, whose love for Jonathan has become a key myth of gay love.

Cruising: Past and Present

As my data show, the synagogue played an important role in the field of mate selection. Nevertheless, that phenomenon was in sharp contrast to the frequent evaluation of the synagogue, by male congregants, as a poor cruising field and claims such as "I never went to the synagogue in order to find a lover." Jeff, for example, who made that statement, had twice been attracted to men who unfortunately were already engaged, but he also met a man at the synagogue with whom he stayed together for nearly two years. When I last encountered him in January 1993 he was dating a Gentile he had met in a bar. After two years with no luck except for brief meetings, mainly at anonymous sex scenes, he was very hopeful.

"This is not a great cruising place" was a phrase often reiterated to me by Leon and Jay (Leon was among the most active congregants and Jay a frequent visitor). They emphasized their own and other members' devotion to CBST in spite of their preferences for sexual partners who they could better find elsewhere. (Leon, for example, was known for his attraction to Asian men). This somewhat patronizing description of the synagogue's crowd, neutralizing its "hidden agenda," was probably the other side of the coin portrayed by Mark, with whom I opened this chapter. I should emphasize, however, that the data for this subject mainly relate to my observations among gay men.

To the extent that CBST was a cruising site, that activity was carried out in a very subtle fashion. I often found in my notes, particularly from the early period of my visits there, my comments to various congregants that the synagogue did not seem to me to represent a cruising scene. But they argued with me to the contrary. They suggested, for example, that certain seats were better positioned to allow a good view of the entrance doors to the sanctuary and therefore enabled an easy observation of latecomers to the service. But blatant cruising seemed inappropriate on the synagogue's premises. Those whose behavior seemed conspicuous in their continuing search for attractive newcomers and their unmasked interest in potential mates were considered in uncharitable terms.

Ron, among my first acquaintances, noticed a man who tried to befriend me in a crude manner, as he did many other newcomers. He was considered a vulgar cruiser, grudgingly tolerated by many congregants. As I have already mentioned in an earlier chapter, another man in his mid-fifties took upon himself the task of welcoming newcomers and actually served as a sort of security man, spending the evening at his desk in front of the entrance door. He was obviously admiring the young and attractive guests, whom he showered with affectionate attentions. His conspicuous behavior was generally ignored, although a few visitors had complained about his demeanor. He was good-natured and served the synagogue in his own special way. I thought he was tolerated in the same fashion as a few other eccentric congregants who displayed their love for the synagogue in special ways that compensated for their "freakish" habits.

203

I first introduced Bill's story in chapter 4, which I wrote soon after I left New York in February 1991, about two months since Bill had joined CBST. I described his self-denial in an unsatisfactory relationship with a Puerto Rican man. Already before I had left Bill had begun to participate in various synagogue activities. I met him once during a meeting of volunteers called by the newsletter distribution committee in order to mail out the monthly issue. As usual during those events the small company of five to eight volunteers (mostly men) were in good spirits, joking and gossiping about the participants and other congregants. They were exchanging information and sharing experiences they had had in other places, at other times, and during their visits to other countries.

On this jovial and somewhat erotically charged occasion Bill added a short handwritten note on the back of the envelope addressed to a man whom he had met during the last service and who had given him his phone number. I jokingly complained that he was misusing his responsibility and intruding upon the privacy of the membership. He laughed as he answered, "Why else should one volunteer?" When I returned to New York for a short visit in November 1991, Bill was happily settled in an apartment he began renting three months earlier together with a new partner. I soon learned he was the man with whom Bill had corresponded through the good services of the synagogue's mailing list.

Joel, whose administrative role in the synagogue and whose continuing involvement with various committees made him a keen observer of its membership, had often commented on the cruising habits of the synagogue constituency. He frequently mentioned in his drashot the phone calls from Orthodox men who inquired about a dating service or sexual activities in the synagogue. He beamed with satisfaction as he related his answers, for example, "One can never know what goes on in the men's room." I assume Joel would not have used that metaphor had CBST a reputation for its busy "tearoom." In a more cooperative mood, he responded to these anonymous callers:

▼

"We are not a dating organization. Come to the synagogue, and if you meet somebody it is none of our business what you do when you go home." I actually met one of these inquirers, who was advised to call on Ben, an Education Committee member who might inform him about some social activities available in New York for gay people. The man was at first disappointed when he discovered he was meeting with a consultant rather than a date, but since then had occasionally attended services at CBST. He told me the story in the presence of Ben who, in his humorous style, added an erotic flavor to the story, claiming that the narrator was "too passionate" for his taste.

One Friday evening Joel couldn't suppress his amusement at the behavior of a board member who seemed excited on meeting a newcomer during a recent service: "His eyes were out of their sockets, but he sent him to me to take care of his transport home!" On that occasion I asked Joel about an Orthodox-looking man we both had seen at the Talmud class whom I had never met before. He had no information to add, but asked me instead if I had noticed the hungry look the newcomer had constantly displayed. Joel, as much as he was engaged in the running of spiritual affairs, was, nevertheless, open and jocular about the power of sexual impulses and fantasies. I heard him shouting before departing from a friend after services: "Are you going home or are you going out fucking?" Joel expressed much skepticism toward the preaching of moral convictions that overlooked the natural needs of gay people. He opposed the suggestion raised during a public discussion about the hiring of a rabbi that the synagogue's rabbi should refrain from visiting gay bars: "If it is good for me it is also good for our rabbi," he explained. But he himself introduced the story of Morris who years ago stopped visiting a gay bar he had often patronized once he was elected chair of the synagogue's board. Morris assumed that in his new position he represented the congregation and thought it might damage the synagogue's reputation had he been exposed under embarrassing circumstances.

Memories of an earlier era were publicly aired during a memorial service held in honor of a deceased female congregant. Penny, among the few active veteran female members, was described by men and women with much love and respect. Never before or after had I attended a public event that commemorated an individual's sexuality openly and adoringly in a similar fashion. The assembled mourners shared their feelings of loss and expressed their nostalgia in a series of evocations. A woman guest, who met the deceased outside the synagogue, told how Penny had taught her to understand her own body. She encouraged her women friends to talk about sex: "I lusted and she lusted and we shared experiences." "It seems we are today more conservative than we used to be in the past," concluded the speaker.

Joel went on to tell how during a meeting of the Community Development Committee that was held in his apartment they somehow reached the topic of cruising in the synagogue. Penny lashed out at the men, obviously annoyed, "How dare you go cruising in the synagogue? This is a place for spirituality." She mocked the men's habits of those days, advertising their sexual preferences through the color of a handkerchief and the side of their trousers it showed from. Everybody in the hall was laughing as Joel continued to relate the details of that lost tradition. "I told Penny, I carry a handkerchief in order to dry up my wet nose, what have I to do with these tricks? Everybody knows I leave the synagogue alone!" Joel was sometimes pinpointed to me as a cruiser, although not a very successful one. No doubt he was as pitiless toward himself as toward his colleagues in his descriptions of their never ending search for a promising mate.

The sketched profiles of both Joel and Penny suggest the uneasy accommodation between the lifestyle endorsed by many congregants, who had grown up with the promise of sexual liberation, and the expectations they themselves have nourished about the ambience and norms of behavior that should separate the synagogue from other gay establishments.

I was often told that in the past there was more cruising in the synagogue, there were more congregational dances, and also that people used to be more provocative in their appearance, attired in tight jeans and shorts, etc. I have no way to confirm these notions, which must be part of a general realization that gay life has changed tremendously in recent years. My friends at CBST were reporting no less on the disappearance of many gay establishments and their own withdrawal from activities they enthusiastically embraced in the pre-AIDS days. At the same time, however, one must consider other changes that might have influenced the actual behavior as well as the memories and perceptions of individuals involved. Simon, for example, often reminisced about the more active sexual life he experienced in the synagogue during the first years: "I slept around" he told me, or cited a friend who claimed that Simon kept a "harem" in those days, when

▼

he must have been more attractive to younger men. That friend compared him to Edward, another prominent congregant who was particularly noticeable for his clique of close mates, with whom he shared an unusual domestic life. Since most members of that group have passed away in recent years, they have become a symbol for the vanishing lifestyle of the 1970s and early 1980s.

Jeff, who told me about his close relationship with another congregant, a victim of AIDS endeared to many for his talents and character, described the man's love habits—for a few years he had shared his life with two other congregants. He would reside three days a week with each, but on Saturdays he used to go to the baths. To my surprised reaction at the last part of his story Jeff answered immediately: "This was a time when it was considered an achievement of freedom." He himself used to go to these places, "It was like going out hunting. It gave you the pleasure of success, and you discovered that men were attracted to you." But after a few years he got tired of it; actually, he confessed, he always looked for a lasting relationship. For that, he thought, he had a better chance at CBST.

But Jeff's first experience at CBST was less pleasant. As he told me at a later stage of our acquaintance, he discovered the synagogue ten years earlier. On that occasion, as he left the sanctuary at the end of prayers and walked around to the community hall, he was soon approached by two men who courted him in a crude fashion. One grabbed his buttocks and the second touched his front parts. He was deeply offended. This was the sort of behavior he would have expected in a gay bar at that time and wouldn't have minded had he met those same men ten minutes later outside the synagogue; this was not what he expected on the synagogue grounds. When he came back a few years later, in 1988, he noticed a considerable change. Not only did the service seem more traditional, but nobody approached him. For a few weeks he stood by himself during the social hour and, as he imagined retrospectively, his appearance seemed to many somewhat threatening, "I looked like sort of a fucking bastard" (in tight jeans, muscular, sporting a mustache and a trendy hat).

But if cruising in the synagogue was much subdued and geared mainly toward mating for a lasting relationship, and although the cruising scene had greatly changed outside the synagogue's borders, nevertheless, CBST members sometimes shared experiences still resembling the old habits. They sometimes met with no prior planning at the surviving or the newly established places for cruising, entertainment, and sex. A few among my acquaintances visited, regularly or irregularly, the three gay saunas left in Manhattan and Queens; others attended the gay cinemas, the new establishments for instant sex,[6] and the many old and new bars, which, however, have mostly closed the back rooms and no longer allow sexual activity on their premises.

207

One day I met Jeff, who was in a depressed mood and worried about the future prospects of gay people: "We'll all soon get out of this world," he exclaimed. I responded in dark humor: "At least you'll meet in paradise with the pillars of the community." His face and mood changed quickly as he gleefully retorted that he was afraid not all among the synagogue's leaders would end up in paradise. He went on to tell me he had seen a past board chair as he was engaged in sexual activity in one of the surviving settings for anonymous sex.

Aaron, who remained with the Talmud circle, often related his vision for a different gay society he had already pictured during the old days of gay liberation. He was not excited with the Friday service mass attendance, followed by the small attendance on the Sabbath morning, "because Friday was a great cruising night." He preached against one-night stands, "the great achievement of gay liberation." However, these habits were not easy to give up completely, even by those who had abandoned that lifestyle long before the AIDS scare. When one among Aaron's disciples visited Israel he was tempted to watch the gay scene in the park that was considered to be the main cruising site in Jerusalem. As he told his friends of that experience, he jokingly reported that only a much older man had tried to seduce him. He allowed his desperate suitor to kiss his hands and arms as sort of a mitzvah.

Talking Sex

The synagogue's public presentation as a place for spirituality rather than cruising was particularly noticeable in the absence of decorations, posters, and pictures that might have indicated its hidden agenda. Only at a later point in my stay had I noticed the absence of a condom vending machine when it was mentioned as a sign of prudence on the part of the board. But I suppose its absence was not resented by the majority of congregants.

The expectation that CBST represent a "different institution" was succinctly expressed by Harry, the artist who designed the syna-

▼

gogue's logo, a star of David delicately composed of six Greek lambdas, which had become a major symbol of gay liberation. He told me he was under pressure to express the synagogue's identity more blatantly. It was suggested, for example, that he introduce one large lambda instead of the six that produced the star's lines in an unobtrusive style that could escape recognition by a stranger to gay culture. Actually, not a few among the congregants have never noticed the gay symbol laced into the synagogue's logo. The artist who, in his words, preferred a subtle symbolic presentation was not prudent in his sexual life; on the contrary, he was proud of the fruits of gay liberation and had fully exploited the opportunities and freedom offered to his generation during the 1970s in particular.

A group of male congregants accepted an invitation extended by Rabbi Marshall Meyer to attend a Saturday gathering at the B'nai Jeshurun synagogue on the Upper West Side. The event was dedicated to developing support activities among the victims of AIDS. Since we arrived somewhat early, we strolled for some time along Riverside Park, which was particularly attractive on a sunny spring afternoon. Somebody pointed to the underground tunnel we were walking above, part of a ventilation system for a defunct railroad line. We stopped and looked at one of the entrances to the tunnel below the walking path where two homeless men were taking a nap. I was told the place was a popular site for anonymous sex during the 1970s. One man in our group claimed he was too scared to go there during those days. But another admitted he did visit it on occasion when he looked for adventure.

Similar reactions were expressed as we sometimes walked before or after services along the bank of the Hudson River in front of the synagogue. After dark but also during daylight hours the river bank near Christopher Street, only a few blocks away from the synagogue, was still a busy cruising scene, but apparently not as popular and crowded as in earlier days. Watching from the pavement, we saw a young man standing on the bank side negotiating with a few drivers who had stopped near him. I commented how risky that activity must be for all involved. Simon confirmed my assumption, but added that risk was part and parcel of the experience. He recalled the days when he and many others in the community participated in those activities along the Hudson River and its out-of-use warehouses, which had become a haven for cruising. True, it involved risk, but also the notion of competition and achievement. He still remembered how fast his heart would beat at the mixed experience of fear, anxiety, and excitement. He used to call that activity "cleaning the system" because of the release of pressure he felt afterward. However, Simon was more cheerful about the lost habits of the 1970s when we met for dinner at Jean's apartment with a few new female congregants. The table linen of various colors instigated a merry discussion on the meaning of colored handkerchiefs among gay men in the pre-AIDS days, from "top" or "bottom" to the "golden shower," etc.

As we assembled in the B'nai Jeshurun community hall, Martin, acting as go-between, told the assembled audience the personal circumstances that led him to become a member of B'nai Jeshurun as well as of CBST. He described his first fascination with the music, particularly the impact of the organ, at B'nai Jeshurun, an innovation he had not previously experienced in a synagogue. As he mentioned the organ, somebody in the audience commented loudly, "a musical organ!" Martin smiled, but the CBST guests at my table reacted in embarrassment. It seemed they did not like the vulgarity, which was meant to express familiarity with the guests' culture, although the comment was made by Rabbi Marshall Meyer himself.

The border between sexual humor and awkward vulgarity was not defined by the content of the discourse and comments, nor by the status of the speaker, but by the forum of its expression. As much as blatant cruising was considered improper on the synagogue's premises, so too was sexual language in a public forum. When the Religious Committee was discussing the purchase of new silver candlesticks and a wine cup, they reviewed a set of photographs that displayed the items being considered. Both men and women commented on the "muscular" appearance of the candlesticks. A member called one example "the penis candlesticks," suggesting they resembled an erection. Somebody else suggested they look for "vagina candlesticks." Nobody was offended, and the meeting was noticeable for its relaxed atmosphere.

The Education Committee was reviewing the list of films to be screened in the synagogue and advertised in the newsletter. The chairman was reluctant to select the Israeli film *Drifting* because it included an extremely graphic cruising scene in a Tel Aviv park. "True, we are a gay congregation, nevertheless, it is improper to show films here which display sexual acts," he exclaimed. The disputed scene showed two men who met in the park, the encounter ending with one partner kneeling down in front of the other. But the chairman remained in the minority. Moreover, the majority on the committee were very amused, and one suggested that the synagogue should implement its own film ratings, for example, "One Tongue," "Two Tongues," "Three Tongues."

Occasionally, as during the newsletter mailing sessions mentioned earlier, somebody would notice the name addressed on an envelope he was putting in the synagogue's mail. That might start a conversation related to the congregant involved, eliciting a jocular-erotic atmosphere. Somebody noticed, for example, the name of a leading personality in another Jewish gay organization who was also distinguished for his good looks. One participant added he was told that the latter's appearance in a red swimming suit was quite sensational, which made him believe he might be endowed with a horse-size erection. That description raised some discussion about the seriousness of the image employed by the narrator.

During a congregational meeting called before the annual elections to the board, I was very impressed by the short presentation made by a young candidate who argued that the synagogue was not doing enough to recruit people in their late teens and early twenties. Ze'ev, a member of the Religious Committee who was sitting next to me, seemed less impressed and said in an amused tone, "You wait and see." As we were ready to leave the young candidate approached us and I congratulated him on his performance. To my surprise he answered me in Hebrew, explaining that his mother could speak that language and adding that he had also learned French from his previous lover. Congratulating him on his linguistic skills, I asked him if it was his custom to choose his lovers by the language he preferred. He answered me immediately, "No, I choose them by their dick size." Since I was not yet familiar with gay slang, I did not comprehend his quick reply. He soon realized my deficiency and added a more graphic indication while looking down his pants. Everybody was amused but not impressed. I could see Ze'ev's look of satisfaction communicating "I told you." I was then told about the young candidate's behavior on other public occasions when he had displayed effeminate mannerisms.

I was not surprised to discover that the candidate did very poorly in the elections to the board. Had he expressed the same language and images in an intimate forum, also in the synagogue, he would not have been sanctioned but considered somewhat freakish. As already observed during committee meetings, mailing sessions, and other convivial occasions in the synagogue or elsewhere, congregants (including leading members) expressed sexual images and figuratively appreciated the physical assets of friends and strangers without causing damage to their reputation. But these jocular incidents always occurred in the company of close friends or a small group.

When we departed after services for a late snack in a Village restaurant, the group of eight congregants included Leon and other influential members. In comparison with his usual reserved demeanor, Leon was much more relaxed. He was complimenting the good looks of men who entered the place and later told us a story about being with a younger admirer who nevertheless was too shy to enjoy sex and made him miserable.

Similarly, when a group of six men came to decorate the sanctuary for the forthcoming holiday of Sukkot, they continuously exchanged jokes and stories, some of which were blatantly sexual. The gourds, fruit, and tree branches that comprised the major decorating materials were compared to fallen organs and physical odors. Joking insinuations were made about the private life of present members. Ben suggested the synagogue's decorations be embellished with small statues of virgins, but concluded immediately: "No, we can't do that, there are no virgins in the synagogue." He later commented that he preferred Gentile lovers, even though they often beat their mates and drag them immediately to bed.

During an antiques sale run by the synagogue to raise money for the victims of AIDS, the CBST volunteers were as usual sharing gossip and jokes. For example, when a newcomer arrived to replace the man at the door somebody asked, "Is he reliable?" "Of course he is, he sleeps with me," answered the first man who happened to be his lover.

Sexual jokes were, however, welcome in public when these seemed to imply an unspecified notion of communal affection. For example, a popular motto ascribed to Morris was the phrase "A family that eats together cleans together!" That phrase was called upon to recruit volunteers to clean up the synagogue after congregational dinners, dances, and other activities. When, at the end of a congregational dinner that preceded a holiday service, Norman raised his voice and

▼

called, "A family that eats together," the crowd shouted back, "sleeps together," and the place roared in laughter. Norman, who was openly gay and among the synagogue's representatives in various gay and nongay organizations, was usually very careful in his public speeches to avoid gay argot. But at home he was far less inhibited. For example, when during a birthday party a guest expressed his surprise at Norman's collection of male nudity in art, he replied immediately, "Of course, I'm a faggot!"

Close friends shared their good luck in erotic encounters as much as they shared their failures and depressions. Joel, who had developed a serious relationship with a Gentile he had met at work, often volunteered information about their plans and outings. At a later stage he was quite open about the growing difficulties in their relationship, particularly around intimate issues. On one such occasion, I heard him commenting to a mutual friend about the good spirits the latter demonstrated during a meeting they attended together. Our mutual friend reacted in a suggestive tone implying that he had had a "good experience" before coming to the meeting. As it turned out, he was referring to a pleasant encounter with a younger man who pursued him as he walked to his car, which had been an unexpected excitement after a session with his analyst that left him depressed. Undecided about the young man's intentions, he entered a nearby drugstore, watching and waiting. As he came out he saw the young man waiting in front of the store. He finally decided to take a risk and asked his pursuer, "What are you up to?" and got for an answer: "You know!" They ended up in his apartment and spent a pleasurable and "safe" afternoon together. His afternoon wooer was an out-of-town musician whom our friend didn't expect to meet again. But it was pleasant to know he could yet attract a nice younger man. It had been quite a long time since he had last met somebody in the synagogue for a shorter or longer affair.

The restrained style of sexual communication in the public forum was striking when compared with other organizations I attended, as, for example, a meeting of the Gay Fathers Forum mentioned earlier in this chapter. The members of that group met on the first Friday evening every month in a large hall (at the Lesbian and Gay Community Services Center) except for special events on other dates. On the Friday evening I attended, in the company of a few CBST members, the atmosphere was more sexually charged than I had ever experienced at CBST. The opening question in the discussion group in which I participated was whether one can find Mr. Right if the first encounter is immediately sexual. The leading speaker argued that one might meet nice men at popular cruising sites. His position was supported by other participants who said that they had met impressive men at the East Side Sauna with whom they continued to meet after the first sexual encounter on its premises. That argument was taken up by another leading member who reviewed a long list of places congenial for meeting men. Many of these sites could be defined as ordinary cruising grounds. He was relating to these gay territories and establishments in a tone greatly different from that prevalent at CBST, which considered this type of gay environment in terms of the pre-AIDS days.

213

The synagogue was not a sex-free environment, but the expression of sexual attraction, sexual language, and erotic demeanor on its premises were contained within clear rules that divided between the public and more intimate forums. In that "noncruising site," cruising was perceived mainly as a means for embarking upon a stable relationship leading toward lifelong commitment. In addition, sexuality was clearly distinguished from affection, which was displayed in the sharing of past and present intimate experiences, the manifestation of fondness and intensely jocular relationships.

The expression of affection through physical contact was usually reserved for lovers and close friends. Men and women would enthusiastically embrace their close friends upon meeting and departing. Hugging and kissing were also common between men and women. Congregants were, however, less reserved in expressing affection and joked around in a more blatant fashion during parties held in private homes.

For many individuals who had no partner for a loving relationship, or even for a fleeting affair, the synagogue offered an arena of intimacy that was not devoid of physical closeness. That widespread generosity in the display of affection supported the idea often promulgated in drashot and at other public events about the congregation's innate qualities as community, as family, and as home. It was a sort of diffused intimacy not often found in the world of mainstream society.

Many other institutions and habits that symbolized and celebrated gay liberation have disappeared or fallen into disrepute. True, congregants have suggested changes that have influenced sexual demeanor at CBST. But the special qualities of the synagogue as a safe gay envi-

▼

ronment were continuously evoked as the congregants recalled old memories or related recent adventures and sensations they were exposed to in other scenes of New York's gay life.

I return to the query I posed at the beginning of this chapter. Why were the congregants reluctant to emphasize the presence of couples? Why have they underplayed the synagogue as a scene for matchmaking? I can only hypothesize about the apparent gap in the congregants' perceptions.

Many female and male members related to the synagogue partly at least in terms of their return to cultural and social roots. But lesbian and gay couples presented a paradox in terms of mainstream Jewish society: they strikingly advertised their sexual preference and repudiated the expectation of reproduction. At the same time, however, contrary to stereotypic views and stigma, they displayed a model of stability in conjugal relationships.

The synagogue in mainstream American society, which has endowed the family with a major social role, introduces a difficult dilemma for CBST's congregants. Do they adopt mainstream synagogue social structures as a model for imitation? Do they endorse the "gay family," with a status equivalent to that of the nuclear family in heterosexual society? Is it appropriate for them to celebrate their emotional and sexual commitments in a style borrowed from the straight Jewish majority? Endorsing the "gay couple" also threatened to divide couples from singles in the congregation. Gays and lesbians had escaped their parents' synagogues and had given up Jewish life in great part because of the discomfort they experienced as individuals who could not accommodate the social expectations of mainstream congregations. Were they now to create new discomforts and raise the painful notion of social failure within their own synagogue? In conclusion, have the oppressors inscribed their mark on gays and lesbians, even in the safe space of the synagogue's sanctuary?

Many participants hoped to find a suitable mate at CBST; nevertheless, they did not evaluate that institution in terms of its success in helping them to fulfill their search for love. They believed CBST was a poor cruising place—that not withstanding the fact that some of their best friends had found their mates there. The issue of matchmaking on the synagogue premises carried a double–edged dilemma. The congregants resented the insinuation that their synagogue was a pick–up site, but they were also ambivalent about its association with the blessed expectation in mainstream society of being a safe ground for young Jewish men and women to find each other. The congregants were homosexuals who happened to be Jewish, but they were no less Jews who happened to be homosexuals. At that junction it seems the presence and the special status of Gentile lovers supported the notion of CBST as a less exclusively Jewish cultural enclave.

Most couples and singles didn't contemplate going through a commitment ceremony. Nevertheless, they were fascinated, moved, and amused by these extravagant events. They appreciated, and many searched for, the security of stable committed relationships; however, many male members were nostalgic for the sexual ethos of a lifestyle stimulated by gay liberation during the pre–AIDS era. The unqualified acceptance of stable pairing, and those straight mainstream rituals as models for CBST congregants, entailed a total debunking of gay male liberation ideology and symbols.

The low visibility of couples, the rarity of couples' bonding rituals, as much as the absence of a clear official policy concerning commitment ceremonies, seemed to demonstrate a stage of CBST's development: oscillating between the yet unresolved Jewish versus gay components of personal identity, collective goals, and political commitments.

▼

CHAPTER ELEVEN

"We Are an Extended Family": Confronting the Rampage of an Epidemic

When I sat down to write this chapter in early 1993, four of the close acquaintances quoted elsewhere in this work, including Martin, had already died of AIDS, and not a few others—among them leading members of CBST—were experiencing its symptoms.

Numbers, Signs, and Metaphors

A permanent reminder of this increasing death toll is the memorial board that has quickly expanded in recent years and threatens to take over one wall of the sanctuary. As Ron scanned the board for the names of AIDS victims, he remarked: "We used to have one death a year, then we had one per month, but now almost one every week. It gets close to home." He remembered there had been only five names when he first arrived, in 1980, but now there were nearly forty, most of them from AIDS. Leon told me, "We have many more deaths than would be expected for the age structure of our congregation." He assumed that about half of the male membership was HIV positive. (Others thought the percentage was considerably higher.) I was present at a discussion in which Morris, himself a survivor of the disease, suggested that the memorial board be immediately expanded while they could still find the same type of wood to match it.

When I first arrived at CBST in the spring of 1989, I was told that the number of congregants who had died from AIDS was about thirty-five. When the synagogue's board decided to contribute to the AIDS

Quilt, Jill, who chaired the Quilt Committee, suggested they order cloth for fifty panels, although by then there were only thirty-two confirmed names. When someone ironically remarked on her "forethought," Jill responded, gravely, "It is real." About three years later, when the names of the deceased were read during the memorial service at Shavuot in June 1992, ninety-five names were called out. Henry, the service leader, conservatively estimated that three-quarters of them had died of AIDS. Dov, looking through the list, confirmed that they were mostly AIDS victims.

Another frequent reminder of the epidemic was the announcement during the service of a recent death. This was followed by a communal memorial adapted from the Israeli Nobel laureate S. Y. Agnon's eulogy, "Kaddish." With the congregation standing, Agnon's words were intoned: "When one of Israel is missing, a diminishing and lessening takes place." Led by Martin, whose own health showed clear signs of deterioration during his two-year service as board chair, this ceremony held a special poignancy.

On one of these occasions Martin came to the bimah with a black ribbon on his sleeve to commemorate a close friend who had died after a two-year illness. The friend's family had refused to visit him before his death, although Martin's lover had informed them of his terminal condition and his request to see them. They hadn't attended the funeral either. Martin told the congregation: "His family was not there, but we, his family, have been with him."

This had been a very difficult week for Martin. He told me of his own family's inability to accept his life. His sister had phoned to tell him not to come to Thanksgiving with his lover if they were going to hug each other in front of her young daughters. Quite hysterical, she told him she was afraid their behavior might influence the girls. Martin's lover then called her and asked how she would react if she had been told to hide her Jewish identity? She was not convinced by that reasoning and Martin canceled the visit. He told me he was tired of his family and wanted to cut off the painful ties.

The role of the family was sometimes problematic, as when members of a congregant's family attended his funeral at CBST. When Lenny passed away his parents, siblings, and children discovered, for the first time, that he was gay and active in the gay world. All the funeral arrangements were made by the synagogue and his close friends there, who were the first informed of his death (and surprised

▼

to learn he had a family.) Lenny was buried next to his lover, a wish the "synagogue family" imposed over that of the biological family. The burial was described as an uncomfortable experience, with the family's anger and resentment obvious.

The synagogue's role as surrogate family was expressed in a prayer written by Ron, who wanted to offer a recitation more specifically directed to the gay community's suffering instead of the universality and uncritical acceptance of death expressed in Agnon's eulogy. "We are a community of strength," was his prayer's refrain, which was often recited by service leaders. It read, in part, "Many of us are infected with HIV. . . . We are a community under attack. Yet we are working, fighting, loving, helping, giving, and praying." Ron told me he wrote it in response to other prayers that related to AIDS victims as a group apart, "as if they are somewhere out there." He wanted to express the sorrow and pain "we all share together."

The issue of AIDS was also often raised in the drashot and other addresses that frequently compared the public's apparent indifference to the disastrous consequences of the disease with the world's indifference to the Holocaust. Norman's Yizkor sermon, quoted elsewhere, for example, began with the cry "Why is the world silent when so many people are dying of AIDS? Isn't it because they want to get rid of gays as much as they want to get rid of drug addicts and Blacks? Why did the world keep silent during the Holocaust?" In the face of these questions he found a note of consolation in mutual responsibility: "We are an extended family and we take care of each other." And he called on the male congregants to take the HIV test and save themselves.

The Holocaust analogy was always made by Ted, an Act-Up member who wore a "Silence = Death" button. His father had escaped from Germany shortly before the Holocaust and, as he told me, Ted could never stop thinking about the world's appalling silence. A former yeshiva student, Ted's discourse was no less with God, who allowed the demise of the gay community and his best friends.

When Bob first expressed his opposition to the festive reception of the Holocaust Torah and its installation in the synagogue, he nevertheless felt it symbolized those murdered without cause, just as the synagogue's memorial board named members who had died for no reason. A year later, when Bob had become reconciled to the installation of the Holocaust Torah, he made a new symbolic association with "our AIDS Holocaust." Just as Jewish survival was a victory over those who sought its annihilation, Bob hoped for a triumph over the AIDS Holocaust now that gays were united in battle.

The frequent comparison at CBST of AIDS with the Holocaust was   219
an evolutionary development. Initially, Larry Kramer's (1981) association of AIDS with the monumental Jewish tragedy was frequently resented. As one speaker explained, "The Holocaust was a man-made atrocity, but HIV is a virus-caused calamity." The adoption of this metaphor appeared to signify a growing awareness of the indiscriminate nature of the disease. The victims were among all ages and ranks, leaders and members alike. Since many of the male congregants had in earlier years engaged in what was now discovered to be unsafe sex, the notion of an imminent disaster that might strike all gay men made the Holocaust comparison meaningful. As custodians of Jewish tradition and partners to the Jewish experience, CBST's leaders and speakers claimed the right to use the Holocaust as a metaphor to express their fear and anger. This association placed the unexplained assault of the disease within a culturally familiar milieu. It also set the congregants' religious discourse within a context familiar from the previous catastrophe: "Why did God allow the annihilation of his people?"

The installation of the Holocaust Torah scroll in a wood and glass case on the same wall as the list of CBST's dead made a strong association between the two disasters.

AIDS and the Leadership

The existence of AIDS at CBST was dramatically revealed by its presence among highly visible members and those in positions of leadership, and suggested the dimension of the epidemic and the congregants' vulnerability. It also produced a constant flow of information about the health of the afflicted and an open discussion of the strategies for life in the age of AIDS.

Ira, the first leading figure at CBST to die of AIDS, stopped appearing in public long before his death. He kept his illness secret until it became visible to those who came to see him. Although he was very active, generous, and popular at CBST, he withdrew from the synagogue. Dov told me he had been open about his illness with his friends in the Gay Men's Chorus, but was probably worried about the reaction at CBST: "Our people didn't know how to behave when it all started." During an innovative Sabbath morning service I attended,

▼

someone asked about the previous night's drashah, which dealt with leprosy and the rules of exclusion surrounding it. Had the speaker been relating it to the issue of AIDS? The question sparked a lively dis-cussion. The service leader reminded the group that when those first afflicted with AIDS came to the synagogue with obvious KS lesions they were shunned by people they considered their friends. They were also seen as notoriously promiscuous. "Nobody thought the day would come when we wouldn't know who might be ill." Another member active in volunteer work responded that many still avoid those with clear signs of AIDS. He thought it was sad that a people with a history of being ostracized and confined to ghettos would victimize its own. It was generally agreed that when someone fell ill with AIDS-related pneumonia he did not generate the same discomfort that would someone else with other symptoms because he bore no outward signs after recovery.

Though he had withdrawn from the synagogue during his lengthy illness, Ira's death was commemorated with a public concert and thus incorporated in the synagogue's history. Since his self-imposed seclusion people with AIDS have taken a visible role at CBST. Particularly conspicuous was Martin, whose last few years were dedicated to fighting the Jewish establishment's indifference to issues involving gays and lesbians. I first became aware of his growing mission when he wrote an article for the *Jewish Week* (February 3, 1989) in which he attacked institutional Jewry's readiness to take contributions from gays but completely ignore their plight, denying support for AIDS victims despite the Jewish tradition of mutual responsibility. As he explained it, he felt compelled to write the piece because of his recent hospitalization for pneumonia. He was in bed when the hospital's Orthodox rabbi came to his room. Martin offered him a seat, but the rabbi remained standing. Martin suspected he was resentful at seeing the Reconstructionist Mordechai Kaplan's book on his bed. When Martin told him he suffered from AIDS, the rabbi nodded and left. Martin was outraged and complained to the hospital's administration. The rabbi called him the same day and asked what the trouble was. Martin told him he was unsuited for his position because he hadn't taken a seat at a sick man's bed, resented the sight of a book on Judaism not to his taste, and took quick leave when he discovered the sick man he had come to comfort had AIDS. Martin went on to say, sarcastically, that his own partner was only a Conservative rabbi, but truly Jewish in his compassion. The Orthodox rabbi explained he had been in a hurry to catch a bus, and the next Friday he came to see Martin with wine and cake, but without apology.

Martin at first intended to sign his article with a pseudonym, in order to save his family embarrassment among friends who subscribed to the *Jewish Week*, but the next day changed his mind. Since then Martin had no more hesitation in publicly revealing his gay identity or his health condition. He seemed almost destined for the role of a gay spokesman. He was an imposing figure, tall and robust, confident in speech and assertive in manner. Martin's association with the AIDS crisis began long before he discovered he was HIV positive. He was a senior administrator with the New York State Health Department and directly supervised its AIDS task force. That job made him only too familiar with the symptoms of the disease. His friends laughingly dismissed his claim that he must be infected with HIV. Nevertheless, he decided to leave his position, which he felt was too demanding. He took another leading job in health services, but soon went on sick leave when his fears were confirmed. Not yet forty, he was financially able to stay out of work and devote his time to his own pursuits, among which was a growing involvement in CBST.

When I visited Martin on Thanksgiving 1989, after my absence from New York, he told me he considered himself a candidate for board chair. I was surprised since I remembered his continuing frustration on the board and his enthusiasm with his dual synagogue membership in CBST and B'nai Jeshurun, whose leader, Rabbi Marshall Meyer, he admired. However, Martin thought it was important that the gay synagogue be represented by someone like himself, a person with AIDS, and one experienced in the public arena. He thought his death, which might occur before the completion of his term, would be a traumatic experience for many congregants, but was adamant that should not deter him from seizing the opportunity to implement his plans for CBST. Supported by Saul, the retiring chair, Martin, a veteran board member, was elected the board's next chair.

Martin's self-assurance and determination in approaching the Jewish mainstream was demonstrated on many occasions before he assumed this position. I mentioned his article in the *Jewish Week*, but a more direct opportunity came through his membership at B'nai Jeshurun. At the special service and dinner for people with AIDS I attended, organized by Rabbi Marshall Meyer to find ways to confront

221

▼

that crisis, Martin, who was among the speakers, told the congregation and their gay guests the story of a patient who had been deserted by the hospital rabbi when the rabbi discovered he was in the room of a person with AIDS. His listeners gasped in surprise when Martin revealed he had been that patient. In spite of the shock Martin had deliberately staged, and the discomfort some may have felt at discovering the deadly disease in their company, he charmed everyone. It was difficult to believe he was really the man in the story. He didn't resemble the stereotypical AIDS victim. He looked too healthy, too robust, solid, and humorous for that role.

As I have described in chapters 3 and 8, one of Martin's major goals as board chair was the appointment of a full-time rabbi. He considered it an urgent need, especially in light of the AIDS crisis. He estimated that about 40 percent of the male membership was HIV positive and thought a rabbi could provide personal and communal support for the sick and their families. His presidency was marked by the pace at which he pushed to complete this goal as much as by the pace of his own illness. His first major setback occurred just before Yom Kippur, 1990, when a lung infection put him in the hospital. His room facing the East River was constantly packed with visitors. His lover and close friends knew he was greatly disappointed with this health failure, but they tried to convince him there was no real danger in the episode. As on many other occasions, Morris's story was raised as proof for hope. As Martin's lover related, it was now four years since Morris had been told by his doctors to call in "the mishpocha" (close family). He was thought near death, but within twenty-four hours received the newly available drug AZT, and was soon back on his feet. Morris had recently made the story known during a public speech urging congregants to take the HIV test. Whatever the personal circumstances that enabled his recovery, he became a living symbol for hope in the face of AIDS, a CBST myth of man against the virus.

Morris himself, in his Yom Kippur address to the congregation, referred to Martin's hospitalization: "It is a small setback, but there are today new drugs," he promised. A close friend of Martin's told me Martin saw his hospitalization as a personal failure. When he was first diagnosed with AIDS he gave himself only eighteen months to live, which was then the average prognosis. He was counting the months. With the development of new drugs, however, he became more hopeful. Although he remained realistic about his long-term prospects and had given up the idea of buying an apartment with his lover, Martin, it appears, came to see this as another fight he could wage, one in which he was gaining a degree of control. As his lover, Job, described it, "It is a step back, but not the end." Emphasizing the lack of gravity in the situation, Job—unique among the many visitors—conspicuously wore no mask.

223

And in fact, on the next Chanukah Martin was able to deliver the Friday drashah. He related the story of his first hospitalization on Chanukah two years before. He had thought he was going to die. He couldn't breathe, but Job, nevertheless, wanted to light the Chanukah candles. "I told him, give me a break, don't you see I'm dying?" But Job was adamant: "If you are really going to die," he said, "it wouldn't be so bad if the Chanukah candles were the last thing you saw in this world." Martin laughed as he added, "This is the situation when you have a rabbi for a lover." He then spoke of his recent Yom Kippur hospitalization, which he described as among the darkest days of his life. He had vowed that if he got out of the hospital he would dedicate his recovery to working on a new drashah. This is how he had come to study the Chanukah myth of light, as compensation for the drashah he had missed presenting on Yom Kippur.

His gradually deteriorating health didn't deter Martin from his single-minded effort to prod the congregation into hiring a rabbi. Joel, who opposed that goal, told Martin that he "better live for another year" if he wanted it to happen. Although Joel meant Martin must stay on for the second year of his term as board chair, the unintended ghoulishness of his comment didn't escape other listeners. Martin remained unmoved, as usual, when the issue of AIDS-related death was discussed in public. He often led the congregation in the Agnon eulogy and lectured on AIDS. Although it appeared that his health was not improving, or even stabilizing, he and Job went ahead with their plan for a commitment ceremony. It was conducted in grand style, in November of 1991, with six rabbis officiating at a service designed for the occasion.

On my return to New York in June of 1992 I phoned Martin. He told me he was tired and dizzy because of his heavy medication. He had lost weight and visited the synagogue only rarely. I was told he had lung cancer; his mood had darkened, and he preferred to spend his time with Job. Close friends now admitted he had only a few months left. His illness was also spoken of from the bimah by Morris, who had been elected as the new chair. Paul, who had been expected to succeed Martin, was himself fighting AIDS and confined by chemotherapy. His resignation from the board was announced by Morris as well.

Martin died early in September 1992, shortly before the fulfillment of his cherished project, the installation of a full-time rabbi at CBST. I did not witness the later stages of the selection process or the inauguration itself of the first official rabbi. Though Martin was not alone in making that possible, without him, I strongly believe—as do many other congregants—it might never have materialized. His affliction with AIDS served him greatly in that goal, not because he played on it, but because of the free time and focus it allowed him in his unwavering dedication. He had no patience with the compromise and delay one might otherwise have accepted. He used all his time, skill, personal charm, and tenacity to realize his project. Such zeal would not have been likely in one, himself included, also pursuing a career.

Among CBST leaders Martin's public confrontation with AIDS had been preceded by Morris's disclosure of his own illness on Yom Kippur, 1989. As reported earlier, he urged the congregation to take the HIV test and avail themselves of new drugs if necessary. "Look at me," he told his audience, "I am sick, but I am in wonderful shape." Naomi, who related Morris's statement to me, was very impressed with his appeal, which ran counter to a common rejection of the test on the theory that in the absence of any treatment, testing positive would only increase psychological stress and risk employment and insurance discrimination. Following Morris's appeal, Naomi, a physician, was approached by at least ten men who inquired about the test. Simon took his close friend Gilbert, whom he suspected was still practicing unsafe sex, along to be tested. The frightening gamble paid off: "We both came out clean."

In his early thirties, Paul was representative of a younger generation at CBST. His rapidly declining health shocked many congregants. He often had unexplained attacks of high fever and lost both weight and the sparkle that so endeared him to many congregants. A friend of Paul's told of happening upon him, apparently distraught, aimlessly walking in the Village. When asked what was wrong, Paul explained that he had seen his doctor, who told him his immune system was close to zero. Along with Martin's, Paul's health situation, about which he was quite open, was often commented on at CBST with growing apprehension. More than with other cases, one heard the painful conclusion that "Paul is dying" (he passed away in June 1993).

225

Lenny's sudden death was probably the most shocking since he had shown no symptoms of the disease and was not generally known to be HIV positive. In a December 1990 board meeting Martin informed his colleagues that Lenny would not be able to attend to his usual voluntary job in the synagogue's kitchen for the next week or so because of a bad winter cold. Only a few days later Lenny was dead, having succumbed to his first attack of AIDS-related pneumonia. Lenny was, no doubt, secretive about his life. (I noted the congregants' surprise that Lenny had children.) He had only told one or two friends about his condition, and had claimed his lover's AIDS death, a year earlier, was the result of a heart attack. Many congregants concluded that Lenny preferred to deny his condition rather than fight it.

Despite Lenny's behavior, which exhibited a somewhat closeted attitude, his death was widely mourned. He was a dedicated member and his passing seemed to manifest the gravity of the threat to the CBST community. During the funeral service Harvey commented that we should expect a growing number of these events in the next few years unless a new drug was developed. Simon told me how painful the funeral service was for him. He couldn't speak but had a need to express the affection he bore for his synagogue friends. He felt for Lenny's loneliness and was concerned about his own future and that of the community. He feared there were not many days left for the synagogue because of the continuing AIDS devastation and the growing conservatism in the country.

Following Lenny's service, David, a board member and generous congregant, was among a small group of Lenny's close friends who accompanied the family to the burial. When they reached the cemetery, he collapsed. David was another active CBST member unexpectedly struck with AIDS. Like Lenny, he tried to deny his illness.

The news of David's hospitalization, some time later, caused great surprise. I first learned of it from Joel, who was told that David was running a high fever and had lost seven pounds. Joel commented that David had been "married" for many years, and he found it hard to believe that he "fooled around." When David returned from the hospital, he looked pale and had stopped smoking. He denied he had

AIDS, although it became known he had been hospitalized with pneumonia. He told me he suffered from nicotine poisoning. His close friends didn't dispute his claim but, when asked about his health, spoke gravely. I was told he refused to take the test until Morris finally convinced him.

Upon his return to the board, David vehemently opposed the Education Committee's plan to show a film, *The Last Laugh*, in which a group of PWAS use humor to document life with AIDS. David considered it an offensive comedy and cited a quip that having AIDS "is a shopaholic's dream. I buy everything on time and credit—two things I don't have." He was neither swayed by Martin's promise of a prefatory address to the audience nor by Paul's obvious anger with him. When a vote was taken David remained the only one in opposition. It was not so much David's stubbornness—which was characteristic—but the degree to which he seemed personally invested in this issue that suggested his own illness. Sometime later he resigned from the board for health reasons. His condition was considered grave. The last time I saw him he was very pale and lacked his usual energetic appearance. Although he was not among the more popular of CBST's active members, his illness carried a compelling message about the ubiquity of the disease. Harvey, in his Rosh Hashanah drashah, no doubt had David in mind when he described a fellow committee member whose presence he could barely tolerate. But when he heard that the man was ill he felt a terrible sadness and would have done anything in his power to see him well again and sitting beside him on the committee.

An End to an Era

A different impact is borne out in the tragic story of five close friends who were united in an unusual alliance of love and sexuality. Two had already died by the time I arrived in the synagogue. Two others, Matthew and Harry, died during my stay. Edward was the surviving member.

When it became known to the Talmud circle that their member Matthew could not attend class because of an unidentified illness, Aaron commented that he hoped it was not AIDS. Edward responded, in an ironic tone, that these days when anyone in his office was sick with a winter cold they immediately suspected AIDS. However, it was not long before Matthew was known, in fact, to have AIDS, and he died shortly afterward of cancer.

Harry's battle with the illness, in particular, captured the sympathy and concern of the congregation. He endured the disease longer than many others, having lived four years after his first bout with pneumonia. Harry seemed to overcome the various attacks, helped with new drugs, experimental treatments, and surgery. But most of all, he was thought to have survived because he was ready to put up a continuing fight. Edward's loyalty was another asset in that long battle. 227

I first met Harry at the Talmud class Purim party, which he attended together with Edward and Matthew. He was very quiet and not among the class regulars. In his mid-thirties, Harry was loved in the synagogue because of his gentleness and creativity. He loved the synagogue, where he had met Edward, and enjoyed its social atmosphere, although he was not religious. When I talked to him sometime later, during a Friday service, he told me he had retired from work and put everything he owned in liquid assets. He had worked all his life saving for the future; now he knew he had no future to consider. He would soon die because his immune system was completely compromised. He tried to enjoy life as much as he could and mentioned a recent Caribbean cruise he had taken together with his parents and Edward. Although he assumed he had no chance for survival, he told me he was optimistic. It had already been two years since his diagnosis and he considered himself in good shape, given that time. His optimism impressed friends like Aaron who told me that Harry's youth overcame the ravages of the disease.

Harry preserved his optimistic outlook for a long time. He talked about his body almost in terms of an old car that needed sensitive care to keep going. He told me that he was careful to track any changes in his body and immediately call his doctor. He could always talk to him by telling his nurse, "I am passing away." He had already been hospitalized three times with pneumonia. Recently, he had been operated on to remove a cancerous growth. As he told the story, it had been a Sunday morning when he felt a scary pain. He called Edward, who, still sleepy, suggested he phone his doctor. But Harry insisted on going to the hospital. He had correctly assessed the urgency of his condition and was soon wheeled into the operating room. Harry assumed that about seventy-five percent of the male congregants were HIV positive because "they were members of a generation which was sexually very active." Was that assumption among the sources of a remarkable equanimity that coexisted with his determination in deal-

▼

ing with the illness? That equanimity in particular endeared him to—
and intrigued—many observers.

Harry's battle with AIDS was seen as a testament to his pride in gay
identity. His longevity was contrasted with other men—Lenny, for
example—who succumbed to their first attack of the disease. Dov
claimed that one can always survive the first assault—to do otherwise
reflects a mental position of self-denial. He told me the story of one
of the first AIDS dead at CBST, who possessed low self-esteem. He had
children and had never fully reconciled with his homosexuality.
Harry's reluctance to give up his independence, despite his worsening
condition and defiance of the inescapable verdict, made his presence
or absence at Friday evening services a matter of public concern. He
attended as long as he could spare the effort. He was not deterred by
his deteriorating body and physical appearance. It was known that
Edward was becoming less enthusiastic about CBST's services, but he
accommodated Harry's wishes. "Harry was very special in his battle
with AIDS," were Joel's words a few months after his death.

But, as Edward told his friends in the Talmud class, Harry was
becoming tired and depressed. He had lost the energy he had in the
past to go on fighting. He was now hospitalized again from drug poisoning caused by the massive medication he was taking. Jeff, a close
friend of his, told me that Harry had recently become edgy, frustrated,
and angry with the doctors and their conflicting opinions about his
proper treatment. "He is fading before my eyes. It will be a funeral I'll
hate to attend," Jeff remarked sadly. Harry was evidently losing weight
rapidly. It was a sad sight only brightened by the affection his friends
showed him in the synagogue, embracing and kissing him as if for the
last time. Harry died in the summer of 1991. I was told by Aaron, who
led the funeral service, that they read Harry's last words: "Life is good."

Edward was the last and probably the most tragic member of that
group of men, who had known many happy days together. He was
considered the leader of a circle that epitomized the extraordinary lost
freedom of the heyday of gay liberation. The men were all very close
but maintained open relationships. Their story, though not clear in its
details to everyone, was often retold. But the description of the
"promiscuity" among this educated and successful group was not
made in a disparaging way. Edward's growing Orthodoxy added to the
complexity, if not mystery, surrounding the life and fate of the disap-
pearing company.

Edward, who had comforted his dying friends, was most likely destined to confront the deadly affliction alone. It was Martin who, already in 1989, told me he suspected Edward had AIDS because he had noticed that his glands were swollen. But it was Jeff who con- firmed Martin's suspicion when we first met after Harry's death. He knew Edward was taking AZT and had already suffered minor complications. Jeff was living with the fear that he himself was HIV positive, but avoided the test because he couldn't face the certain knowledge. He was convinced that most PWAs were doomed to endure a painful death and spend their last days in loneliness. He empathized with Edward, Harry, and other friends with whom he shared the memories of a generation and an era he had witnessed only in its last days. Sad and reflective, Jeff told me,

> We had sex without hesitation with everyone we were attracted to. We met our tricks in the supermarket, the department stores, the bars, and the baths. I sometimes miss those days of complete freedom after so many generations of repression. But now it is all over, except for some young kids who do silly things.

But sometime later I discovered Jeff was not all that careful in his sexual life. He succumbed to temptation and retrieved a taste of the good old days, though he assumed he maintained the less risky role in a new relationship (he started outside the synagogue) that seemed satisfactory for a while.

Edward passed away in June 1993. Many CBST veteran members attended Edward's funeral, which was organized by his family at an Upper West Side chapel. He was eulogized by the family's rabbi, by Aaron, and by another close friend from the Talmud class. Edward's devotion to his sick friends was mentioned by the family's rabbi, but the Talmud class colleague made a more direct and poetic reference to Edward's lost circle of intimate friends and lovers as he quoted from David's eulogy for King Saul and Jonathan, who had not parted in life or death (II Samuel 2:23).

Jeff, in his mid-thirties, who had seen the decline and death of men to whom he had been attracted, felt a growing loneliness. "I see the angel of death moving around whenever I come to the synagogue," he told me. Believing that half of New York's gay males were HIV positive, he claimed that two hundred CBST members had already died. He thought I didn't realize the extent of the loss because new members were always joining CBST and the congregation was apparently growing. One of the first acquaintances Jeff made from the synagogue was, in fact, a person with AIDS. Jeff met him one Friday evening as he was waiting for the train to Manhattan. A good-looking young man approached him and asked, "Haven't I seen you in the synagogue?" Jeff, somewhat surprised, replied cautiously, "In the Village?" The man then introduced himself but added, immediately, "and I have AIDS." Jeff was shattered, but maintained a friendship with him until he died, continuing to visit his parents, Holocaust survivors whose lost son was their only child.

Jeff sometimes wondered why he had survived. More than once his dead mother's voice had stopped him on the way to the Mineshaft, a place, viewed in retrospect, of notoriously unsafe sex. That feeling of miraculous survival was publicly expressed by another member in his early forties who related that two of his close friends had died the summer before. For the first time he felt an urge to celebrate his birthday. There was a reason to celebrate, he realized, "I am alive!"

PWAS on the Bimah

When I first arrived at CBST the AIDS rhetoric I heard struck me as a form of Jewish benevolence reminiscent of the support for Russian Jewry, Ethiopian Jews, the old, and the poor. No doubt, as a novice to the scene, I may not have grasped the urgency of the words spoken from the bimah. But I was not alone in sometimes tiring of the frequent metaphors "We are a community" or "We are an extended family." But when Lenny, whose sentimentality about the synagogue's community was often dismissed, suddenly died, CBST's response bore out his words. An enormous crowd made the effort to attend his funeral, which lasted several hours. The crowd was engulfed with sadness and the sense of an unknown destiny. Collectively they shared the fear that they too could suddenly fall ill to AIDS. After the service I went to lunch with a group of congregants. The mourners seemed reluctant to leave one another's company for their daily affairs. They didn't want to lose the comfort of communitas.

My perception of the resonance of certain metaphors changed not only with the passage of time, but with a change in the bimah's leading actors. The healthy and always easygoing Saul was replaced by the imposing and driven AIDS advocate, Martin. Paul, his close friend and board ally, was also battling AIDS, as was David, a third and visible member of the board. Morris, who replaced Martin as board chair, was also counted among those personally dealing with AIDS. People with AIDS were no longer an isolated category "somewhere out there," as Ron contended. They had literally moved up from the corners of the sanctuary to the center of the bimah.   231

The discourse on AIDS changed when those speaking about the epidemic were themselves infected. When Martin, referring to a friend whose family rejected him in his mortal illness, declared, "But we, his family, have been with him," it carried a more profound resonance. When Morris called on the congregants to take the HIV test, they were shocked, but they responded to his heartfelt plea, which was rooted in his own experience. PWAs were not being talked to, they were talking, and talking from a position of leadership.

The growing presence of PWAs in the synagogue's leadership increased CBST's visibility and reinforced its demand for legitimacy as an institution, one dealing with a major challenge of the day. The congregation was not hiding the victims or ashamed of the behavior whose unintended consequence encouraged the epidemic. As witnessed by its presence in the AIDS vigil, to the wider gay community, CBST was taking its place—at least symbolically—on the battle line.

But more important, it appeared, was the increased claim made on the Jewish establishment. Martin's article in the *Jewish Week* and his appearance at B'nai Jeshurun became part of the synagogue's legacy. The installation of CBST's first rabbi—conducted by the president of the Union of Hebrew [Reform] Congregations of America—could not have occurred without the process being greatly energized by Martin and his colleagues' concern with AIDS. Having added AIDS to homosexuality, Martin, Morris, and Paul were acting out their "stigma" with a bravado they had not displayed heretofore. There was no longer any way for them, or for those they were dealing with, to evade their sexual identity. The irreversibility of their health condition, one that they openly advertised, made their claim more compelling. By expanding the dimension of the stigma they negotiated with the Jewish establishment, they raised the stakes—elevating their expectation for return in terms of acceptance and legitimacy. The exposition of the brutal finality of their situation made their plea more powerful and, in spite of the stigma, their goals more realizable.

CHAPTER TWELVE

A Gay Space, a Jewish Space, a Safe Space

Gay Versus Jewish

In recent years anthropologists have become accustomed to describing the difficulties they experience on entering their "fields" and the research strategies they employ throughout "fieldwork." They also turned to look into their practice of writing during fieldwork— their fieldnotes.[1] Their critics, however, have gradually become more interested in the means and processes by which anthropologists construct their ethnographic texts.[2] Anthropologists have by and large adopted Crapanzano's depiction of fieldwork and the writing of ethnographic texts as a confrontation with "otherness,"[3] but they have mainly expanded in their presentations on the early stages of that confrontation. They have far less engaged themselves in describing their feelings, on the political, intellectual, and other personal influences that affected the writing of their ethnographies.[4] Equally significant, how did they come to compose the chapters of their books? Does the order in the published table of contents actually represent the chronology of writing? In sum, readers are mostly uninformed about a crucial stage in the creation of an anthropologist's work.

Beyond my comments in the opening chapter about the conditions of my work, I stress the fact here that I first wrote up my observations of the Talmud class. Although I enjoyed the authoring of all other ethnographic chapters, there was, nevertheless, something about the Talmud circle that intrigued me in particular. True, I was fascinated by Aaron's special position in the story of CBST. I was flattered by the warm hospitality he and his friends extended to me. I assume I could also better grasp the overall agenda of that company and the lives of its participants, who formed a close–knit society. But, most of all, I felt that group, and the changes its members had undergone since their first days at CBST, epitomized some major issues pertinent to the phenomenon of a gay synagogue in America.[5]

233

The people whose religious organization and personal experiences are described in these chapters represent an intersection of the profound developments engaging two social minorities in modern history. First, the majority of CBST members were children and grandchildren of immigrants who escaped the poverty, discrimination, and persecutions typical of Jewish life in Eastern Europe and, more recently, in Central Europe as well under the vestiges of World War II. Never before have Jews experienced the security, affluence, and influence they came to enjoy in America, "the *goldene medina*"—"the land of gold" (in Yiddish), as that country became known among the masses of Jews in Eastern Europe.

The dramatic reversal of Jewish fortunes in the United States was soon expressed in the organizational and spiritual life of American Jews. Jews have been among the strongest ethnic groups in the United States in terms of their creativity in establishing a wide variety of viable communal institutions and national organizations. American Jews have displayed a remarkable cultural continuity, but they also proved to be imaginative and prolific in innovating religious and social patterns of congregational life. In my introduction I briefly presented the major forms of organized Jewry in the United States. If the ultra-Orthodox, Modern Orthodox, and Reform movements had their roots in Europe, and the Conservative movement emerged almost simultaneously in Europe and America, the Reconstructionist and Havurah movements originated in America. The firm support of the State of Israel represents a symbolic expression of American Jewish solidarity and self–assertion (also influenced by the impact of the Holocaust).

The founding of CBST and other first gay synagogues, in the early 1970s, happened at a time when that creativity and expansion seemed to have reached its peak but also when the "turbulent sixties" had introduced deep cleavages, instability, and loss of confidence in mainstream religion. American Judaism was not spared these developments. Among the issues affecting major religions at that time, Wertheimer (1993) observed: "In Jewish religious life, as in Christian America, gender and sexual issues have been at the center of much of the maelstrom—within each of the movements and between them" (190).

Second, the founding of CBST was also part of the "explosion of gay things" in the wake of gay liberation since the late 1960s. Those who came to write the history of that movement have often related it to World War II, which mobilized millions of men and women out of their native communities, enabled new forms of social bonding, and opened new occupational opportunities for many women. That immense mobilization and the vast socioeconomic changes in recent decades greatly affected major urban centers where gay and lesbian communities could take shape, develop services to satisfy the special needs of their people, and promote political action.[6] American Jews who actively participated in other social, political, and intellectual movements that emerged on the American scene became visible in that growing movement as well. As I have noted, the gay synagogues were initially encouraged by the successful debut of gay churches. In sum, the founding of gay synagogues seems to have been deeply related to the recent histories of both Jews and homosexuals in America.

"We're gay!"

"We're Jewish!"

"And we're proud!"

These phrases were uttered and written down for me by Simon, among my closest friends in Congregation Beth Simchat Torah. He went on to explain each phrase:

"The [American] mainstream would have us closeted."

"The [Jewish] mainstream would have us assimilate."

"But we are proud of our double identity—we are twice blessed."

Simon's presentation of himself as part of a collective project emphasized his deep feelings of involvement in the history and experience of both Jewish and gay people. For many observers, however, CBST might appear as just "another American synagogue," Reform or Conservative in particular. From that point of view, the gay and lesbian congregants display an impulse familiar among American Jews, to build a synagogue comfortable for its particular constituency, in a style borrowed from mainstream Jewish society. Thus the gay synagogue movement represents another case of creativity and diversity typical to American Jewry, namely, a new institution that contains elements from both an ordinary synagogue and a Havurah minyan. That, however, was not the perception of most congregants themselves.

Why was I so impressed by the Talmud class? Aaron and his close friends, who stood at the cradle of the gay synagogue, appeared to me authentic representatives of the story of the gay revolution of the 1960s and 1970s. Arriving from an Orthodox background, Aaron's search for gay life led him to find spiritual comfort in a gay church, engaging him to a Gentile lover. What more could symbolize his withdrawal from Jewish life? But from that radical departure Aaron made it all the way back to Jewish Orthodoxy. His teaching and his own journey "from Brooklyn to Manhattan and all the way back to Brooklyn," were sometimes comprehended in mystical terms, revealing the dramatic conflict between personal desire and cultural commitments. Although introducing the Orthodox pole of Judaism, that extreme position chosen by formerly active congregants seemed to encapsulate the incongruity embedded in the attraction of homosexuals to mainstream religious life.

The dilemma of 'gay versus Jewish' components of identity and modes of behavior, first exposed by Aaron and his supporters, could be traced, though in a less dramatic fashion, throughout CBST's later history, as often observed here. While Aaron gradually came to advocate the development of a *Jewish community* whose members happen to be gay and lesbian, the lay leadership wished to promote a *gay* and *lesbian community* whose members were Jews.

The "gay–Jewish" confrontation (sometimes related to in terms of a "synagogue" versus a "social center") took on various shades in later years, often displaying inconsistent results. Those deliberations in the various synagogue forums engaged major issues of liturgy, ritual, and recreation, from the adoption of a new prayer book to the question of food catering. The last-mentioned problem, for example, was expressed during the events reported in chapter 8: "If we are the shul that we are, we have to address the issue of kashrut," an emphatic statement made at a board meeting but dismissed for what seemed a more urgent social consideration—the ticket price. Or the frustrated plea voiced at a Religious Committee meeting on the issue of a musical troupe: "We are the seven rabbis of the synagogue and we have a responsibility. We want a Jewish place, we want a Jewish feel." But

235

against the obvious resentment of many (if not the majority of the
active membership), CBST, under the leadership of its forceful chair,
appointed an ordained rabbi, the most visible symbol of Jewish main-
236 stream communal life. At the same time, however, the synagogue did
not join a Jewish denomination open to them.

The issue of commitment ceremonies, for example, was sort of a
ball game between the "principles" of Judaism versus gay life. That
issue directly addressed the values and position of the family, a major
institution in Jewish communal life. Gay "weddings" apparently supported mainstream ideals of stable bonding relationships but challenged them no less in what might appear to outsiders to be camp
mockery. After a few locally created ceremonies (during the early days
of Aaron's radicalism), which, however, were careful to avoid close
imitations of a Jewish wedding, the congregation refrained altogether
from an encounter with mainstream culture. More recently the synagogue opened its doors, albeit unwillingly at first, to the performance
of commitment ceremonies that integrated much of Jewish traditional
marriage ritual, adopted to the special needs of lesbians and gays. In
the final account, it seems, these ceremonies were equally supporting
the Jewish and gay agendas at CBST.

Aaron's return to Orthodoxy also involved his separation from a
Gentile partner. Gentile lovers remained a permanent phenomenon at
the synagogue, often as partners to leading CBST congregants; their
very existence formed a kind of balancing weight against the Jewish
pole. However, the Talmud class was not homogeneous in its
gay–Jewish theological position either. Gentile lovers were equally
observed among core members of that group.

The gay-Jewish discourse was often expressed in the rhetorics and
symbols of "diversity." It echoed in the frequent announcements from
the bimah as well as in conversations: "We are not a neighborhood
shul"; "We are a diverse congregation"; "our unity within diversity";
"What is our theology?"; "The synagogue is more than its parts."
These compact phrases, picked up from among many other references to the synagogue, advocated the nature of a mixed audience
and its manifold aspirations for CBST's position on theology, ritual, gay
ideology, and practice. "Our unity within diversity" was a kind of
refrain in a CBST collective prayer.

No doubt diversity is not only typical to gay synagogues. But while
resentful individuals in mainstream synagogues can easily opt out for

other more suitable congregations, that option is not equally available to lesbians and gays. "Diversity" at CBST was the symbolic cement and a kind of "sentimental education"[7] evoked to fill in the sometimes immense gaps between the different types of joiners and their expectations on the gay–Jewish continuum.   237

The convergence of the history of the Jewish and gay people found a powerful expression in the AIDS epidemic. Male members from all ranks and groups (the Talmud circle included) were wiped out at the prime of life. That calamity was gradually conceived at CBST in terms of current Jewish Holocaust imageries. The tragic destiny of infected homosexual men was associated with the Jewish experience of stigmatization, indifference, and persecution. Board chair Martin, struck with AIDS, as well as other speakers, attacked the Jewish establishment for neglecting the victims of the epidemic. The accusation might have raised among the more liberal sectors the guilt of having been silent during an earlier disaster. That affliction was also a major rationalization for the hiring of a rabbi.

The relationships between men and women at CBST formed another stage for the convergence of developments in both the Jewish and homosexual constituencies. Both supporters and opponents of Aaron's religious transformation often contemplated his position on women's participation. As he increasingly turned to Orthodoxy, could Aaron endorse women's growing equality in ritual affairs? Thus remained untested the likelihood of gay Orthodox Jews accommodating Jewish feminism. The lesbian membership has gradually moved from the periphery of the synagogue to greater involvement in ritual and the running of the synagogue organization. Feminism, which was making its mark in mainstream Jewish religious life, gained considerable achievements at CBST within a short period of time. The appointment of Rabbi Sharon Kleinbaum stamped that process.

The hiring of a rabbi, celebrated in grand style in the presence of leading figures in the Jewish world at large, signified the durability of CBST also as part of an expanding gay synagogue movement. In the American scene of voluntary associations and claims for minority rights, "gay Jews" have emerged as a strong and viable group. They rallied for the legitimacy of their identity not only as part of the overall gay and lesbian national front, but have concentrated their battle in a continuing confrontation with the Jewish establishment. The effi-

▼

cacy of their efforts became dramatically evident in 1993, when, under the leadership of their recently appointed rabbi, the synagogue requested to take part in the annual Salute to Israel Parade, organized by the Orthodox and other mainstream Jewish denominations and official organs. The complicated negotiations, the final denial, and the consequent split within the Jewish establishment got much publicity in the national media and bestowed upon CBST the exposure and public sympathy it had never gained before.[8]

The emergence of gay Jews seemed to become a visible social category that was heretofore nonexistent. It strikes one as fitting to apply in this context Goffman's pioneering understanding of the behavior of stigmatized people and their display of militancy: "In drawing attention to the situation of his own kind he is in some respects consolidating a public image of his differentness as a real thing and of his fellow–stigmatized as constituting a real group" (1963:139).

Repairing a Cracked Identity

Probably banal yet inescapable remains the query I addressed early on: Why do people who seem "liberated" from primordial loyalties of kinship, ethnicity, and other "premodern" ties and lifestyles recall the label and obligations of a traditional religion, hostile to homosexuals, and of what often had been considered a problematic and demanding ethnicity? Exploring the membership, ritual, and other activities at CBST, I avoided the ongoing debate in sociology on the role of religion and the nature of secularization in modern society.[9] Since the majority of congregants were familiar with synagogue life, which many had initially rejected as part of coming out, I did not consider their return to Judaism particularly revealing on these issues. My treatment of the behavior I observed was basically "secular," as I concentrated on the impact and reflection of synagogue affiliation on the congregants' lives as gays and lesbians. But I am not denying the relevance of these observations to a position rooted in the tradition of the sociology of religion. However, the approach I employed might raise suggestions of the following nature: Is this choice of sanctuary mainly a strategy to lighten the burden of the stigma of homosexuality? Is this part of the search for a new communitas in the urban metropolitan jungle? Or are these the paradoxical emblems of postmodern men and women?

I assume we can consider all three suggestions true to some extent. But there was another element, often expressed by congregants, which related to the broken image of one's identity. Joining CBST was for many an act of restoring their cracked self–image and identity, combining its divided parts into one meaningful entity. Separating themselves from Jewish life freed their sexuality, but, for many, left them devoid of emotional, cultural, or social commitments. Those individuals, it seems, were unable to reconcile with their homosexuality until they had regained their lost sense of Jewish affiliation. "What is gay identity? Gay bars, Betty Davis?"—the articulate expression of malaise by a man who left the mecca of gay life in California to join the gay Talmud circle at CBST.

I refrained all along from imposing a formal definition of identity.[10] I empathize with Weeks' following conclusion: "Identity may well be a historical fiction, a controlling myth, a limiting burden. But it is at the same time a necessary means of weaving our way through a hazard–strewn world and a complex web of social relations" (1991:85). I related to that term mainly as it was conveyed to me by the congregants who, much like most of our generation, have integrated "identity" as a major idiom to express feelings of belonging and their position in the various worlds meaningful to them.

As for the origin of gay identity, we know it has been a dramatic process of only a few decades since a desire—for centuries considered an individual pathological and moral deviancy—has been transformed into a social movement. That phenomenon reveals the dependence of destinies binding the individual to the group he or she chooses to identify with.[11]

Very different, however, has been the transformation of what we might call Jewish identity in contemporary society. As observed by a leading figure in world Jewry: "The premodern Jewish world, then, was one in which much else was problematic but Jewish identity was not. To be a Jew was to be born into a society, history, destiny, and way of life whose content was coherent and shared by other Jews across space and time" (Sacks 1991:24). But the end of the eighteenth century saw the beginning of a process of "civility" that transformed an almost compulsory total definition of self and destiny into a condition in which "to be a Jew was now only one aspect of personal identity, not its totality" (24).

The construction of gay identity, as much as of a *gay/lesbian Jew*, could not be imagined before the restoration of the image of the individual, man or woman, as a member of a group that represented the

▼

totality of one's being and aspirations. But *gay–Jewish* identity could not develop before the collapse of a new ethnocentric idea typical to a revolutionary movement, perceiving gay identity as the embodi-

ment of the totality of one's self, cravings, and dreams. From another perspective, though closely related to this position, Fitzgerald (1993) has argued:

> Where sexual preference is forced to take on a power of its own, there is always the danger of making gay identity so central that this "master status" can overshadow all other identities. . . . Such a view of self is often negative rather than positive precisely because the category tends to inhibit the individual's capacity to fashion other identities. (136)

However, homosexuality has never been part of the positive repertoire of values and images one has grown up with. And once the enthusiasm, defiance, and bravado of acting out one's homosexual desire have lost their first taste of liberation, the notion of loss, intuitively suggested by reflective congregants as the need for "boundaries" or "stability," took place. It is not a coincidence that the emergence of gay synagogues has been observed mainly in the United States, where the majority of organized Jewry is affiliated with a synagogue movement, from the ultra-Orthodox to the Reconstructionist and Havurah congregations. But, as contemplated by a leading CBST congregant, when people reconcile with their identity as gay Jews, they can be content without a synagogue too, and "then it is enough to visit CBST once a year and feel it is still there." Thus CBST itself has become a shrine that symbolizes a culture and an identity similar to other ethnocultural historical and sacred monuments and spaces offering a map of pilgrimages and imageries for experiencing and reinventing one's primary affiliations.

As I have already suggested, the emergence of the gay synagogue and its survival should be understood within the evolutionary trends affecting the two major domains and constituencies relevant to the population engaged. American Jews have continually experimented with "a Judaism" pertinent to their changing life situations. Judaism in America has adopted more than ever before to the changing structure of the Jewish community as well as to new ideologies and other novel expectations generated among the Jewish constituency. It is true that I am considering that segment for whom a visible and active Jew-

ish communal association remained a potent goal as vehicle of sociability and identity.[12] The gay synagogue's eclectic and innovative style
as well as its remarkable volunteering tradition combined some of the
fundamental characteristics of Havurah ideology. But, in spite of the   241
revolutionary elements it exhibited, no less cogent were the forces
from within exerting pressures toward its institutionalization. The gay
synagogue appeared as a far stronger institution than the Havurah
minyan. It revealed itself viable enough to contain the ongoing discourse about its special streak of Judaism.[13]

On the gay front, the creation of communal gay space adept at fos-
tering communitas and gay political action could no longer be
molded by "sexuality stripped of social condition" (mainly in the male
scene) as perceived by Newton (1993:184) in the pre–AIDS Meat Rack
of Fire Island. The early gay territories have nourished a short-lived
utopia that might have proven illusionary even without the epidemic.
"Sexuality stripped of social condition," its experiential communitas
reached through the shared destiny and the ecstasy in back rooms of
gay men's bars, the baths and dark bushes, could not carry the gay
movement much beyond the liminal stage of a rite of passage for the
creation of whatever one might consider "gay nationalism." Already at
the heyday of gay liberation one of its authors expressed the following verdict of mixed glory and gloom: "At its best, the gay experience
is liberating, adventurous, righteously daring, revolutionary, and
beautiful in its sexual abundance. At its worst it is a dark vision of
hell" (Rechy 1977:242).

The pre–AIDS popular gay territories have fallen into disrepute,
often closed down by the local authorities (most noticeable the
demise of gay baths). They became part of a lost world, also challenging the ethos and strategies of gay liberation. But the gay and lesbian synagogues and churches have survived as alternative safe
spaces. Not having constructed their agenda primarily on the free
expression of sexuality, they have paved the way for gay communitas
in an era of plague, and most probably for the days after. Religion or
ethnicity, as much as other mainstream affiliative categories, could
offer a framework for stable lesbian and gay associations surpassing
the ephemeral nature of sexually based alliances. If the framing of gay
spaces at an earlier stage offered protected zones for the affirmation of
sexual preferences and fostered social action, the deframing of experiential realms stimulates the spilling over out of the gay into the non-

▼

gay. That convergence of spaces not only reveals new options but also poses acute dilemmas engaging constituencies from both sides of the hitherto bounded sociocultural territories.

This exploration into the politics of identity, suggesting a mainstream social landscape as vehicle for the construction of gay identity and collective action, might disappoint or even antagonize many gay and lesbian activists. Yet I do not claim that gay militancy and fellowship cannot survive unless embedded within another pregay ascriptive category. But "pure" gay political activity cannot provide for the needs of identity and social affiliation of all lesbians and gays. Moreover, the challenge a stigmatized minority might maintain vis-à-vis mainstream society and the sources of its discrimination is far more effective when directed from territories familiar and shared with the dominant majority.

Most people are not born into a socially constructed "gay ethnicity," and not many can completely erase and transform the deep layers of social messages, emotional traps, and symbolic conditioning implanted by society since infancy. These remain, for better or worse, indispensable components of one's core identity. Inevitably, we are all—heterosexuals, homosexuals, Jews, Gentiles, and the rest of humanity—part of a "text" we can write in only a few lasting novel notes. The emergence of a new self–assertive social persona and a new type of communitas of gay and lesbian Jews, initiated from the "safe space" of the sanctuaries of gay synagogues, is not a meager achievement in the annals of both contemporary homosexual and Jewish society. I quote Eric Rofes in a gay activist's confession: "I find a great deal of pleasure and happiness in realizing my identities as a gay man and a Jew. I feel satisfaction and comfort in attending services at a gay *shul*. . . . I feel special strength in naming myself publicly as a gay Jew" (1989:204).

Much of the ethnographic work on gay men has been limited to their behavior in secluded and covert spaces where they could mainly express their sexual orientation. The gay synagogue, a place and a "field," offers a far more complex context: it is a gay men's space, but no less a Jewish space, and a lesbian space as well. The development of modern Jewish society entailed the physical, legal, and emotional breakaway from the ghetto walls. Gay liberation was conceived metaphorically as "coming out of the closet." The emergence of gay and lesbian spaces, more visible and familiar to the world outside, where *gay* and *lesbian* encodes more than sex,[14] carries profound consequences for the current living of gay and lesbian communities as well as for the meaning of their identities.

243

Ne'ilah not only signals the end of our role in the spiritual drama of these Days of Awe, it likewise signals the beginning of a new role for us in living the drama of our everyday lives. Ne'ilah is one last act after which the curtain does not fall; it goes up!—to which one hardly knows whether to say "Amen" or "Break a leg!"

—From Gilbert's Ne'ilah drashah for the 1990 Yom Kippur concluding service. The full name of the service is Ne'ilat She'arim—"closing of the gates"— associated with the symbolic closing of the heavenly gates at the end of the period of God's yearly judgment.

▼

Ethnographic Texts as Layered Ethnographies— CBST Ten Years Later

Ethnographies of our generation age very quickly, to an almost disconcerting extent. They are outdated the minute they first appear in print. That realization struck me most vividly with this book. First published in 1995, it presents observations made during a twelve-month stay in New York in 1989–90 and later short visits. Even as it was being proofread, I knew that my account of CBST chronicled an era in the synagogue's life coming to a close. The curtain was ringing down on the story of a lay-led congregation. The September 1992 installation of Sharon Kleinbaum as its first paid full-time rabbi would inevitably begin a process destined to profoundly transform the institution.

I have had the opportunity to confirm that assessment during subsequent visits to New York. Indeed, Rabbi Kleinbaum was only the first of a growing list of paid appointees to the synagogue organization. To date, these include a full-time assistant rabbi, two rabbinic interns (on an annual funded invitation), an executive director, a music director, a children's program coordinator, four office and maintenance employees, two part-time cantors, and a part-time development consultant. By 2002 the synagogue's annual budget had grown to $1,250,000. From an association led by volunteers, CBST has become an institution under the increasing control of salaried officers. The roles of service leader, cantor, and drashah presenter are now regularly (though not exclusively) performed by the rabbi or her assistants, the trained cantors, and interns. Skilled "professionalism" has become the watchword for services as well as for social and educational events, supplementing to some extent the egalitarian ethos of "unity within diversity" that had formerly been negotiated by the rank and file.   245

But not only are the routine running of the organization and its spiritual leadership greatly changed, the synagogue population itself has been transformed from a male majority to almost an equal number of men and women. New circumstances at the synagogue as much as the consequences of feminist influences among Jewish women, promoting their self-assertion in religious terms, encouraged many women to join CBST during the 1990s.

At the same time, many close friends as well as major figures in the ethnography are gone. A number had died of AIDS by the time I dedicated the book to them—Martin, Edward, Harry, and Paul. Others followed. Morris, the twice board chair and CBST benefactor whose public disclosure of his illness opened the door to the discussion of AIDS in the synagogue, himself succumbed. Though not unexpected, his death nevertheless shocked the congregation.

Other absences have less tragic causes. My first informant, Simon, and my close friends Naomi and her partner are less involved with the synagogue and attend only irregularly. Both Martin's partner and Dov, experts in Judaism, moved to California. Saul, the board chair who welcomed me during the first phase of my work, left for Florida. Others, like Henry, Gershon, Zeev, and Jeffrey, became estranged from the new leadership or lost interest in the synagogue's life and turned elsewhere to pursue their social and spiritual needs. Sheila, the forceful board chair who dominated the last period of my observations, joined a mainstream congregation welcoming to gays and lesbians. Although quite a number of my old friends and acquaintances remain in the synagogue, an ethnographer today would encounter a very different social milieu.

Another significant change is the relocation of the weekly services to a new, larger space. The premises leased since 1975 in the West Village became too small to hold the crowded services along with the new staff and expanded educational program. In November 1998, I attended the last congregational service at Westbeth. A week later, services were initiated at the Church of the Holy Apostles on 9th Avenue and 28th Street in Chelsea. This is the church intimately associated with the synagogue's founding myth, the place where its first services were held. But whereas the legendary founders met in an anteroom used by the church kindergarten, CBST now returned in style as a mature society to take up residence in the main sanctuary. Modestly decorated with Christian iconography, the space receives a weekly makeover shortly before the Friday night service, when CBST's new ark, Torah scrolls, bimah table, prayer books, candlesticks, wine cup, and so forth are set in place.

Moving the services to the church was considered the most attractive alternative for dealing with the space problem. Owning its own premises remains a cherished ideal for the synagogue, but its realization still seems far off. Yet the move was not an easy one and not without opposition. As with earlier major changes at CBST, it involved a long and hectic process of congregational decision making. And in the end it prompted a split. A minority of congregants adamantly refused to move from their "home" to a church.

The rift, however, did not develop into a formal partition. The Westbeth space, which was refurbished to accommodate the administrative and educational activities, still retained the old sanctuary. Those opposed to the transfer were able to stay on and conduct their own lay-led services, where they are occasionally joined by members of the "Chelsea congregation." In any case, both congregations come together in prayer for the High Holiday services, which are still conducted in other yet larger spaces, such as the Javits Convention Center. These venues also accommodate the many visitors who take advantage of the synagogue's open door policy during these major events in the Jewish calendar. 6000 members and guests attended the Yom Kippur services in 2001, two weeks after the attack on the World Trade Center.

The opposition to moving the weekly services to the church was about more than venue. It represented a broader protest by a group of veterans—headed not surprisingly by Norman—to the quick pace of change transforming CBST into a complex organization, one closer to a typical American synagogue. Norman—who had often stood as the custodian of CBST's "tradition"—and his close friends felt their synagogue was being "hijacked" by the rabbi and the strong female leadership claiming authority in both administrative and spiritual matters. Though this opposition was largely male, it was not exclusively so. Some women remained ambivalent about the rabbi's agenda.

Some felt the need for more social services and typically expressed a preference for a smaller, more intimate community.

From their base at the Westbeth sanctuary, this group of men and women try periodically to regain influence on the board by running for office at annual elections. Their repeated attempts have yielded little success, but their feelings of frustration and loss continue to find voice, often in complaints of discrimination. One such conflict erupted when a new executive director, unaware of local sensitivities, suggested cutting the budget for the caretaker who cleans and locks up after the Westbeth Friday service.

In a 2001 *Ethnos* article, "'The Women Are Coming': The Transformation of Gender Relationships in a Gay Synagogue," I discuss in some detail the emergence of female leadership at CBST. I observe that despite vocal opposition, the majority of male congregants—including the remaining leadership core, which ceded a good deal of its long-held authority—accommodated themselves to this and other dramatic changes. Many, in fact, were instrumental in them. Martin orchestrated the appointment of a rabbi—it was his cherished last wish. Others were on the committee that selected Sharon Kleinbaum. Morris and Larry—before their untimely deaths—Harvey, Leon, Simon, Jack, Abe, and Joel have been continuously supportive. Indeed, the service move and the expansion of the professional staff were made possible, in part, by generous donations given by influential male congregants.

The magnitude of this change was visible at the 28th Anniversary Service I attended in February 2001. It was a joyous event whose energy evoked CBST's early days, but with a polish then unknown. The service, conducted almost three decades after the synagogue's founding, could compete with that of B'nai Jeshurun, the Conservative synagogue widely admired for its lively yet spiritual atmosphere. The performance of male and female cantors, supported by the synagogue's chorus, introduced a musical refinement lacking in the services I attended in 1989–90. In all, it was a far more gentrified event, one firmly directed by the professionals.

At the celebration, the rabbi called on the chair and vice-chair (female and male respectively) to read excerpts from my book recounting CBST's first service, which took place on February 8, 1973 in the same Church of the Holy Apostles. They repeated the story of Jacob Gubbay, whose minyan went on to become the world's largest

▼

gay and lesbian synagogue. Gubbay, who disappeared before the end of the first year, had still never returned to see the results of his initiative. But he had been located in Australia, and the chair reported she had phoned him the evening before.

During the service, I could not avoid reminiscing about my earliest days in the field. When I first encountered CBST—this creation of volunteers managing to run an institution without professional support—it seemed more exotic. I wondered whether, if I had arrived for the first time at this now "fully fledged synagogue," as a congregant described it to me, it have captured my anthropological imagination to the same extent.

The following Sunday, I attended CBST's Shabat Shira concert, which, timed to the Torah reading cycle, commemorates the song of liberation sung by the ancient Israelites following the Exodus from Egypt. For this occasion, CBST leased the impressive sanctuary of Congregation Ansche Chesed on the Upper West Side to host a concert devoted to Jewish liturgical music. The program featured three leading cantors active in major American synagogues and concert halls, a celebrated klezmer artist, and CBST's community chorus. The site, magnitude, and pomp of the performance would have left Jacob Gubbay speechless. Referring to prominent artists of the Jewish liturgical world performing under the banner of a gay synagogue, one veteran congregant told me later: "It's an achievement we can draw people from the outside to join us."

Indeed, the concert was emblematic of CBST's changed position in New York's Jewish landscape. Now fully credentialed with a professional rabbi who can act as its spokesperson, CBST, though still unaffiliated, is a far more visible institution among mainstream Jewish organizations. The more liberal elements of the Jewish establishment in New York have accommodated themselves to its presence and come to acknowledge its role in contemporary Jewish life. Evidence of CBST's growing visibility and acceptance are a $250,000 grant from the Ford Foundation in 2000, as well as a three-year grant from the United Jewish Appeal for developing educational programming and other services for the gay Jewish community.

Yet, despite the profound changes CBST has undergone in recent years, in many respects it remains the society I first studied in the late 1980s. There are still many familiar faces and a strong core of active members from the old "regime," enough to make me feel I am not a

stranger. They include past chairs Leon and Norman; religious committee chair Jack and his partner Ron; dedicated congregants Joel,
Arnold, Daniel, and Tom; and the somewhat eccentric survivor of the
1973 founders who for many years has made it his labor of love to
bring flowers to decorate the bimah, always arriving late for the Friday service. Among the women, the continuing presence of active
congregants is most noticeable. In particular, there are Annette, Carol,
Jean, and Rebecca, who became board chair after Sheila. But even in
the unfamiliar faces of the newcomers to this somewhat "transient
community," as Rebecca once defined it (as most voluntary organizations seem to be), there is something of the familiar. As much as they
are transforming the institution, in their dedication to CBST they are
following the path formed by its previous generations of stewards and
builders.

Be that as it may, an ethnographer embarking on a fieldwork project at CBST today would observe an organization run by a charismatic
rabbi with a professional staff and a strong cohort of dedicated female
and male volunteers. He or she would likely be told of a heroic past
when untrained congregants—many of them newcomers to
Judaism—acted as service leaders, cantors, and drashah presenters.
The ethnographer might meet a few of these surviving strong-willed
organizers and record their stories—relieved, nostalgic, or bitter—
about the days when, with a very modest budget, they worked hard
to welcome hundreds of gay and lesbian Jews searching for religious
and social life. The resultant ethnography would no doubt be different from that based on observations recorded ten years earlier.

But even that "current" ethnography will soon need updating.
Within a few years another chapter will be required to present the
changes continuing to reshape and remodel CBST, its community, and
its culture. One can already glimpse the gradually emerging impact of
a younger cohort of gay and lesbian congregants. Commitment ceremonies are increasing, as is the parenting of children—particularly by
lesbian couples, but by gay males as well. In the leadership domain,
with the takeover of the organization by professionals, one can foresee a change in the traits required for board members and chair.
Instead of the assets of "personality," the preferred candidates may be
those with specific managerial skills or social and business connections that can benefit the synagogue. There is evidence of this already.
Broader changes in Jewish institutional and religious life may also

▼

affect CBST. In particular, there is increasing acceptance of gays and lesbians by mainstream synagogues. A number of congregations currently engage in outreach and have encouraged gays and lesbians to join and develop social activities tailored to their specific needs.

Mindful of the temporal nature of our work, I suggest we perceive our ethnographic texts as "layered ethnographies" (a metaphor borrowed from archaeology). Rather than attempt to rework the 1995 CBST ethnography into a new text more suitable to a changing style of narration and more reflective of the current situation in the field, I have chosen to present the work intact. I treat it as at once an artifact of its time and an excavation of a field that has embedded within it past layers of history and signs of future strata. The original text, I believe, presents a story of community building whose issues have not lost their relevance or moral implication. To the original I have appended this epilogue—another stratum—sketching out in broad outlines some of the subsequent changes at CBST. For a more detailed view of the major issues that have affected the organization and the public discourse at CBST in recent years, I would direct the reader to the *Ethnos* article.

Anthropologists often speak of the impact of their work on their personal lives. I have written how, after my first research project, I changed my name to one adopted from the subject of my study, Atlas Mountains immigrants in Israel. Subsequent projects have not prompted such a dramatic act. But with the hindsight of a fairly long career, I can appreciate that my work at CBST afforded me a satisfaction unique in my experience and rare in the field: recognition and appreciation by the subjects of my observation. I gained their approval without attempting to flatter them.

I discuss some of the interaction between informants and ethnographer in the introductory chapters of the book. In a 1997 article, "Negotiating Multiple Viewpoints: The Cook, the Native, the Publisher and the Ethnographic Text," I detail the impact of insiders on the final stages of the production of my ethnography. I present our exchange of views on a number of observations and issues prominent in the text.

The exploration of this process seemed relevant to contemporary issues of reflexivity in anthropological work and the discourse raging in recent years on ethnographic authority. It also seemed likely that, as anthropologists turn to fields closer to their own society, their subjects will have an increasing impact on their final product. I assumed that the complex web of interactions between the ethnographer and his subjects described in detail—some positive and other problematical—will be more frequently encountered in future studies. It would 251 not be the first time in the history of anthropology that circumstances transforming the encounter between the partners to the ethnographic project affect the construction of the ethnographic text.

The *Current Anthropology* article with commentary by colleagues familiar with that field and the methodological issues it raised (Esther Newton, Virginia Dominguez, and Leonard Plotnicov) came to the attention of *Lingua Franca*, which wrote a piece on it. Its report included interviews with the protagonists in my presentation— "Return of the Natives: What Happens When the Anthropologist's Manuscript Is Edited by His Subjects?" (Nussbaum 1998). No doubt, my CBST engagement had initiated many unforeseen tests and gratifications.

Finally, as I was preparing for the new edition, I enjoyed the opportunity of discussing recent developments and future trends with a number of congregants from various generations and roles in CBST society. I am grateful to all those who shared with me their thoughts and feelings.

▼

NOTES

1. A Journey to CBST

1. See Shokeid 1971b; 1989.

2. Samuel Heilman, author of *Synagogue Life*.

3. I studied, however, Moroccan synagogues. See, for example, Shokeid 1971a.

4. See in particular Gregor (1985), who admitted: "My material on female sexuality seems limited in light of the villagers' openness about sexual intimacies. Much of my information on this topic was elicited by my wife. . . . Coming from a culture where such topics are approached delicately did not prepare me for the villagers' candor and unembarrassed accounts of sexual conduct" (15).

5. Hastrup (1993) made a relevant comment on the possible discrepancy between the ethnographer's and the "native's" understanding of the dialogues observed in the field: "But native voices never tell the full story about the world, because 'the native point of view,' precisely, is a point of view" (176).

6. I used pseudonyms for all participants, except for two men who insisted on being introduced by their real names. I followed that anthropological tradition in spite of its deficiency when applied to individuals whose identities are difficult to conceal.

2. From Tearoom to Sanctuary: Introduction

1. See, for example, Humphreys 1972, Enroth 1974, Irle 1979, Gorman 1992.

2. See Cooper 1989; Magid (1989) discusses the influence of MCC on the founding of the first gay synagogues.

3. There are about twenty additional gay Jewish organizations internationally; most of these are not synagogues, however, but social networks and associations, such as the Israeli Society for the Protection of Personal Rights (SPPR).

4. *Nice Jewish Girls* (Beck 1982), *Twice Blessed* (Balka and Rose 1989), Brick on gay Jews in *Positively Gay* (Berzon 1979), Leipzig and Mabel on their Jewish union in *Ceremonies of the Heart* (Butler 1990) have taken lesbians and gays out of the Jewish closet.

254

5. The fall 1983 issue of *Judaism*, for example, was devoted to the question of gay participation in the Jewish community.

6. Rabbi Yoel Kahn of Sha'ar Zahav, the gay synagogue in San Francisco, has been particularly active in presenting this position. See his paper prepared for the Reform Movement's Central Conference of American Rabbis' Ad-Hoc Committee on Homosexuality and the Rabbinate, 1989 (also published in the *Journal of Homosexuality*, 1989). See also Schwartz 1988, Eron 1993.

7. "This constant insistence upon the value of the family as a social unit for the propagation of domestic and religious virtues and the significant fact that the accepted Hebrew word for marriage is *kiddushin* 'sanctification,' had the result of making the Jewish home the most vital factor in the survival of Judaism and the preservation of the Jewish way of life, much more than the synagogue or school." *Encyclopaedia Judaica* (1971), 6:1172. See also a recent debate on that issue: Kimelman vs. Levado (1994).

8. The available data on American Jews' denominational preference is Reform, 41 percent, Conservative, 40 percent, Orthodox, 7 percent, Reconstructionist, 1.5 percent, and the others, unidentified (Kosmin et al. 1991:33) See also Wertheimer's (1993) description of the divisions among American Jews.

9. *News from Agudath Israel of America*, June 30, 1993. See also Zwiebel (1985).

10. Unidentified male respondent. Calls to other Orthodox organizations were unanswered.

11. For example, in his Park Forest study Gans (1958) reported higher attendance at lectures sponsored by the synagogue than at religious events. See also Hertzberg 1981, Moore 1981, Wertheimer 1987.

12. About 60 percent of American Jews are affiliated with a synagogue. See also Waxman's exposition (1983) of American Jewry.

13. The Havurah movement attracted a number of researchers interested in observing religious innovation in vivo: Reisman (1977) documented its emergence; Weissler (1989), though an anthropologist, viewed it, more than Prell, from the vantage of the sociology of religion.

14. See, for example, Davis and Whitten 1987, Tuzin 1991, Vance 1991.

15. Much of this literature, as well as that by related disciplines, is accessible in comprehensive texts, such as Greenberg (1988).

16. Newton described the "camp" expressed in these performances as a philosophy of transformation and incongruity; as an ethos or style, she compared it to "soul" in the African American subculture.

17. Weinberg and Williams (1975), as well as Style (1979), studied gay baths. Style emphasized the diverse expectations of the participants, observing that not a few hoped to find a lover there. Some did develop continuing ties with men they met at that scene of "anonymous sex."

18. The bar patrons Read studied earned minimum wages when employed and were otherwise "living by their wits or on welfare and social security . . . the majority have not completed high-school education . . . some are alcoholics for whom the tavern is virtually their only `home.' " (1980:14)

19. *Sambia* is a pseudonym.

20. Among them were Blackwood's collection of worldwide homosexual studies (1986), Williams's seminal work on the Berdache in American Indian culture (1986), Shepherd's work in Mombasa (1987) and Lancaster's study in Nicaragua (1988). These studies revealed the many faces of homosexuality, demonstrating the sociocultural variability of its practice and meaning. See also Carrier (1980).

21. For example, Bolton 1989, Feldman 1990.

22. Two recent books have dealt with gays in the workplace. Woods and Lucas (1993), in corporate America, and Leiner (1993), in the New York City Police Department. Woods and Lucas interviewed seventy gay men, concentrating on their strategies for concealing their identity at work. Leiner interviewed forty-one gay and lesbian police officers of different ethnic backgrounds. These interview-based studies differ from the ethnographic approach, which observes its subjects on a continuing basis in a broader context of activity and interaction.

23. See, for example, Adam (1987) and Weeks (1991) on the role of gay territories in the development of gay identity.

24. See Newton 1993:10.

25. See, for example, Epstein 1992.

26. See Turner 1969:96–97.

27. On June 27, 1969, the police raided the Stonewall Inn in Sheridan Square. The patrons, described as "drag queens," barricaded themselves inside the bar until the arrival of more officers, when a few arrests were made. The next night crowds of homosexuals and sympathizers gathered nearby to protest the vice squad's action. Confrontations with the police continued for four more nights. Within a month after the Stonewall riots the Gay Liberation Front was organized in New York City (Humphreys 1972:5–6).

28. See Zerubavel's exploration (1991) of frames and distinctions.

29. See Rabbi Alexander Schindler's rebuttal (1986:93).

30. See, for example, Davies's commentary (1992:77) on that issue.

31. See Geertz 1973:448.

32. I borrow Turner's idea (1969:131–40) of the elements of existential, normative, and ideological communitas, by which inwardly shared existential experiences organize into a perduring social system.

3. The History of CBST

1. *Synagogue News*, February 1993

2. The early congregant's reminiscence continues, providing the most concrete detail of Jacob's later travails:

Jacob had only temporary alien-resident status in this country. Because of his gay activism, he had protracted legal difficulties with the Immigration and Naturalization Service, which eventually commenced deportation proceedings. Jacob's distinguished relatives, who were his employers in the publishing industry here in New York City, also eventually dismissed him. In the midst of these difficulties, Jacob lost his lover to their unscrupulous therapist-counselor and Jacob suffered a nervous breakdown requiring hospitalization.

Following his namesake, Jacob, who fled Canaan and Esau, Jacob subsequently moved to Bondi Beach, Australia, where he founded another gay synagogue called Beth Simcha! At this point our shul lost contact with him.

3. *Synagogue News*, September 1975.

4. As later described, Sharon Kleinbaum was installed as CBST's first official rabbi in 1993.

5. This arrangement was not acceptable to the Orthodox organizers of the Salute to Israel Parade to which CBST applied in 1993 for the first time.

4. Why Join a Gay Synagogue?

1. Morris related that comment to our earlier discussion about my research among Israeli immigrants (yordim) in New York (1988).

2. In fact, no specific reference to homosexuality is made in the Al Chet confessional, but the Leviticus portion relating to that offense is read on Yom Kippur.

3. See Rabinowitz 1983:434.

4. I can suggest that not a few women of the founding generation were less likely to have been exposed to the traditional religious education that engendered this conflict, and point to the fact that the Levitican injunction against homosexuality is expressed in male terms. But some men also reported having experienced no conflict. Mark, a notably inactive CBST member, insisted that in his experience of Judaism in a suburban Conservative temple—including a prepubescent Hebrew school education that ended at age thirteen—religion had not been "a vehicle for the transmission of the popular customary antipathy to homosexuality" of which he was keenly aware. Believing Jews to be "essentially liberal and tolerant," he was "amazed and mortified, not as a homosexual but as a Jew," when he read a *New York Times* report of the Conservative movement's vote against ordaining gay and lesbian rabbis. In an allusion to a chain of "family" restaurants that refuses to hire homosexuals, Mark heatedly declared: "They [Conservative's leadership] are cheapening my religion—making it the moral equivalent of Cracker Barrel."

5. The Ritual Process

1. The Amidah is the core and main element of each of the prescribed daily services. It is said silently and no interruptions of any kind are permitted. It must be recited standing as its name indicates.

2. The Hallel is comprised of psalms expressing thanksgiving and joy for divine redemption. It is recited on all major biblical festivals (except for Rosh Hashanah and Yom Kippur, because of their solemnity) and on Israeli Independence Day.

3. See, in particular, Plaskow (1991).

4. Ibid.

6. The Drashah: Negotiating Multiple Realities

1. "Homiletic Literature" in *Encyclopedia Judaica*, 8:946–60.
2. The *teru'ah* (alarm) is a series of staccato blasts on the shofar on a lower note.

257

7. The Talmud Circle: Identities in Conflict

1. Tzitzit (Hebrew) are ritually tied fringes worn by observant Jewish males on four-cornered garments.
2. The earlier interview with Ralph ("Rami" in the original text from 1983) appeared in a symposium on Judaism and Homosexuality. See Rabinowitz 1983.
3. See Geertz 1973.
4. See Turner 1957, 1974.

8. The Politics of a Lay-led Synagogue

1. Literally, "pleasure" or "comfort." Abbreviated from *Oneg Shabbat*, a term applied to Friday evening parties that include lectures, sing-alongs, etc.

9. Getting Around the Gender Issue

1. The AIDS disaster carried, however, a far-reaching influence on the synagogue's social structure. The epidemic, which afflicted only male congregants, at once divided but also brought together gay men and lesbian women at CBST. That sudden misfortune revealed a weakness in men and an urgent need for help that could not, in the long run, be provided without increased involvement by women. I felt the new vulnerability of men eroded considerably the patriarchal image and dominating position of men in CBST's affairs.

The growing presence of women on the board, for example, seemed a clear sign of the changing balance of power in the synagogue stimulated by the epidemic. Men in leading positions expected women to take a greater share in the emotional burden and the activities designed to offer various services to the population with AIDS. When I last met with Job, in the summer of 1993, he expressed disappointment in the synagogue's engagement—now under the leadership of a female board chair and a female rabbi—with programs for the HIV and AIDS congregants. He thought the new leadership was too much invested in political achievements (such as the fight for CBST's participation in the annual Salute to Israel Parade). No doubt the growing parity between men and women under the vicissitudes of the epidemic was destined to raise shared interests and sentiments but also rifts and tensions.

10. The Social Component at CBST: Couples, Gentiles, Cruising, and Talking Sex

1. See Leipzig and Mable 1990.
2. Not all among those who had been involved in committed relationships, including those who went through the commitment ceremonies, have been openly gay and lesbian. Job, Martin's mate, as well as Alice, Jill's partner, were closeted in their respective careers in the rabbinate. Both have been engaged in mainstream, sensitive jobs and had reason to believe they might lose their positions had their sexual orientation been revealed. Martin and Job, for example,

retained their separate apartments but lived together on the weekends. However, while the majority among male and female couples resided together, there were a few more couples of long-standing who have preferred to reside separately. In most cases that decision was not influenced by external constraints.

Harry was an artist who worked at home. He preserved his independence until his last days, although Edward, his lover of fourteen years, wished to take care of him at his own apartment. (They both had come out to their families. About a year before Harry died they went for a cruise with his parents to celebrate the latter's fiftieth anniversary.) Another couple in their sixties, who had been together for fifteen years, retained separate apartments. They used to meet every day for an early breakfast. One of them told me he would have preferred a joint residence but he respected his lover's reluctance and concluded that this might be the reason that kept them happily together for so long.

Joseph and his lover, who met at the synagogue, have been together for nearly ten years. They both have been fully accepted by their families. They were regularly invited as a couple to all family events and, as emphasized by Joseph, they received and reciprocated gifts as a couple. They lived separately. Among the advantages of that arrangement, Joseph elaborated on the benefit of cooling off at home after a disagreement instead of consummating a conflict under the same roof.

3. See, for example, Weston (1991:161), who introduced the controversy over gay weddings, focusing on the question whether such ceremonies breach community solidarity and promote assimilation to a "straight model."

4. The relationships between couples and their "in-laws" was a common subject of conversation among congregants. Martin, for example, was proud to tell his friends how much his lover's father was fond of him. He used to kiss Martin on his mouth, while he wouldn't kiss Job, his own son. Job, however, carried on a stormy relationship with Martin's own mother. She couldn't reconcile herself to Martin's homosexuality, which she perceived as a personal assault. She was even less accommodating when she discovered Martin's public acknowledgment of his affliction with AIDS. Defending Martin against her bitter reactions, Job often called her up "and gave her a lesson." He told her "to shut up" when she aggravated Martin after he referred to his situation in a feature in the *Jewish Week*. She claimed he humiliated her, since many among the family acquaintances would read it.

5. See, for example, my observations of strong ethnocentric expressions in a New York hasidic environment (Shokeid 1988a:139–160).

6. The "jerk off" clubs.

12. A Gay Space, a Jewish Space, a Safe Space

1. See Sanjek 1990.

2. See, for example, Clifford and Marcus 1986, Atkinson 1992.

3. See Crapanzano 1977.

4. See Rosaldo 1989.

5. I am not claiming, however, my work represents all lesbian and gay synagogues in the United States. No doubt studies in other synagogues might reveal

different characteristics in the composition of congregations and identify various ideological or theological discourses being waged on their premises.

6. See, for example, Humphreys 1972, D'Emilio 1983, Adam 1985, Weeks 1991, Kennedy and Davis 1993.

7. See Geertz 1973:449.

8. See extensive coverage in *New York Times*, March 23, 1993; April 21, 1993; May 5, 1993; May 8, 1993; May 10, 1993. *Daily News*, May 8, 1993; May 9, 1993; May 10, 1993. *Newsday*, May 8, 1993.

9. See, for example, Berger 1969, Deshen 1972, Hammond 1985, Weissler 1989, Davidman 1991.

10. See Fitzgerald's review (1993) of the academic construct of identity.

11. That conclusion could equally engage our observations in the debate on biological essentialism versus social constructionism. See, for example, Weeks 1991, Stein 1992, DeCecco and Elia 1993.

12. The issue of Jewish identity in a secular society raised hectic debates and involved extensive research among scholars from various disciplines. See, for example, the sociological perspective in recent work by Cohen 1983, Goldscheider 1986, Liebman 1983, and Furman's ethnographic work (1987) in a Reform synagogue.

13. I am not implying that the major Jewish denominations are characterized by internal homogeneity and consent on matters of ritual. As already observed by Sklare (1972), Conservative Judaism, for example, is highly pluralistic. However, the dynamics and content of that kind of pluralism are not comparable with the diversity, in practice and in rhetorics, observed at CBST.

14. See Bech's suggestions (1992:138–39) about the particular characteristics of the "modern homosexual," including his "ways of experiencing"; see also Dowsett 1993:703.

▼

REFERENCES

Adam, Barry D. 1985. "Structural Foundations of the Gay World." *Comparative Studies of Society and History* 27:658–71.

―――― 1987. *The Rise of a Gay and Lesbian Community*. Boston: Twayne.

―――― 1992. "Sex and Caring Among Men: Impact of AIDS on Gay People." In Kenneth Plummer, ed., *Modern Homosexualities*, pp. 175–83. London: Routledge.

Alpert, Rebecca T. 1989. "In God's Image: Coming to Terms with Leviticus." In Cristie Balka and Andy Rose, eds., *Twice Blessed: On Being Lesbian, Gay, and Jewish*, pp. 61–70. Boston: Beacon.

Atkinson, Paul. 1992. *Understanding Ethnographic Texts*. Newbury Park, Cal.: Sage.

Balka, Christie and Andy Rose, eds. 1989. *Twice Blessed: On Being Lesbian, Gay, and Jewish*. Boston: Beacon.

Bech, Henning. 1992. "Report from a Rotten State: 'Marriage' and 'Homosexuality' in 'Denmark.' " In Ken Plummer, ed., *Modern Homosexualities*, pp. 134–47. London: Routledge.

Beck, Evelyn Torton. 1982. *Nice Jewish Girls: A Lesbian Anthology*. Watertown, Mass.: Persephone.

Berger, Peter. 1969. *The Sacred Canopy: Elements of a Sociological Theory of Religion*. Garden City, N.Y.: Anchor Books/Doubleday.

Berzon, Betty, ed. 1979. *Positively Gay*. Los Angeles: Mediamix.

Blackwood, Evelyn, ed. 1986 [1985]. *The Many Faces of Homosexuality: Anthropological Approaches to Homosexual Behavior*. New York: Harrington Park.

Bolton, Ralph, ed. 1989. *The AIDS Epidemic: A Global Emergency*. New York: Gordon and Breach.

Brick, Barrett L. 1979. "Judaism in the Gay Community." In Betty Berzon, ed., *Positively Gay*, pp. 79–87. Los Angeles: Mediamix.

Brodsky, Joel I. 1993. "The Mineshaft: A Retrospective Ethnography." In John P. DeCecco and John P. Elia, eds., *If You Seduce a Straight Person, Can You Make them Gay? Issues in Biological Essentialism Versus Social Constructionism in Gay and Lesbian Identities*, pp. 233–51. New York: Haworth.

Butler, Becky, ed. 1990. *Cermonies of the Heart: Celebrating Lesbian Unions*. Washington: Seal.

Carrier, J. M. 1980. "Homosexual Behavior in Cross-Culture Perspective." In J. Marmor, ed., *Homosexual Behavior: A Modern Reappraisal*, pp. 100–22. New York: Basic.

Clifford, James. 1983. "On Ethnographic Authority." *Representations* 1:118–46.

Clifford, James and George E. Marcus, eds. 1986. *Writing Culture: The Poetics and Politics of Ethnography*. Berkeley: University of California Press.

Cohen, Steven M. 1983. *American Modernity and Jewish Identity*. London: Tavistock.

Cooper, A. 1989. "No Longer Invisible: Gay and Lesbian Jews Build a Movement." *Journal of Homosexuality* 18(3–4):83–94.

Crapanzano, Vincent. 1977. "On the Writing of Ethnography." *Dialectical Anthropology* 2:69–73.

Davidman, Lynn. 1991. *Tradition in a Rootless World: Women Turn to Orthodox Judaism*. Berkeley: University of California Press.

Davies, Peter. 1992. "The Role of Disclosure in Coming Out Among Gay Men." In Kenneth Plummer, ed., *Modern Homosexualities*, pp. 75–83. London: Routledge.

Davis, D. L. and R. G. Whitten. 1987. "The Cross-Cultural Study of Human Sexuality." *Annual Review of Anthropology* 16:69–98.

DeCecco, John P. and John P. Elia, eds. 1993. *If You Seduce a Straight Person, Can You Make Them Gay? Issues in Biological Essentialism Versus Social Constructionism in Gay and Lesbian Identities*. New York: Harrington Park.

Delph, Edward William. 1978. *The Silent Community: Public Homosexual Encounters*. Beverly Hills: Sage.

D'Emilio, John. 1983. *Sexual Politics, Sexual Communities: The Making of a Homosexual Minority in the United States 1940–1970*. Chicago: University of Chicago Press.

Deshen, Shlomo. 1972. "The Varieties of Abandonment of Religious Symbols." *Journal for the Scientific Study of Religion* 11:33–41.

Dowsett, G. W. 1993. "I'll Show You Mine, If You'll Show Me Yours: Gay Men, Masculinity Research, Men's Studies, and Sex." *Theory and Culture* 22:697–710.

Duberman, Martin Baumel. 1990. "Twice Blessed or Doubly Other?" *Tikkun* 5(2):102–5.

Dumont, J. -P. 1978. *The Headman and I: Ambiguity and Ambivalence in the Fieldworking Experience*. Austin: University of Texas Press.

Encyclopedia Judaica. 1971. "Homiletic Literature." 8:946–60.

Enroth, Ronald M. 1974. "The Homosexual Church: An Eccleslastical Extension of a Subculture." *Social Compass* 21:355–360.

Epstein, Steven. 1992. "Gay Politics, Ethnic Identity: The Limits of Social Constructionism." In Edward Stein, ed., *Forms of Desire*, pp. 239–93. New York: Routledge.

REFERENCES

Eron, Lewis John. 1993. "Homosexuality and Judaism." In Arlene Swidler, ed., *Homosexuality and World Religions*, pp. 103–34. Valley Forge, Pennsylvania: Trinity Press International.

Feldman, Douglas A., ed. 1990. *Culture and AIDS*. New York: Praeger.

Fitzgerald, Thomas K. 1993. *Metaphors of Identity*. Albany: SUNY Press.

Forrest, David. 1994. " 'We're Here, We're Queer, and We're Not Going Shopping': Changing Gay Male Identities in Contemporary Britain." In Andrea Cornwall and Nancy Lindisfarne, eds., *Dislocating Masculinities: Comparative Ethnographies*, pp. 97–110. London: Routledge.

Fortes, Meyer. 1978. "An Anthropologist's Apprenticeship." *Annual Review of Anthropology* 7:1–30.

Furman, Frida. 1987. *Beyond Yiddishkeit: The Struggle of Jewish Identity in a Reform Synagogue*. Albany: SUNY Press.

Gans, Herbert J. 1958. "The Origin and Growth of a Jewish Community in the Suburbs: A Study of the Jews of Park Forest." In Marshall Sklare, ed., *The Jews: Social Patterns of an American Group*, pp. 205–48. New York: Free.

Gates, Henry Louis. 1991. " 'Authenticity,' or the Lesson of Little Tree." *New York Times Book Review*, November 24.

Geertz. Clifford. 1973. *The Interpretation of Cultures*. New York: Basic.

Glazer, Nathan. 1957. *American Judaism*. Chicago: University of Chicago Press.

Goffman, Erving. 1963. *Stigma: Notes on the Management of Spoiled Identity*. Englewood Cliffs, N.J.: Prentice-Hall.

Goldscheider, Calvin. 1986. *Jewish Continuity and Change*. Bloomington: Indiana University Press.

Gorman, Michael E. 1992. "The Pursuit of the Wish: An Anthropological Perspective on Gay Male Subculture in Los Angeles." In Gilbert Herdt, ed., *Gay Culture in America*, pp. 87–106. Boston: Beacon.

Greenberg, David F. 1988. *The Constuction of Homosexuality*. Chicago: University of Chicago Press.

Gregor, Thomas. 1985. *Anxious Pleasures: The Sexual Lives of an Amazonian People*. Chicago: University of Chicago Press.

Hammond, Phillip E., ed. 1985. *The Sacred in a Secular Age*. Berkeley: University of California Press.

Hastrup, Kirsten. 1993. "The Native Voice—and the Anthropologist's Vision." *Social Anthropology* 1:173–86.

Heilman, Samuel C. 1973. *Synagogue Life: A Study in Symbolic Interaction*. Chicago: University of Chicago Press.

———— 1983. *The People of the Book*. Chicago: University of Chicago Press.

Herdt, Gilbert H. 1981. *Guardians of the Flutes: Idioms of Masculinity*. New York: McGraw-Hill. Reprint 1987. New York: Columbia University Press.

Herdt, Gilbert, ed. 1992. *Gay Culture in America*. Boston: Beacon.

Hertzberg, Arthur. 1981. "Introduction." In Mordecai M. Kaplan, *Judaism as a Civilization: Toward a Reconstruction of American-Jewish Life*. Philadelphia: Jewish Publication Society of America Reconstructionist Press.

REFERENCES

Hoffman, Martin. 1968. *The Gay World*. New York: Basic.
Hooker, Evelyn. 1967. "The Homosexual Community." In John H. Gagnon and William Simon, eds., *Sexual Deviance*. pp. 167–84. New York: Harper and Row.
Humphreys, Laud. 1970. *Tearoom Trade: Impersonal Sex in Public Places*. Chicago: Aldine.
_____ 1972. *Out of the Closets: The Sociology of Homosexual Liberation*. Englewood Cliffs, N.J.: Prentice-Hall.
Irle, Roger D. 1979. "Minority Ministry: A Definition of Territory." *International Review of Modern Sociology* 9:197–213.
Kahn, Yoel H. 1989. "Judaism and Homosexuality: The Traditionalist Progressive Debate." *Journal of Homosexuality* 18(3/4):47–82.
Kennedy, Lapovsky E. and Madeline D. Davis. 1993. *Boots of Leather, Slippers of Gold: The History of a Lesbian Community*. New York: Routledge.
Kimelman, Reuven. 1994. "Homosexuality and Family-Centered Judaism." *Tikkun* 9:53–57.
Kleinberg, Seymour. 1980. *Alienated Affections: Being Gay in America*. New York: St. Martin's.
Kosmin, Barry A. et al. 1991. *Highlight of the CJF 1990 National Jewish Population Servey*. New York: Council of Jewish Federations.
Kosmin, Barry A. and Seymour P. Lachman. 1993. *One Nation Under God: Religion in Contemporary American Society*. New York: Harmons.
Kramer, Larry. 1981. *Reports from the Holocaust*. New York: St. Martin's.
Krieger, Susan. 1983. *The Mirror Dance*. Philadelphia: Temple University Press.
Lamm, Norman. 1974. "Judaism and the Modern Attitude to Homosexuality." *Encyclopaedia Judaica Year Book*, pp. 194–205. Jerusalem: Keter.
Lancaster, Roger N. 1988. "Subject Honor and Object Shame: The Construction of Male Homosexuality and Stigma in Nicaragua." *Ethnology* 27:111–26.
Leiner, Stephen. 1993. *Gay Cops*. New Brunswick, N.J.: Rutgers University Press.
Leipzig, Rosanne and Judy Mabel. 1990. "Tikkun Olam: Healing of the World." In Becky Butler, ed., *Ceremonies of the Heart: Celebrating Lesbian Unions*. pp. 289–305. Washington: Seal.
Levado, Yaakov. 1994. "Family Values: A Reply to Reuven Kimelman." *Tikkun* 9:57–60.
Levine, Martin P. ed., 1979. *Gay Men: The Sociology of Male Homosexuality*. New York: Harper and Row.
Liebman, Charles S. 1983. "The Religion of American Jews." In Marshall Sklare, ed. *American Jews: A Reader*. pp. 245–74. New York: Behrman House.
Magid, Aliza. 1989. "Joining Together: Building a Worldwide Movement." In Christie Balka and Andy Rose, eds., *Twice Blessed: On Being Lesbian, Gay, and Jewish*, pp. 157–70. Boston: Beacon.
Mains, Geoff. 1984. *Urban Aboriginals: A Celebration of Leathersexuality*. San Francisco: Gay Sunshine.
Malinowski, Bronislaw. 1967. *A Diary in the Strict Sense of the Term*. London: Routledge and Kegan Paul.

264

Matt, H. J. 1978. "Sin, Crime, Sickness, or Alternative Life-Style? A Jewish Approach to Homosexuality." *Judaism* 27:13–24.

Melville, Herman. 1961. "Bartleby." In *Billy Budd and Other Tales*, pp. 103–40. New York: New American Library.

Moore, Deborah Dash. 1981. *At Home in America: Second Generation Jews in New York*. New York: Columbia University Press.

Murray, Stephen O. 1984. *Social Theory: Homosexual Realities*. New York: Gai Saben Monographs no. 3.

Newton, Esther. 1972. *Mother Camp: Female Impersonators in America*. Chicago: University of Chicago Press.

———— 1993. *Cherry Grove, Fire Island: Sixty Years in America's First Gay and Lesbian Town*. Boston: Beacon.

Nussbaum, E. 1998. "Return of the Natives: What Happens When an Anthropologist's Manuscript Is Edited by His Subjects?" *Lingua Franca* 53–56 (February).

Petuchowski, Jacob J. 1985. "The Impact of Beth Gneva Chadasha." *Journal of Reform Judaism* (Summer), pp. 125–27.

Plaskow, Judith. 1991. *Standing Again at Sinai: Judaism from a Feminist Perspective*. New York: Harper Collins.

Plummer, Kenneth. 1975. *Sexual Stigma: An Interactionist Account*. London: Routledge and Kegan Paul.

Plummer, Kenneth, ed. 1992. *Modern Homosexualities*. London: Routledge.

Prell, Riv-Ellen. 1989. *Prayer and Community: The Havurah in American Judaism*. Detroit: Wayne State University Press.

Rabinow, Paul. 1977. *Reflections on Fieldwork in Morocco*. Berkeley: University of California Press.

Rabinowitz, Henry. 1983. "Talmud Class in a Gay Synagogue." *Judaism* 32:437–39.

Read, Kenneth E. 1980. *Other Voices: The Style of a Male Homosexual Tavern*. Novato, Cal.: Chandler and Sharp.

Rechy, John. 1977. *The Sexual Outlaw*. New York: Grove.

Reisman, Bernard. 1977. *The Havurah: Contemporary Jewish Experience*. New York: Union of American Hebrew Congregations.

Rofes, Eric, E. 1989. "Living as All of Who I Am: Being Jewish in the Lesbian/Gay Community." In Christie Balka and Andy Rose, eds., *Twice Blessed: On Being Lesbian, Gay and Jewish*, pp. 198–206. Boston: Beacon.

Rosaldo, Renato. 1989. *Culture and Truth: The Remaking of Social Analysis*. Boston: Beacon.

Sacks, Jonathan. 1991. *Arguments for the Sake of Heavens: Emerging Trends in Traditional Judaism*. Northvale, N.J.: Jason Aronson.

Sanjek, Roger, ed. 1990. *Fieldnotes: The Making of Anthropology*. Ithaca: Cornell University Press.

Schindler, Alexander M. 1986. "Communication." *Journal of Reform Judaism* (Winter), pp. 92–93.

Schwartz, Barry D. 1988. "The Jewish View of Homosexuality." In Harry Brod, ed., *A Mensch Among Men: Explorations in Jewish Masculinity*, pp. 124–42. Trumansburg, N.Y.: Crossing.

Shandler, Jeffrey. 1988. *Now You See Us, Now You Don't: The Self-Presentation of Gay Synagogues in America*. Paper presented at the Sixtieth Annual YIVO Conference (October). New York: YIVO Institute for Jewish Research.

Shepherd. Gill. 1987. "Rank, Gender and Homosexuality: Mombasa as a Key to Understanding Sexual Options." In Pat Caplan, ed., *The Cultural Construction of Sexuality*, pp. 240–70. London: Tavistock.

Shokeid, Moshe. 1971a. *The Dual Heritage: Immigrants from the Atlas Mountains in an Israeli Village*. Manchester: Manchester University Press. [1985 augmented ed. New Brunswick, N.J.: Transaction Books].

_____ 1971b. "Fieldwork as Predicament Rather Than Spectacle." *Archives Europennes de Sociologie* 12:111–22

_____ 1988a. *Children of Circumstances: Israeli Emigrants in New York*. Ithaca: Cornell University Press.

_____ 1988b. "Anthropologists and Their Informants: Marginality Reconsidered." *Archives Europennes de Sociologie* 29:31–47.

_____ 1989. "From the Anthropologist's Point of View: Studying One's Own Tribe." *Anthropology and Humanism Quarterly* 14:23–28.

_____ 1992. "Commitment and Contextual Study in Anthropology." *Cultural Anthropology* 7:464–77.

_____ 1997. "Negotiating Multiple Viewpoints: The Cook, the Native, the Editor, and the Ethnographic Text." *Current Anthropology* 38 (4): 631–45.

_____ 2001. "'The Women Are Coming': The Transformation of Gender Relationship in a Gay Synagogue." *Ethnos* 66 (1): 5–26.

Shokeid, Moshe and Shlomo Deshen. 1982. *Distant Relations: Ethnicity and Politics Among Arabs and North African Jews in Israel*. New York: Praeger and J. F. Bergin.

Sklare, Marshall. 1972. *Conservative Judaism*. New York: Shocken.

Stein, Edward, ed. 1992. *Forms of Desire: Sexual Orientation and the Social Constructionist Controversy*. New York: Routledge.

Stocking, George W. 1992. *The Ethnographer's Magic and Other Essays in the History of Anthropology*. Madison: University of Wisconsin Press.

Style, Joseph. 1979. "Outsider/Insider: Researching Gay Baths." *Urban Life* 8:135–52.

Thumma, Scott. 1991. "Negotiating a Religious Identity: The Case of the Gay Evangelical." *Sociological Analysis* 52:333–47.

Travers, Andrew. 1993. "An Essay on Self and Camp." *Theory Culture and Society*. 10:127–43.

Turner, Victor. 1957. *Schism and Continuity in Ndembu Society*. Manchester: Manchester University Press.

_____ 1967. "Betwixt and Between: the Liminal Period in the *Rites de Passage*." In *The Forest of Symbols*, pp. 93–111. Ithaca: Cornell University Press.

_____ 1969. *The Ritual Process: Structure and Anti-Structure*. Ithaca: Cornell University Press.

_____ 1974. *Dramas, Fields, and Metaphors: Symbolic Action in Human Society*. Ithaca: Cornell University Press.

Tuzin, Donald. 1991. "Sex Culture and the Anthropologist." *Social Science and Medicine* 33:867–74.

Vance, Carole S. 1991. "Anthropology Rediscovers Sexuality: A Theoretical Comment. *Social Science and Medicine* 33:875–84.

Warren, Carol A. B . 1974. *Identity and Community in the Gay World*. New York: Wiley.

Waxman, Chaim I. 1983. *American Jews in Transition*. Philadelphia: Temple University Press.

Weeks, Jeffrey. 1991. *Against Nature: Essays on History, Sexuality, and Identity*. London: Rivers Oram.

Weinberg, Martin S. and Colin J. Williams. 1975. "Gay Baths and the Social Organization of Impersonal Sex." In Martin P. Levine, ed., *Gay Men: The Sociology of Male Homosexuality*, pp. 164–81. New York: Harper and Row.

Weissler, Chava. 1989. *Making Judaism Meaningful: Ambivalence and Tradition in a Havurah Community*. New York: AMS.

Wertheimer, Jack. ed. 1987. *The American Synagogue: A Sanctuary Transformed*. Cambridge: Cambridge University Press.

_____ 1993. *A People Divided: Judaism in Contemporary America*. New York: Basic.

Weston, Kath. 1991. *Families We Choose: Lesbians, Gays, Kinship*. New York: Columbia University Press.

Whyte, William F. 1955. *Street Corner Society*. 2d ed. Chicago: University of Chicago Press.

Williams, Walter. 1986. *The Spirit and the Flesh: Sexual Diversity in American Indian Culture*. Boston: Beacon.

Wolf, Deborah Goleman. 1979. *The Lesbian Community*. Berkeley: University of California Press.

Woods, James D. with Jay H. Lucas. 1993. *The Corporate Closet: The Professional Lives of Gay Men in America*. New York: Free.

Zerubavel, Eviatar. 1991. *The Fine Line: Making Distinctions in Everyday Life*. New York: Free.

Zwiebel, Chaim Dovid. 1985. "Fighting City Hall—When 'Gay Rights' Collide with Religious Rights: Agudath Israel's Decision to Challenge New York City's Mayoral Executive Order 50." *Jewish Observer*, March, pp. 28–31.

▼

INDEX